Secret Leaves

Secret Leaves

THE
NOVELS
OF
WALTER
SCOTT

Judith Wilt

THE UNIVERSITY OF CHICAGO PRESS
CHICAGO AND LONDON

Judith Wilt is professor of English at Boston College

Parts of "Introduction, with Aftermath" are taken from my article "Steamboat Surfacing: Scott and the English Novelists," in *Nineteenth-Century Fiction*, vol. 35, no. 4, pp. 459–86. Permission to reprint has been granted by The Regents. © 1981 by The Regents of the University of California.

The University of Chicago Press, Chicago 60637
The University of Chicago Press, Ltd., London
© 1985 by The University of Chicago
All rights reserved. Published 1985
Printed in the United States of America
94 93 92 91 90 89 88 87 86 85   5 4 3 2 1

Library of Congress Cataloging in Publication Data
Wilt, Judith, 1941–
  Secret leaves.

  Bibliography: p.
  Includes index.
  1. Scott, Walter, Sir, 1771–1832—Criticism and interpretation.   I. Title.
PR5341.W55 1985   823′.7   85-8615
ISBN 0-226-90160-2
ISBN 0-226-90161-0 (pbk.)

Dedicated to

Novelist Dorothy Dunnett, who wrote

"There is a divine solution, but we
are only human, and Scots at that.
Which means we dote on every complexity."

Contents

Acknowledgments ix

Introduction, with Aftermath: Scott and the Victorians 1

1 Coming Home: *Waverley* and *Ivanhoe* 18
        Waverley: The Kidnapped Romantic 26
        Ivanhoe: Arrows Out of Secret Leaves 37

2 A Destiny of Choice: *Rob Roy* and *Quentin Durward* 49
        Rob Roy: Proper Names 61
        Quentin Durward: The Authority
        of Revolution 70

3 The Language of Carnal Reason: *Old Mortality,*
The Monastery, The Abbot 80
        Old Mortality: The Muffled Man
        at the Bridge 95
        The Monastery/The Abbot: The World
        Upside Down 105

4 "This Confused Waste": Gender and Imposture in
The Heart of Midlothian, The Pirate, Redgauntlet 116
        Jeanie Deans, Prince Errant 129
        Brothers and Sisters 142

5 The Salted Mine of History: *The Antiquary,*
Woodstock, The Talisman 153
        Kunst Macht Gunst: The Stuart Matter 164
        Chivalry: Cutting the Cushion 176

Conclusion, with Prefaces: "The Author of Waverley" 185

Notes 205

Index 229

Acknowledgments

I went to Scotland to meet the novelist Dorothy Dunnett and found the books of Scott at every turn there; that is how I came to love the country, to read Scott seriously, and eventually to write about his novels. I am grateful for early encouragement to work on Scott from F. R. Hart and Alexander Welsh, and later to Thomas Crawford, David Hewitt, and Jill Rubenstein, among others who welcomed this tardy reader to the community of Scott critics. Officials at the Library of Edinburgh University extended important courtesies to me when I worked there, and a fellowship from the American Association of University Women enabled me to spend a semester reading the Waverley novels and planning this work. I thank both institutions, as well as my own, Boston College, for research aid. Thanks also to Lady Patricia Maxwell-Scott for hospitality at Abbotsford. Some sections of the Introduction first appeared as part of a larger essay on "Scott and the Victorians" in *Nineteenth Century Fiction* (March 1981); I also gave a portion of Chapter 3 as a talk at a conference on literature and language sponsored by *Boundary 2* in the fall of 1980, and a portion of Chapter 4 as a talk at the Scott Conference at Aberdeen University in the summer of 1982.

Abbot's bellies and arrows out of secret leaves . . . [fiction] has always been strongly linked, at least in my own experience, with the notion of retreat, in both the religious and the military sense; of the secret place that is also a redoubt. And for me it is here that the Robin Hood—or greenwood—myth changes from merely symbolizing folk-aspiration . . . to enshrining a dominant mental characteristic, an essential behavior, an archetypal *movement* . . . of the English imagination.

John Fowles, *Daniel Martin*

I walked out to-day to the western corner of the Chiefswood plantation and marked out a large additional plantation to be drawn along the face of the hill. It cost me some trouble to carry the boundaries out of the eye for nothing is so paltry as a plantation of almost any extent if its whole extent lies defined to the eye.

Walter Scott's *Journal*, 1 May 1826

There is no reply, in clear terrain, to an archer in cover.

Dorothy Dunnett, *Queen's Play*

Introduction, with Aftermath:
Scott and the Victorians

To see Walter Scott through the eyes of the great Victorians is to see a figure whose life constituted apparently a more significant and influential narrative than his works. No doubt they were taught partly by Wordsworth's, and from another perspective Byron's, Romantic enactment of life into art. Scott himself, in that carefully low-mimetic personna he created to talk about his art even in his personal journal, visualized the "magnum opus" of the collected Waverley novels as incomplete without this last narrative: "Death (my own, I mean) would improve the property, since an edition with a Life would sell like wildfire."[1] Five years after this came Lockhart's *Life* (1837–38) to improve the estate. This was a tale of a crippled child in love with the great outlaw deeds of aristocratic forbears who did not grow up to be Byron; of a solitary boy in love with the trees and streams of his childhood who did not grow up to be Wordsworth; of a passionate teenager harnessed to routine work by his loved father and painfully rejected by his first love who did not grow up to be Charles Dickens; of a writer with a famous nom de plume, intimately and finally ruinously engaged with the printing and publishing side of his art, who did not become Mark Twain. In Lockhart's narrative, Walter Scott, like his own fictional heroes, struggled to combine the most recent familial destiny, the farm, the law, with the ancient, more tragic, choices of his family, high rank and bold deeds. In his "anxiety to realize his own ancestry to his imagination"[2] he wrote (wrought, in Scott's own telling term) stories from ancestral times at a brain-killing rate, first to amass the expensive lands and goods of the Tweedside "Lairdship" he called Abbotsford, and then to save that house of his imagination from the financial ruin in which his publishing house fell.

It is a satisfyingly Victorian narrative Lockhart tells in his *Life of Scott*. A young man of great gifts overcomes major obstacles and wins

1

fame by tenaciously holding onto a dream; the dream acquired becomes
the reality, the man becomes "the dupe of his own illusions" (p. 649);
the illusion, expanded obsessively, crashes in pieces. The man, scorning
the crass temptations of escape or misanthropy, meets his agon with the
epic arousal of moral strength, working without cease to the end of his
life to pay his and his partners' debts and leave an honorable name to his
children. What could be lovelier, more Victorian, more novelistic, than
Lockhart's shaping of the ending: "It is the fond indulgence of gay fancy
in all the previous story that gives its true value and dignity to the
voluntary agony of the sequel" (p. 650).

For Carlyle, writing his crochety review of the *Life*'s early volumes,
without intimate acquaintance with the journal entries of the "sequel,"
the story was a pitiable melodrama: "Walter Scott, one of the gifted of
the world . . . must kill himself that he may be a country gentleman, the
founder of a race of Scottish lairds . . . —why, it is a shabby small-type
edition of your vulgar Napoleons, Alexanders, and conquering heroes."[3]
In this sorry life there is an idea that Carlyle can use, and does, for his
continuing adventure with the Idea of the Great Man. But in the works
themselves, Carlyle claims, there is no "idea," no "gospel," only one
truth which is a truism, "that the bygone ages of the world were actually
filled by living men" (p. 456), and one fact, "The great fact about them is
that they were faster written and better paid-for than any other books in
the world" (p. 452).

For the great novelists who came after, it seemed also the life and not
the works of Scott which gave them ideas, cautionary gospels. For
Dickens it was Lockhart's picture of the written-out and dying Scott
setting out in the last years of his hagridden life to visit Italy at last that
confirmed him in his own restless urge to travel and experience while he
was young and strong, and acted as both caution and secret goad to his
own obsessive writing.[4] For George Eliot it was Scott's lawyerly defense
of his own right to anonymity that provided a crucial aid in her own
passage from Mary Anne Evans to "George Eliot."[5] Virginia Woolf,
reviewing the Tait edition of Scott's journals in 1940, is fascinated by
Scott's chairmanship of the Oil Gas Committee, a mark of his apparently
duplicitous or schizophrenic investment in nostalgia and progress, in
romance and commerce. Noting his early use of gaslight at Abbotsford
entertainments she muses, as she does in her novels, on the life and
half-life, the truth and the ventriloquism, of parties, when the "tiny red
beads of light in the chandeliers blossomed into splendour." But as for
the works, well, her 1924 essay on *The Antiquary* begins, "There are
some writers who have entirely ceased to influence others . . . Among
them is Scott."[6]

From Carlyle's complaint that the Waverley novels have no message to Twain's accusation that they shaped a nostalgic Cavalier culture in the South which caused the American civil war, from Dickens's silence on them and Thackeray's parodies to Woolf's serene dismissal/acceptance, the sublimation of the Waverley novels as the ground of the English novel proceeded down the generations. It surfaced in a fascinating topos: Scott's novels did not influence the authors; they influenced the authors' characters, especially the autobiographical ones, from Arthur Pendennis, Mr. Micawber, and Maggie Tulliver, to Lord Jim and Mr. Ramsay, in a process of misreading, Bloom's clinamen or "swerve," more profound than the simple rises and falls of reputation.[7] The community of the Waverley novels and the community of their readers created each other as an enabling environment for the whole century, precisely because the great fact about them was that they were faster written and better paid for and more widely read than any books in the world. Their abundance, their pervasiveness, seemed to fashion again, as a media event, that community which, as Scots peasants, as chivalric brothers, the plots of Scott's novels hinted was lost and must be found. The older, simpler emotions which bound communities occurred in subplots and secondary characters, which readers, and later critics, insisted on seeing as primary, to get what the new urban fragmented masses needed from a great public artist, a domain of the imagination in which great and simple truths should be true. The Johnsonian warning about the dishonesty of fiction no longer answered human desire. Romantic theories of the imagination as primary truth teller sought to ameliorate the crisis, but as Alexander Welsh remarks in his classic study of *The Hero of the Waverley Novels*, no theory, no individual work of art, nothing less than the Waverley novels themselves, a continuing presence, a lengthy validation, "could bring about the compromise between truth and fiction that was evident by 1832," a compromise utterly necessary to liberate the moral energy behind the fictions of the great Victorians.[8] To Scott's works is owed that "sense of plot" and story as "more truthful than fictional" whose rise in the nineteenth century and fall in our own Robert Caserio traces in his important new study, *Plot, Story, and the Novel*.[9]

As truth tellers, Scott's novels are even admitted as evidence in the trial of Trollope's Phineas Finn. Old lawyer Chaffanbras, no fancier of fiction himself, calls the novelist Bouncer to affirm that no novelist taught by Shakespeare and Scott, "those great masters of human nature, those men who know the human heart," would sanction as credible fiction so contradictory a melange of spontaneity and contrivance as the plotters of the persecution ascribed to Finn as the accused murderer of

Bonteen.[10] Never mind that Scott (not to mention Shakespeare) actually excels at portraits of men and women whose lives and deeds emerge from their weaving with a warp of spontaneity and a woof of contrivance, that this dilemma is in fact the central material of the central plot in many a Scott novel. The later novelists—Thackeray, Eliot, Woolf— believe they are working *toward* this and other sophisticated truths; it is to become the special territory of the early modernists. They cannot afford, quite, to find it behind them. And so, in the artists' memory of Scott, the center of Scott's novels, where young men and women fight for identity on the slippery interface between destiny and choice, history and desire, contrivance and spontaneity, suffers a curious whiting out, and the brillant periphery of the novels, where regional characters display unguardedly their almost obsolete emotions and ideas, retains its hold on the fond memory's eye. It is typical of works of criticism like this one to claim that their subject is more "modern" than has been seen before. My claim throughout this book will be only slightly more modest: that the Waverley novels are more "Victorian" than has been seen. (So, of course, is modernism.)

The life which produced this community of books, and books of community, was in many ways a Victorian life, though the mind formed by his teachers had a typical eighteenth-century rationalist consciousness guarding romantic and Gothic intensities. Scott was born in 1771 and died in 1832, the year of the First Reform Bill. His father was a lawyer, his grandfather a merchant-farmer and drover, his great grandfather a lord and his grandfather's great-great-grandfather a legendary Border outlaw. His attempt to acommodate his identity as an artist to his desire to shape his life as a Professional, a Businessman, and a Gentleman succeeded wonderfully for so diverse and Victorian a project. Yet his success was compromised by that Victorian love/hate for the vanishing Gentleman and for the new minted Captain of Industry. An infant illness left him for three crucial years half-paralyzed among the grassy hillocks and speaking waters of his grandfather's farm in the Southern uplands; these Wordsworthian communications, confirmed by the animist tales of servants and peasants and later by his education in the mingled fantastic-historic record of great deeds written in every rise and cleft of his native land, translated themselves in a very Victorian way into a kind of land hunger. At fifteen he was a law clerk, apprenticed to a rigorous but loved, he says, father.[11]

Like Fielding and Richardson and later Thackeray and Mary Ann Evans, he trained himself in one kind of professional journal-based writing so that the slide into self-generated fictions would happen naturally: as with Dickens and his Parliamentary reporting he learned a kind of professional speed writing which made the physical act virtually automatic and made rewriting, or self-editing, an impossibly onerous task. At twenty-four he had found the baronet's daughter he passionately loved, Williamina Belshes, engaged to the son of a wealthy banker. Around this episode he seems to have constructed a temporary fantasy of parental pressure on a weak and giddy woman, of an epic male love betrayed by a shoddy female mind, which faded in time to more generous and rational feelings. Scott's modern biographer, Edgar Johnson, suspects that the fantasy lived on not only in figures like *The Bride of Lammermoor's* Lucy Ashton, where the collision of female high romantic feeling with parental materialist pressure produces madness, but also in the severe restriction on high romantic feeling evident in most of his upper-class protagonists, especially the women.[12]

The legacy of all this was a reinforced stoicism, and an indifference which guarded a newly triggered ambition to excel in both love and public life, a legacy whose ultimate expression was the consciously rational, accidental, and deprecated public achievement which at bottom he both desired and deserved. He began writing lyric verse and translating horrific German ballads at this time. Two years later he met and aggressively won Charlotte Carpenter in a romantic three-week campaign-courtship he later characterized as a rational mating of two companions and, as a simultaneous and perhaps causal act of Waverleyan manhood, moved out of his father's house to organize his own home. In the next three years he consolidated this victorious manhood with a rising lawyer's income, the Sheriffdom of Selkirk, and the publication of his German translations. Some attempts at prose tales were abandoned, like the first try at *Waverley* was to be: prose tales, though a good business, were not quite for the Professional he was becoming, let alone for the Gentleman he had in him. By 1802 he was writing essays for the *Edinburgh Review* and had published to great public excitement his collection of historical and legendary ballads called *Minstrelsy of the Scottish Border*. In 1804 he wrote the *Lay of the Last Minstrel*, embellishing an ancient tale of his own ancestors with his own verse and his own extra characters. Simultaneously he made his first move to take back the land of his verses, leasing the "legend haunted region" (Johnson, p. 228) of Ashestiel (steep bank of Ash trees). And six months later he accomplished the third archetypal act of his life, responding to the need of his publisher for money by consummating a sleeping partnership, instead of a loan, with James Ballantyne Co.

These three acts, closely related in time and theme, seem emblematic, even constitutive, of that powerful dynamic of gain through loss, of expression through concealment, the public spectacle which is really a retreat to the "sacred coombe" beneath the Greenwood Tree, which John Fowles argued in *Daniel Martin* was the great enabling myth of the British writer.[13] If he is right, we should expect to find the myth powerfully enacted in the works which open the great century of the British novel, and I will make that argument, the foundation one for this critique, with *Waverley* and *Ivanhoe* in Chapter 1. For now it should be noted that the achievement-advancement of the *Lay* featured a minstrel who refused the lure of "southern" fame and apparently vanished from the bright hall after his tale; that the single most powerful topos of Scott's land hunger, repeated over and over as he moved from Ashestiel to "Clarty Hole," summoning around him the acres, 1400 at last, which became Abbotsford, is his passion to cover the acres with trees;[14] that the clearest indication of the real purpose of his investment in the Houses of Ballantyne and then Constable lies not in his frequent calculation of their joint financial position but in his still more frequent references to the projects that *had* to be dreamed up to fill pages ("leaves," in Scott's own phrase) so as to keep Ballantyne's presses busy.[15] The vision of himself as virtually kidnapped by, in service to, turning into, the printing machine, is the obverse of the lordly vision of trees rising again to adorn (but also to hide) the legendary lands, his trees, his cover.

This is not to minimize the impact on Scott's life of his family history, of his desire to restore to visibility the cadet "house" of Scott which had lapsed, or of that continual totting up of his "stock" of moneys which often reminds one of Moll Flanders's poignant equation of her withheld goods with her defended self. Indeed I want to suggest in Chapter 2 that several of the Waverley novels work out with considerable clarity the psychic and social consequences of the movement from a "blood" to a "money" economy, from an "honor" to a "credit" psyche—work them out and accept them. This acceptance requires an acceptance as well of that dreamy individual "anomie" which, as Avrom Fleishman correctly notes, invisibly edges in black all the reconciliations of the Waverley novels.[16] One of the consequences of the conscious acceptance of this movement is an almost intolerable heightening of the conundrum of free will in a universe of process, of the old negotiation of "choice" with necessity. The first two chapters of this study show the Waverley novels constructing, through the motifs of "kidnapping" and of service "under" the king, a foxy modern form of this negotiation. And I would suggest that in these crucial acts of 1804–5, almost literally binding himself to the crass necessities of the machine and the land while creating this alter-ego of the vanishing minstrel, Scott was at some level performing this negotiation, maneuvering circumstance so that destiny should force upon him what was his choice.

As an artist, under cover of the emerging gentleman-merchandiser, Scott's choice seemed at first to have been poetry: in *The Lay* (1805), *Marmion* (1808), and *The Lady of the Lake* (1810), he had already invented the Byronic hero and established that conflict of young right with old right, the public and private "fell encounters of mighty opposites" (Johnson, p. 355), which was to be the spine of all his future plots. With *Rokeby* (1812), written as he moved out of leased Ashestiel into purchased (on credit) Abbotsford, he had even made that crossing of the border into English myth-history that was to take place again significantly in *Ivanhoe*. He has given us disarmingly a number of reasons for the turn to prose in 1814. He had written some early chapters of *Waverley* in 1809 and forgotten them until he found them while looking for some fishing tackle in 1813. James Ballantyne had been bored with the chapters in 1809 but in 1813, made rich and famous by his friend, partner, and "property," Walter Scott, Ballantyne thought the work would find its audience. *Rokeby*, though it sold off the shelves in a month, did not have the shocking financial or critical success of the first three poems, and, as a gentleman businessman, but even more as a jester-artist, Scott was drawn to make another cast for "novelty."[17] *The Bridal of Triermain*, issued anonymously the summer he found the *Waverley* chapters, had completely fooled friends and critics; he had tasted in the secrecy, the baiting and baffling, the being suspected but not proven, not "known," a satisfaction for which, even after the eleven-year masquerade of "The Author of Waverley" was over, he could not quite understand or account for, and which I shall try to account for in the Conclusion.

But I should like to suggest an additional motive for the move to prose. Prose seems the inevitable medium for the artist interested in multiple authentic voices, in the clash and absorption of different modes of discourse, different languages. Metrics absorbs those differences. Even if Scott had intended to work only with the two "languages" of Scots dialect and contemporary English, this move to prose would have been necessary; since he is drawn rhythmically and thematically to work with at least four characteristic kinds of speech, as I shall argue in Chapter 3, the move seems inevitable.

As a novelist Scott found himself engaged with the central matters of character and action as the eighteenth-century novel had established them; the crisis of identity that occurs in the "history" of late-adolescent protagonists by which they are propelled out of neutral childhood and toward the community's definition of man or womanhood. Fielding's exiled Tom Jones, drifting, joins the king's soldiers marching north to put down the Jacobites "out" against the Hanoverian government in "the forty-five," but his journey and his manhood Fielding sees as purely private. Though Scott, like Fielding and later Austen, will establish Prudence as the grail for his heroes, the crisis of passion for Scott will include the matter of kings as well as the matter of mates, the achievement of national as well as personal erotic security. These two passions often, as I hope to show in Chapters 3, 4, and 5 on language, gender, and history, respectively, dynamically ignite or sublimate one another in the Waverley novels, providing one of the many unifying strands in the long tale these novels tell of the vanishing (fictional) distinctness of primitive life and the emergent nausea of modern freedoms. The much-studied "journey north" taken by several of Scott's male protagonists, from a supposed civil "reality" and a lady "fair" to a supposed "dream-state" of intensity and individual power represented by a "dark" male and female alter ego, is itself more complicated than would first appear. Scott's psychogeography also includes in the non-Scottish or "chivalry" novels a male journey south to Palestine that contains similar complex and at times reversible elements, not to mention key journeys by such female protagonists as Jeanie Deans and Mary Queen of Scots, from a northern identity of real, if embattled power, to a southern dream-state of mythic "influence."

The stable nationhood that the Tory Scott proposes as the frame for domestic-erotic security is ultimately traceable to some terrible tableau of homicide. Robert the Bruce himself, standing over the prone form of his murdered rival the Red Comyn, supplies, as we will see, the key topos of the illegitimate "red-handed" king, and the self-slaughtering brother-kings of Christendom's Crusades undermine the notion of divine legitimation of current authority. And behind the stable domesticity that Scott proposes as the nucleus for national security lie muted, or even explicit, dramas of parricide and sterility explicitly worked out in the chivalric novels, muted but still present in the more "modern" or Scottish ones.

As Scott supplied the element of political conflict, of the history of national ideas, missing from the Edenic epics of private conscience which constituted the "history" of the protagonists of eighteenth-century novels, so Scott's own heroes and heroines surface over and over in the works of the great nineteenth-century writers, obliquely paying the debt. Directly they extend and deepen the analysis they had received in the Waverley novels of the modern dilemma—how to harmonize the public/private life of the individual in a community moving visibly in all its parts from an organic to a mechanic model. Indeed it was Scott's apparent capitulation to that movement that profoundly alarmed his first major Victorian interpreter, Carlyle, and intrigued and alarmed Thackeray too. With a brief look at some of Carlyle's and Thackeray's uses of Scott and Scott's characters, and a hint at the surfacing of Scott in *David Copperfield*, I want to complete my introductory case for the proposition, elaborated in the following chapters, that the debt of all the novelists who followed Scott is considerable.

As a notability, a "lion," Scott is for Carlyle one of the pregnant curiosities of public life, great with lessons on the spirit of the age. Like the giant stuffed "Pope" of Rome, or the seven-foot-high cardboard advertising hat of London, Scott exemplifies the great incursion of the mechanical into the properly organic; he was a "novel-manufactory." As a historian, Carlyle says in the 1837 essay, Scott worked by "Contrasts of costume" only (p. 455), dazzled, and dazzling his audience, by the multiplex tailoring of the ages, uninterested in the Carlylian Mystery of life, the world as vestment of the divine. As a narrator, Carlyle thinks, Scott like his protagonists "went forth in the most determined manner, nothing doubting," yet the moral or even psychological center of the narrator, "the thing he had faith in, except power . . . even of the rudest sort," is hidden or absent (p. 413). So his message to his fellows was not a draught of the feverish purgative fire, "enough to burn up all the sins of the world" (p. 414), nor even the misguided enthusiasm of a Morrison's pill slinger, but the merely genial warmth of the candy man; he was "the spiritual comfit-maker of this my poor singular age" (p. 427).

Never mind that disease, not health, is Caryle's own major value: "We find it written, 'woe to them that are at ease in Zion': but surely it is a double woe to them that are at ease in Babel, in Domdaniel" (p. 413). Or that it was surely Scott's Covenanters in the many volumes of the Waverley novels who taught Carlyle to talk that way on the printed page and prepared his readers to listen to him. What Carlyle needed he took properly, without scruple, from the great romantic episodes of Scott, the search through time, space, and race for the decisive man and moment, the recognition of chivalry's reality of human bond despite the fantasy of ritual surrounding it, the remorseless "tending hitherward" of history, the prophetic stance itself. Above all, Carlyle learned from Scott the supreme importance of the striking collision not of right with wrong only, but of right with right, in the making of identity, national and personal.

But it is neither Covenanting Prophet nor colliding heroes that Carlyle finds directly useful from Scott in his own retelling of history. Whatever the past needed, the epic for England at present is no longer Arms and the Man, but rather "tools and the man."[18] And as he arrives in the final pages of *Past and Present* at this formulation, two images from Scott's *Ivanhoe* come into prominence. The first is of "Gurth born thrall of Cedric," brass-collar Gurth who went out to tend pigs, and ate with them, and drove them home to be food for his master. "Gurth was hired for life to Cedric, and Cedric to Gurth" (p. 275), Carlyle argues. The nexus went both ways, and was organic and not cash-mechanic: "Gurth born thrall of Cedric, it is like, got cuffs as often as pork-parings, if he misdemeaned himself, but Gurth did belong to Cedric: no human creature then went about connected with nobody; left to go his own way into Bastilles or worse, under Laissez-faire; reduced to prove his relationship by dying of typhus-fever!" (p. 244). The second, crucial for our purpose, is of Robin Hood and his rebellious outlaws, pictured forever "living, in some universal-suffrage manner, under the greenwood tree" (p. 71).

What makes *Ivanhoe* the imaginative ground of *Past and Present* are the figures of Gurth and Cedric, Robin Hood-Locksley and Richard, bound to each other subtly, beyond all genuine hostilities, by the prime Spirit at work in man, the Spirit that gets Work done, gets the pigs to market and the country governed, whether in the court or under the greenwood tree. Scott's working Gurth, his dog-helper lamed by arrogant Normans, Scott's managing Locksley, his talents cheapened and limited by his outlawry, match Carlyle's mute, angry, spellbound English worker-hero pent up in workhouse-bastilles, his "cunning right-hand lamed" by a game preserving system too witless to see that its own future lies in the freeing of that hand to work, too irresponsible to grasp that hand in human bond to save that freed worker from "liberty when it becomes the 'liberty to die by starvation'" (p. 211).

This muted, managed, freedom, this heroism of resistance, of regulation, that the well-known Great Unknown bequeathed to his successors, is welcomed by Carlyle. The heroism of aggression and conquest sketched by Scott in such personalities as the beloved but eventually "useless" Richard the Lion Heart, appears in the figure of "Landlord Edmund," actively threatening ill-doers, hanging "minatory on the horizon" (p. 113), and in other conqueror figures—William himself, Cromwell, the Duke of Weimar—hanging more than minatory, inviting, at the rim of reality, always bidding to take over the center.

The case is more complicated with Carlyle's contemporary, Thackeray, whose most famous novel was written ostentatiously, "without a hero." *Vanity Fair* does have a heroine, however, named after Thackeray's favorite heroine, *Ivanhoe's* Rebecca. In a famous little satiric fairy tale, we recall, Thackeray affects to rescue Rebecca from the undeserved obscurity which Scott's novel had provided for her by rewarding that "rashly-formed and ill-assorted passion" for Wilfrid of Ivanhoe which Scott had shown Rebecca gracefully repressing.[19] Yet, of course,

Thackeray is nowhere a serious champion of passion; passion always sorts ill with life, whether it is Rawdon's for Becky, Dobbin's for Amelia, or Amelia's for George, whether it is, in some less purely clownlike situations which Thackeray shows us in later novels, Pendennis's for Blanche Amory or Henry Esmond's for Beatrix. When Thackeray, twenty-five years after falling in love with Rebecca, brings her together with Ivanhoe in "Rebecca and Rowena," the heroine and hero marry, to be sure, but neither his passion for them, nor theirs for each other, survives: "but I don't think they had any children, or were subsequently very boisterously happy. Of some sort of happiness melancholy is a characteristic, and I think these were a solemn pair, and died rather early."[20] From work to work, major and minor, the sigh of the narrator of "Rebecca and Rowena" sifts down over what Thackeray calls the spangles and tights, the brilliant mechanics and lusty stage business of romance: "a dismal illusion! Life is such, ah, well-a-day! It is only hope which is real, and reality is bitterness and a deceit" "Rebecca and Rowena," chap. 1). It is as though Scott deceived Thackeray twice, once by denying the schoolboy-reader his Romantic Rebecca, and again by anticipating the mature melancholy author's rejection of romance.

As with romance and heroism, so with narration, and so, finally with history, all for Thackeray is artifice, all is self-reflexive circle rather than genuine contact with truth or reality. As a narrator, Thackeray seems in his early novels to have suffered badly from what Carlyle termed the disease of the age, the appalled vision of life as mechanical. The mechanical quackery of this life, "Vanity Fair," disturbs the "spectator" of the opening passages of that novel, but the narrator, bitterly undeceived, adopts it for his own work, calling attention to the outer paint and inner wood of people, and authors, the unwilled jerking and twitching of motive and obsession, not only in the front and back matter of *Vanity Fair* (1846–48) but all through the narration. But a greater narrative simplicity and confidence emerged during the writing of *Pendennis* (1848–50), a history of "a gentleman," if not exactly of a hero, by a "brother and a friend," not a man in a mask and motley. Generated during the writing of *Pendennis*, to be thus thrown aside, is the mask and motley of "Rebecca and Rowena,"acquired, as the narrative makes clear, from what Thackeray imagines Scott to have been.

Finishing Scott, in both senses of the word, in "Rebecca and Rowena," Thackeray takes leave of Scott the caricatured technician of Romance, and receives him again, as a melancholy model of realistic narration, deflated and deflating, in the title character of *Pendennis*. The young Pendennis himself named his horse Rebecca "after his favorite heroine," rode her through his teenage romance with the actress Miss Fotheringay, and galloped her "fiercely" through the dismal aftermath of that rashly formed and ill-assorted passion, trading her in, during his dandaical phase at college, for a more powerful and expensive beast.[21] Wrecked by imprudence at Oxbridge, Pendennis turns autobiographical novelist, and "Walter Lorraine" is pronounced by partial readers to be "a happy mixture of Shakespeare, and Byron, and Walter Scott." As such, the author is teased by his stronger-principled friend Warrington for selling his feelings for money, to which Pendennis replies with what the Victorians took to be Scott's own equanimity that a man must sell, after all, whatever it is he has—one his feelings, another his scientific curiosity, another his legal knowledge. Warrington plays Carlyle to Pendennis's Scott at another crucial moment late in the novel when the protagonist considers marrying for rank, fortune, and comfort. Accused of worldliness, Pen argues that his skepticism is toleration, his irony truth seeking, his self-satisfaction a refusal to persecute. "Why, what a mere *dilettante* you own yourself to be," retorts Warrington in the language of *Past and Present*; "Were it made of such *pococurante* as you, the world would be intolerable; and I had rather live in a wilderness of monkeys, and listen to them chatter, than in a company of men who denied everything "(*Pendennis*, chap. 61). "Were the world composed of Saint Bernards or Saint Dominics, it would be equally odious," answers Pendennis, leaving the argument where Carlyle imagines Scott leaves it, stuck on dead center. But of course, Scott does not leave it there, even in *Ivanhoe*, where the great-souled Rebecca and the nobly inclined Ivanhoe both lay their lives on the line for passionate, not self-satisfied, moderation, for vital and dangerous, not comfortable, tolerance. Both the man and the woman keep their lives and attain this object, though they do not attain each other, nor is it right, says Scott the moralist, or necessary, says Scott the artist, that they should.

With Scott's moderate heroism set aside, his history undermined as pageant, his judicious and flexible narrative absorbed into the younger novelist's single voice, Thackeray is ready for the masterful ambiguities of *The History of Henry Esmond, Esquire*. This novel, in connection with which Thackeray remarked, demurely, that Scott was for him one of the "most important English benefactors," surrenders both heroism and history to the skeptic monologist Esmond, himself subject, through his daughter's curiously unsettled Preface, to the oblique and corrosive gaze of posterity. Early critics, noting Thackeray's apparent reconciliation with Scott in this novel of Hanoverian-Jacobite clashes One Hundred and Fifty Years Since, called it Thackeray's *Waverley*. This obscures a number of issues.[22] If Thackeray has a *Waverley*, a novel detailing a young man's movement from romantic self-absorption through rash commitment, doubt, and confusion, to moderate adoption of his public and private heritage, the "real history of his life" as Waverley calls it, it is *Pendennis*, where the protagonist settles down to write middle-rank novels and essays somewhere between the mechanical vulgarity of Wagg and the high-minded sharp-tongued self-denying Enthusiasm of Warrington. *Esmond* is, if anything, Thackeray's *Redgauntlet*. Like Darsie Lattimer's Redgauntlet one, Esmond's Castlewood heritage is hidden from him at first, then offered to him in such a way that he cannot take it, then baited with a woman's bright eyes for a dishonorable taking. In both novels the great public act of Stuart Restoration which is to anchor the private reception of heritage comes, and comes, and fizzles out at the crisis—in both cases, at least proximately, because the Stuarts have only one eye on history and the other on amour. Scott's hero ends up safely at home in history, in the new Hanoverian world of sanity and compromise, however, while Thackeray's flees that same world for the new Old World of Virginia.

Does Thackeray's great contemporary Dickens, the inheritor of Scott's place as media hero, have a *Waverley*, a flirtation with, a sublimation of, Scott and Scott's characters? The answer must be tentative, for Dickens is unusually silent in his novels about Scott. One can perhaps detect a resemblance between Nicholas Nickleby, his first serious male protagonist, and such uncle-pursued self-paralyzed young Scott heroes as Henry Morton; between Edward Chester, the genteel hero of his first historical novel *Barnaby Rudge*, and such father-fighting self-doubters as *Ivanhoe's* Wilfrid or *Waverley's* Edward or *The Pirate's* Mordaunt Mertoun. It is curious to note in this context, though, the almost simultaneous running publication in 1848–49 of two quasi-autobiographical novels about novelists by the two competitors for Scott's fame; if we look for it, I think we will find the oblique presence of Scott in *David Copperfield* as well as in *Pendennis*.

In the latter novel Thackeray had looked very closely at the compromised and factory-ized world of London writers. Though Arthur Pendennis might have cut his authorial teeth on verses and epics in his teens, the path to the profession of novelist lies through the wilderness of City journalism, a wilderness explicitly characterized by the alarmed yet fascinated idealist Warrington as a machine:

> They were passing through the Strand . . . by a newspaper office, which was all lighted up and bright. Reporters were coming out of the place, or rushing up to it in cabs; there were lamps burning in the editors' room, and above where the com-

positors were at work: the windows of the building were in a
blaze of gas.
"Look at that, Pen," Warrington said. "There she is—the
great engine—she never sleeps." (*Pendennis*, chap. 30)

Dickens's David Copperfield, on the other hand, chose deliberately
not to look at the great engine of his profession. In line perhaps with his
"golden rule" "never to affect depreciation of my work" he tells us
nothing of its nature and little of its process, only that he did not let the
production of his fictions "interfere with the punctual discharge" of the
journalistic duties which laid the groundwork for his professional career,
as they did Pen's, without, apparently, giving rise to any of the inner
debate about selling one's feelings for money that enlivened the pages of
Pendennis.[23] For the upper-middle-class Thackeray, as for Scott, class
was still a vital concern: Thackeray's scorn for the workless aristocrat was
intimate and nervous, as the lower-middle-class Dickens's was abstract.
Nevertheless Pendennis, the son of an apothecary on the rise, tells us all
about the underlife of literary men, while David Copperfield, the son of
a gentleman, evades it: there is even a hint that after his first novel he
depended on his lawyer friend Tommy Traddles to handle his dealings
with publishers. And though his emotional attitude toward his fame, "in
very self-respect" (p. 686), is a privately pleased modesty, the final
words about it, spoken by the parent-figure Micawber, "Go on, my dear
sir, in your Eagle course" (p. 865), are surely acceptable to him.

Micawber is one of the potent-impotent fathers of David Copperfield. In the dark balance he moves industriously, as Dickens saw
Scott moving, toward ruin, bankruptcy, and prison, and finally exile. In
the light he embraces, drinks, loves, boasts—and obsessively writes ("I
believe he dreams in letters!" Aunt Betsy Trotwood cries, exasperated
[p. 770])—and quotes the Romantic poets from the Scots Border. It is
Burns who provides the verses that ring in Micawber's jovial hard-
drinking "something will turn up" moods (see, for instance, pp. 268,
420, 709). But it is Scott's Rob Roy MacGregor who supplies the famous
quotation on which Micawber departs London for Canterbury, his
home, and David's—"my foot will be on my native heath—my name,
Micawber" (p. 536). Micawber-MacGregor is one of the paternal warning figures in *David Copperfield*; he speaks by negative example of the
need not only for heart but for "disciplined' heart, of the desire not only
for letters but for disciplined letters. The primary source for this figure is
surely Dickens's own inept father. Yet it seems possible that the warn-
ings embedded in his peculiar relationship to work have something to do
with David/Dickens's writing life as well as his nonprofessional man-

hood. The same is true of his childhood terror at the possibility that the road to greatness and distinguished accomplishment would end at the blacking factory, and his long-term horror at the duplicitous path to power by "humility" exemplified by his secret sharer, Uriah Heep. Work is all around and yet Micawber can't succeed: David masters the mechanized routine of the blacking factory because "I knew from the first that, if I could not do my work as well as any of the rest, I could not hold myself above slight and contempt" (pp. 169–70). Micawber invents masterful mercantile enterprises and waits for one of them to turn up in reality: David masters the routine of transcribing other men's Parliamentary speeches in shorthand to demonstrate his fitness as a suitor for Dora. Micawber went astray when he tried to work independently and became efficient in the service of somebody else: only after careful study and collecting and transcribing of Mr. Wickfield's papers does Micawber enter into the hidden Australian adventure in which he is finally successful. Originality, it seems, is bankruptcy: copying is the road to identity.

Or even sanity. The key fostering father in *David Copperfield* in this connection would seem to be Aunt Betsy's other protege, the man of her house, Mr. Dick, who lost his wits and is busy writing a "Memorial," an original work which sounds like a historical novel. It flies off in unfinished tangents everytime he attempts to complete it, because another story, the great English revolution against Charles I and the Stuarts, keeps invading it and demanding to be copied. When Dick, like David and Micawber, is set to copying, first the Dictionary researches of Dr. Strong and then the briefs of lawyers, he is on his way to sanity, or at least useful normality, calmness, fruitful work. For if he makes his work up out of another man's head instead of out of Dick(ens)'s head, then King Charles's (Dickens) head will not come invading.

Mr. Dick, like Micawber, probably has his primary source in Dickens's own childhood traumas of neglect and betrayal. Yet here too there may be a surfacing of Scott, the prolific creator and bankrupt, the historian-copier, whose Memorial works record the continuing angst of the British over the criminal expropriations on which present society's gains are based, records the guilty but necessary cutting of the string that bound the accusing kite of King Charles's Head to the moral life of the land.

As Dickens writes it, David Copperfield accomplished, with some caution, the movement through the discipline of copying and toward originality. He wrote his first fiction still under the discipline, not letting it go until his future in the new form of writing was assured by success. He wrote his second as a means of recovering from, and recovering, the deaths of Dora and Steerforth—"I wrote a Story, with a purpose growing, not remotely, out of my experience" (p. 811)—and with the third took full possession of the "fancy" which begets fictions or, rather, put himself unreservedly into its possession (p. 811), a copier no more.

As for Charles Dickens, he was never the copier, the parodist, the struggler with the eidolon of Scott that Carlyle was, or Thackeray, or even George Eliot, whose quasi-fictional self Maggie Tulliver thought in her bankrupted family's crisis and her own adolescent female misery that she would go to "some great man, Walter Scott, perhaps," who would see that she was clever, like him, and help her.[24] Carlyle, the Scotsman with a message, took on the Scotsman with "no message" as a national and moral duty. The upper-middle-class schoolboy Thackeray fell in love with *Ivanhoe's* Rebecca in the costly early editions. The bookish teenaged Mary Anne Evans fell in love with a library copy of *Waverley* which had to be returned before she could finish it, so that she began her writing career copying out for consolation the parts she remembered.[25] The eleven-year-old Charles Dickens frantically reread the only books he knew, cheap editions of the eighteenth-century novelists, until they had to be pawned, and came out of the pawnshop and later the blacking factory determined to depend on no one but himself forever. Yet even here the works which never "influenced" him contain, as I hope these readings will show, much that we think of as characteristically "Dickensian"—the innocent discovery and weary shrinking from the tangle of public issues, the flight to domesticity, the strangely liberating self-Conviction which expresses itself through an identification with a psychic double who is a dark outlaw or murderer. The relationship is not, could not be, with an ego like Dickens's, influence. Rather it seems proper to suggest that Scott's works, like the chivalric and romantic modes of thought which they "kidnapped" and rationalized, "Victorianized," are the enabling environment for the form itself of the nineteenth-century novel.

In the chapters ahead I want to examine three main forces in this enabling environment. Chapters 1 and 2 find the ground of the Waverley novels in the changeling protagonist and his fight with the fathers of his vanishing or corrupted home, and follow Scott's steady enlargement of this ground from the narrow Scottish space time of "sixty-years since" to the British and then Euro-Christian space time between feudalism and the always receding "now." "Coming home" is always, for the hero, coming forward looking backward; the choices that make him both historically "progressive" and personally recessive (freedom's just another word for nothing left to choose) are always felt as counterpunches to an outside antagonist because he makes them in/as a "dream" and comes to consciousness afterward. And the choices which reveal both historical process and personal desire always, in an impulse politically conservative and personally romantic, are choices of "service"—man to man, captain to king. In Scott's protobourgeois world, the one lasting from 1200 to 1800, the ancient kings of honor are giving way to the new kings of money: the only place where these two competing values empower, rather than destroy one another, is the domain, avowedly mythic at the very moment of its invocation, of the outlaw king, the archer in cover, the Robin Hoods of Scotland in *Waverley* and *Rob Roy*, of England in *Ivanhoe*, even the Robin Hood of all Christendom, *The Talisman's* Saladin.

This is the ur-situation, Arthurian and Shakespearean (the Henry plays) in its literary roots, refined and redefined with the tools of eighteenth-century historiography in Waverleyan venues ranging from Scandinavian Orkney and feudal Byzantium to France, Switzerland, Britain, and Arabia. Within it, Scott dramatizes in ways that seem quite recognizable to contemporary thought the victory of two linked "modern" principles, male rationality and textualized language, over their progenitors, female enchantment or mystery and performative speech. Chapters 3 and 4 locate the Waverley drama of changes and choices in these issues of language and gender.

Chapter 5 and the Conclusion, which takes up Scott's prefaces and his commentary on his own art, attempt with, I think, Scott's secret connivance, to double back on this argument. Do the Waverley novels indeed, with whatever regret or bewilderment, present the modern journey from mystery to history, from "romance" to "real life" or realism, from the unknowable past to the knowing future where even the past is known? Then what is behind the loving but unsparing mockery of history and historians, of realism and of "knowing" itself, in such novels as *The Antiquary, Count Robert of Paris, Woodstock, The Talisman*? What seals the envelope of mockery around the whole enterprise of the Waverley novels, constructed by Scott as a giant tautology—the author of the Waverley novels is . . . "the author of the Waverley novels," the "great unknown?" Perhaps the most difficult claim this book makes is that Scott laid these mines under history, rationality, knowability, textuality, the novel, and himself, half-consciously, in a drama of relinquishment and achievement which the facts of his life engender and imitate. The dynamic is a mystic one, with, I believe in Scott's own mind, Christian sanction. Scott was an ambitious man; intellectually, emotionally, materially, he craved territory. But one thing he knew. That which you lay claim to, that shall you lose. Conversely, that which you hide from, hide from yourself, consent to lose, that shall you secretly, in the outlaw kingdom of spirit, have at, if not in, hand.

1   Coming Home:
Waverley and *Ivanhoe*

Abbot's bellies and arrows out of secret leaves . . . I had failed to
see why we have turned this archetypal national myth [of Robin
Hood], perhaps the only one, outside the Christ story, that literally
every English person carries in his mind all through his life, into a
matter for afternoon TV serials and the sides of breakfast-cereal
packets; for the Walt Disneys and Errol Flynns of this world. It is a
myth based on hiding, and therefore we have hidden its true importance ever since it first balladed and folk-rumored its way
into being.

John Fowles, Daniel Martin

In every period of history certain ascendant values are accepted
by society and are embodied in its serious literature. Usually
this process includes some form of kidnapped romance, that is,
romance formulas used to reflect certain ascendant religious or
social needs.

Northrop Frye, The Secular Scripture[1]

As the origin of much that is central to the tradition of nineteenth- and
twentieth-century English fiction, it is perhaps inevitable that Scott's
fiction would somehow, in the teeth of his fame, remain "unknown."
The novelist took this sign for his name: the artifact itself expressed this
sign, as well as other crucial signs about the fiction, from the very first.
The initial manuscript fragment of *Waverley* so alarmed, or eluded, its
creator, that he mislaid it in a drawer for nine years until sufficient
"cover" had been provided, by the poems of Walter Scott, for its
discovery. Later the "author of Waverley," having kidnapped Spenser
and Shakespeare and Ariosto and the Scotch Bards and distributed their

riches to the poor for four wildly successful years, took a second anxious and cunning step out of cover, and deeper into it, to produce in *Ivanhoe* the definitive treatment of the definitive national myth of Robin Hood, welding it to, seeing it through, the Scottish experience of "Britain."

The two contemporary thinkers about the novel quoted above have recently supplied us with provocative new motifs—kidnapped Romance, the arrow in the secret leaves—around which to generate new understanding of this genre, motifs which lead us straight back to Scott and especially to the two novels which were his beginning and rebeginning. While it is not universally applicable, Frye's claim that Romance is the fundamental condition of storytelling, related to all further modes (realism) or genres (realistic novel) not by replacement or even transformation but rather by kidnapping, seems utterly appropriate to *Waverley*, which is, as artifact, who is, as character, the very type of kidnapped romance. And again, Fowles's location of the English artist's predicament and his strength in a "myth of hiding" not only from "the world that is the case" but also, as he goes on to say even more tellingly, from the imagined world of his own creation, puts *Ivanhoe*, by "the author of Waverley," at the productive heart of the myth.

The apparent critical preference for the periphery over the center of Scott's fictions, for their "life" over their plots, for Scottish-based reality over chivalric romance, traditionally translates into a preference for *Waverley*'s sober colloquialism over the "tushery" of *Ivanhoe*.[2] Yet the so-called wrong turning of the race-identified "author of Waverley" into the field of national mythmaking was of crucial import for the English novel. In that sense *Ivanhoe* was an arrival, not a departure, for the author of *Waverley*. The two novels belong in the same chapter, in the same focus, at the same point of origin in a study of Scott's fiction.[3]

In this chapter, and the four following it, I have adopted the perhaps peculiar technique of talking about each set of novels twice, offering in the first section a brief reading of a significant moment in each text which grounds the major argument of the chapter and forwards the major arguments of the book, and in the second section a more comprehensive treatment of each novel. I do this as a way to dramatize my conviction that the Waverley novels stand not only as a series of individual works, many of which are well worth the traveling through for their own sakes, but also as a single, though not seamless, body of work mysteriously united by a continuing return to a number of key images and ideas. Running through the novels as a whole are figures generated by a powerful sense of the "original sin" of civilization, which is violent usurpation; figures from "real" history like the red-handed king, the reluctant soldier, the corrupted priest, and from the quasi-Gothic domain of fantasy like the spellbinding lady, the Protean outlaw, the shape-shifting minstrel-author of Waverley himself. The violence of infanticide and parricide within the family, or greed and guilt in the soul, are mediated through subtler forms of usurpation—kidnapping, borrowing, disguising, imposture—which are themselves often masked in the protective coloration of "dreaming." These illegitimate actions enable the construction of those modern fictions of legitimacy, the state, and the self. And the more I read Scott the more convinced I am, as my argument moves between the Protestant clerics of the Scottish novels and the less disguised priests of Catholic Europe, toward the climactic priest–king–Robin Hood of the Waverley novels, as I take him to be, Saladin, that the fragmentation and virtual disappearance of the kingdom called Christendom which is part of the construction of state and self causes him the greatest unease of all, is at the very root of the long Waverleyan dream/history of the loss that gains.

A number of things invite us to look at *Waverley* and *Ivanhoe* as repetition and extension of the same act of imagination in Scott. Consider, for instance, the peculiar (and similar) music of their heroes' names, names that the author was at pains to give purely musical, not significatory, identity. Unwilling to kidnap the romantic-historic associations of names like Howard, Mortimer, or Stanley for his first prose hero, the author of *Waverley*, "like a maiden knight with his white shield," has taken for his hero and himself a name unknown to herald or historian, he says. This makes it, in a crucial phrase we shall return to often, "an uncontaminated name, bearing with its sound little of good or evil," a blank space waiting to be filled in, a series of notes to be given what melody and words "the reader shall hereafter be pleased to affix to it" (*Waverley*, p. 1). This attempt to explain and de-mythologize his title in the first paragraph of the first chapter points to an anxiety about origins, and their contamination, which is intrinsic to Scott's vision. Since no one discovers faster than the historian that all origins are lost, and become visible only in the act of contamination ("of good or evil"), we see Scott, once he arrives at his own origin, the novel where he can write directly of knights, exchange his white *Waverley* shield for the silver and gold one of *Ivanhoe*, which bears as its device the uprooted young tree, violently dis-origined, or as the explanatory legend says, Desdichado—disinherited, ill-fortuned. "Ivanhoe" too was a name chosen for its colorless quality: "it conveyed no indication whatever of the nature of the story," Scott says in the novel's preface, a secrecy "of no small importance" in the esoteric game of choosing titles. Without meaning, "Ivanhoe" has its origin, like "Waverley," in sound: "the Author chanced to call to memory a rhyme recording three names of the

manors forfeited by the ancestor of the celebrated Hampden, for striking the Black Prince a blow. . . .

> Tring, Wing; and Ivanhoe,
> For striking of a blow,
> Hampden did forego,
> And glad he could escape so.

(Ivanhoe, pp. xvii, xvi)

The conceit that these men, these words, these book titles, are
originless and carry no contaminating meaning becomes playful almost
at once. The narrator and the characters of *Waverley* capitalize on the
in fact highly meaningful pun of the hero's name all through the narrative. And the antiquarian reader didn't have to wait even the thirteen
years between the novel and the preface to "call to memory" the
forfeiture, the pulling up from its proper family, that the name Ivanhoe
expressed. Even with no notes or preface today's most naive reader
would rather quickly notice that the "of Ivanhoe" refers not to the
protagonist's forfeited patrimony, which is Rotherwood, but to no dis-
cernible property at all, a vanished origin, a missing natal place. Nevertheless, the power of these two "taking titles," as Scott puts it, initially to
duplicate their own blankness in a reader's mind and thus to seize
independent hold on a public mind now newly cluttered with "associations" from a wildly expanding literary culture, links them as an important clue both to Scott's aesthetic, and to the individual and national
process of self-creation his fictions contain.

A second interesting link, musical and meaningful, between
Waverley and *Ivanhoe* is provided by the phrase "splendid yet useless"
(*Waverley*, p. 22), first applied to the "imagery" or memory of the
chivalric doings of young Waverley's ancestors, which at first glance
seems to have warped the character of the hero. It is then applied,
slightly exacerbated as "brilliant but useless," to the reappearance
of the "character of a knight of Romance" in *Ivanhoe*'s Richard the
Lionhearted (p. 409). It was of course the conscious business of poets (I
have Wordsworth, Austen, and Scott in mind here) to warn against the
splendors of pure Romance, while they returned kidnapped romance to
the public at gratifyingly high ransoms. They warn against the memory
trance which undermines the useful present with a fixation on the
splendid past, while at the same time they dramatize the process by
which memory recaptures the dynamic hope and dread of earlier years,
or earlier ages, and animates the imagination thereby.

Now, what is useless, pure infantile fixation, for Scott, so he says in
Ivanhoe, are the meteoric deeds "furnishing themes for bards and

minstrels." What is useful are the less spectacular, often hidden actions which afford "those solid benefits to the country, on which history loves to pause, and hold up as an example to posterity" (p. 409). What lends the splendor, and uselessness, to certain memories for Scott is their example of human unyieldingness, fatedness, mythic unchangeability. What is brilliant in the human situation of the past, so that one's heart yearns toward it, but is useless in the sense that it cannot be used as a model, is that scene, or sentiment, or figure, which expresses the fullness of a single static principle. What is useful is the memory of compromises, of waverings, or struggle against "the inevitable"—but struggle in such a mode that struggle does not itself become an "inevitable," not abstract but human struggle, wry, confused, disoriented, but not disembodied.

Of this peculiar unfatal struggle of the so-called passive hero of the Waverley novels I shall have more to say in Chapter 3. For now let it be noticed that in using the "splendid but useless" gambit Scott is playing more games with the reader, as he does with the "ex-nihilo" origin of "Waverley" and "Ivanhoe." For not only is Scott well aware of the material and inspirational indispensability of "bards and minstrels" to the hardworking historian-novelist, he is also much more subtle in his treatment of the usefulness of the splendidly schematic scene or senti-ment, the brilliant radical of character, than he pretends to want us to believe he is. It is rather as if these schemas and radicals hang as permanent signs, half created and half perceived, in the view of vision-ary men and women, who don them and doff them, often half con-sciously, when the time is right and the use is apparent. It is the kings and prophets of Scott's world who play most dangerously, and usefully, this game, reaching for their fructifying signs as far back as the Old Testament. It is the captains and the congregations who awake to sudden action, bemused, temporary, in borrowed robes. Waverley fights in Fergus MacIvor's coat with the King-Pretender-Chevalier's weapon: Ivanhoe in Isaac the Jew's Patriarchal and Pawned armor. Brilliant, but useful only if temporary: none of it is to keep.

A third quality that links *Waverley* and *Ivanhoe* as the mutual single expression of Scott's narrative heart is the living, almost self-per-petuating quarrel of languages which the novels embody. The battle-fields of *Waverley* see the advance and destruction of a northern army in which the Babel of Highland Gaelic and Lowland middle-Scots, with its rich infusion of lawyerly Latin from the Baron of Bradwardine and Irish from the Prince's advisors and French from the Stuart and his mercenary captains, has already created its own punishment, even had it not had to encounter the united and fluent and flexibly absorbent

English tongue of the southern army. One incident from a multitude may suffice to expose how close to the center of Scott's purpose in *Waverley* the drama of languages is. On the eve of battle the smoldering alienation between Fergus MacIvor and his temporary clansman, Edward Waverley, breaks out openly in the embarrassing presence of Bradwardine and threatens to divide the army itself. Prince Charles Edward evades the explosion by suddenly putting a Frenchman in charge of the Scots-Highlander troops to ready them for battle. The Frenchman cannot make himself understood: they know they must understand him if they are to keep face in the presence of the Prince. Thus Bradwardine is obliged to obtain inexpert translation assistance, and thus, "in the eagerness to hear and comprehend commands issued through such an indistinct medium in his own presence, the thoughts of the soldiers in both corps [took] a current different from the angry channel in which they were flowing at the time" (p. 357). This whimsical avoidance of conflict by the clever crossing of languages is a princely quality and a perfectly useful one always in Scott: one has only to add that the "indistinct medium" whence the commands issue is named M. de Beaujeu to see what serious beautiful play Scott is engaged in here. In *Ivanhoe* too the races, Norman and Saxon, have already met on the field of Hastings, with what results all know. Yet the crossing, the mutual changing, the advance and retreat goes on, two hundred years later, at the level of language. This novel's M. de Beaujeu, the clown Wamba, notices in the very first chapter how words reflect, or create, political reality:

> There is old Alderman Ox continues to hold his Saxon epithet while he is under the charge of serfs. . . . Mynherr Calf, too, becomes Monsieur de Veau in the like manner: he is Saxon when he requires tendance, and takes a Norman name when he becomes matter of enjoyment. . . . pork, I think, is good Norman French, and so when the brute lives, and is in the charge of a Saxon slave, she goes by her Saxon name [swine]; but becomes a Norman and is called pork, when she is carried to the castle hall to feast among the nobles. (P. 817)

Ivanhoe responds tenderly to the unknown melody of Rebecca's Hebrew when he is wounded; seeing that, she switches to English and tells him the meaning of that melody—"your handmaiden is a poor Jewess"—and his gaze changes from the tender to the "cold, composed and collected" (pp. 259, 260). Distinctness of language forces distinctions of class and even of feeling. Language as indistinct medium, on the other hand, is a kind of password in the melting time of races, where we often find Scott's narratives situated: the Saxon Wamba finds his way into besieged Norman Torquilstone Castle with his important message, the Saxon Cedric his way out with *his* important message, by garbling French and Latin words in Saxon accent, a fair disguise for a monk of that time.[4]

I want to return to this drama of language in Chapter 3; for now it should be noted that in compelling us to take the beaujeu of language seriously Scott is following the Shakespeare of the Henry plays, which are, after all, the begetters of the Waverley novels. "Under which King, Besonian?" is the quoted banner, the originating sign, for the narrative of Waverley, a sign which continues, we sometimes forget, "Speak or die."[5]

The Henry plays expose another link, perhaps the crucial one for my purposes, between *Waverley* and *Ivanhoe*. The Henry plays are about the reconstruction of national and personal identity after a cataclysmic and unretractable act of violence has broken the given order and thrust principles and persons who were at the periphery of the nation suddenly to the center. So are the Waverley novels. They are about the demise of kingship as a myth, and the rise of kingship as a political fiction, splendid and useful. So, as I want to argue explicitly in the next chapter, are the Waverley novels. They are about the desirability of living in exile or hiding with genuine thieves and outlaws for a time as a means of facing and assessing the thievery and outlawry on which the rock of "home" and "throne" is built. They are about fathers bewildered by "change-ling" sons, and sons harassed to "pay the debt I never promised."[6] They are about the actual exclusion of women from the hidden and corrupt reality of history—and about the ritual en-witching of the women who do enter the secret world of history: the young Henry VI with Shakespearean hindsight dissents from his nation's necessary en-witching of Joan of Arc, but his own soldier-wife, Margaret of Anjou, becomes a genuine witch in *Richard III*. I will return to this gender drama in Chapter 4.

The Henry plays show England awakening from the dream of legit-imacy to real life in the usurper's world and making tenuous peace with the fact that no "restoration" is possible, so lost is the origin of the king, so self-canceling is the wrongness of the right side, the rightness of the wrong side. And they are about what every man's son meets in the Jerusalem chamber of the brain—usurpation as his desire, his duty, his sin, the original sin of history. This is also the key theme of the Waverley novels, where the struggle for "Jerusalem," the supernational and su-pernatural territory and idea, lies behind much of the secular action. The English kings never got to Jerusalem—scene in chivalric terms of the ur-usurpation. Even Richard the Lion-Hearted never got there. The Jewish myth of Jerusalem is of getting there, but the English, Western, Christian myth is of not getting to Jerusalem, of not restoring that usurped kingdom. The enterprise of the Crusades, that hopeless attempt to recover the Origin of Christianity, the self-corrupted failure to open the sealed Holy Place, plays intimately and malignly around the edges of the Henry plays and their distracted quest for stability at "home." The same is true of the Waverley novels.

Given the Henrys' sponsorship of *Waverley*,[7] given Scott's dilemma greater than Shakespeare's (it's hard enough to build a recovery myth around the Tudors in the age of Elizabeth, but around the Hanoverians in the age of George IV?),[8] we will not be surprised to see the Waverley novels heading for the time and territory of *Ivanhoe*, where all the great usurpations are present in palimpsest in one field. Normans sit in Saxon castles, but the Plantagenets are visibly headed for the Baronial usurpation of Magna Charta. The younger brother sits on the older's throne; Cedric's son has joined the invader-Norman court and the English have laid siege to the usurper Arab in the name of that New Testament religion which took Jerusalem from the people of the Old Testament. They, in all the sharply angled pride of their ancient dispossession, are here on English soil as the bottom layer of the palimpsest.

Scott's special appropriation of perhaps the longest-lived Western archetype, the Coming Home topos (I think here of *The Odyssey*, especially), links the very action of *Waverley* to its fuller expression in *Ivanhoe*. Early in the first novel, in the chapter called, importantly, "Castle-Building," the teenaged Edward Waverley begins dreamingly to rebuild his family's history and his own identity, castle upon castle, through the generations. The farthest back he goes is to "the deeds of Willibert of Waverley in the Holy Land, his long absence and perilous adventures, his supposed death, and his return in the evening when the betrothed of his heart had wedded the hero who had protected her from insult and oppression during his absence" (p. 20). This "origin" was to become the subject of the narratives of the *Tales of the Crusaders (The Talisman, and the Betrothed,* 1825) once Scott had arrived, in *Ivanhoe*, at the Jerusalem chamber of his narrative identity. Still later, in the weird and whimsical *Count Robert of Paris* (1832), he attempted to go further along the Crusaders' way to Jerusalem, and found himself engaged, beyond fiction or myth, with parody, completing at the end of his life the movement from romance through displaced and kidnapped romance (realism) to parody which critics like Northrop Frye and George Levine have seen as nearly inevitable.

Thus the coming home topos, the recovery myth, links all Scott's narratives from start to finish: the move from Scots bard-critic to English chronicler to Western Christian chivalry's memorialist makes psychic sense for a Scot tracing "home" back through the fruitful catastrophes, the happy falls, of the nations of Scotand and of Christendom itself. Avrom Fleishman has argued for the importance of *Ivanhoe* as an enshrinement of the primal English myth of the "Norman yoke," that ancient blocking of the "true" (mythic) English nature (*The English Historical Novel*, p. 27). But it is more complex than this. Scott's vision of his island, of the Western world, has an Arthurian core, of the sort dramatized in C. S. Lewis's *That Hideous Strength*, where the nation that goes by the name of "England" holds hidden, almost forgotten in its sacred combe, in its tombs and burrows, the real powers which are its gateway, powers represented in the crossover Celtic pagan-Christian figure of Merlin.

This resounding fall, of "Logres," of "Rome," of Jerusalem even, surfaces only halfway through the long, linked narrative of the Waverley novels. First Scott chose to build in narrative the second of the originating castles which young Waverley spent time on, the castle of Stuart Scotland, the great Civil War and its eighteenth-century aftermath, the unsuccessful attempts of the Stuart kings to duplicate the seventeenth-century "coming home" of the prototypical Waverleyan hero, Charles II. I will study this topos at the level of kingship in Chapters 4 and 5, though Scott's main concern, and his achievement, as I hope these first two chapters will show, is his elaborate establishment of this "coming home" pattern as the desire and doom of the ordinary Western man, the soldier as well as the ruler.

Waverley itself builds, as we shall see, toward a grand finale of three homecomings, to a destroyed and usurped Tully-Veolan, thence to a familiar and now possessed Waverley-Honour (but Edward himself has had physically to change for this homecoming) and finally to a beautified Tully-Veolan whose restoration has all the secret comic "plottiness" of a fairy tale. But Ivanhoe *begins* with the Coming Home moment and invests this profoundly important topos with full and troubling dramatic ambiguity.[9]

Waverley: The Kidnapped Romantic

The novel developed in the eighteenth century to adapt, or "displace," the structures of romance storytelling to a new social demand for greater conformity to ordinary experience, says Northrop Frye, and then, importantly, "The Waverley novels of Scott mark the absorption of realistic displacement into romance itself" (*The Secular Scripture*,

p. 40). Now, we can be sure, if only from the time/space continuum Scott occupied, and from the volume of attention he created in it, that something crucial was happening in his narratives between "romance" and "realism." What that was is still a matter of debate, as we can see if we look more carefully at Frye's searching but oddly ambiguous description of the Waverley novels. Both "displacement" and "absorption" are tricky operations to track.

One could take Frye to mean here that in Scott the older realism as disguise, as covering for romance formulas, becomes realism more confident of its own inner structure, a realism which now absorbs, or uses, romance itself as a disguise, as a cover for *its* formulas. If this is true, and a number of modern critics who are working to restore Scott to the literary canon as a great realist believe it is, then Carlyle is right to have seen Scott as essentially a worker in costumery, wrong to have resisted seeing underneath a genuine achievement, a new secular, not divine, wearer of the re-tailored romances. On the other hand, more profoundly, and closer to the truth, I think, Frye's phrase suggests that in Scott romance *structure*, widening, snatching back, now accommodates as one of its phases or trappings or disguises it own displacement, "realistic" displacement.

The precariousness of realism as an originating structure is evident when we consider Scott's discussion of the subtitle of *Waverley*. Claiming what can be claimed for realistic displacement, Frye goes on to note that Scott's opening chapter "outlines a number of facile romance formulas that he is *not* going to follow, and then stresses the degree of reality that his story is to have" (p. 40). But what Scott stresses in fact is not the realism of his story but, again, the effort he must make to define his tale in such a way that it can tell itself on its own, without being immediately displaced or absorbed by the hundreds of formulas already supplied to the reader's mind by other people's subtitles. "A Tale of Other Days," "A Romance from the German," "A Sentimental Tale," "A Tale of the Times"—all of these formulas stand ready to kidnap his own *Waverley*, except that he holds them off (a while) with his own blocking subtitle, a thing of genius almost matching his "Waverley"—"Tis Sixty Years Since." The prosaic number enclosed by the antiquarian time-language expresses exactly the limitation and the fragility of the realism upon which Scott was structuring, or pretending to structure, his narrative. For it was, of course, first composed in 1805 as a tale "fifty years since"; and one of the reasons Scott decided to publish it nine years later when he rediscovered it was surely that, did any more real time elapse, he would be forced into a defining subtitle dangerously near the kidnapping expectations raised by "A Tale of Other Days." Fifty or sixty years seemed the safest distance between "other" and "now," those two domains of time which romance formulas seem to dominate. As the case of Edward Waverley shows, each man's own "now" is romance time inevitably, as is his great-grandfather's time. His father's and grand-father's time is "real" time, not "my story" but "history." Edward decides that "the romance of his life was ended, and that its real history had now commenced" (p. 371) after he witnesses the death of his commander, Col. Gardiner, and the first event that occurs after his decision is the news of the death of his father. With that decision, we are made to feel, he has entered into the world and the worldview of the grandfatherly narrator of *Waverley*.

In a crucial sense, then, the passage from "romance" to "real history" in the Waverley novels is by way of ritual deaths. Yet this famous structure of passages is itself a romance formula—moreover, the for-mula contains its reversal too. Death, or exile, is the gateway from ordinary to ideal or Romantic life as well as to "real history." Indeed the model case of Shakespeare's Hal, so far as it applies to Scott's protago-nists, suggests that the passage from romance disguise and freedom through battlefields to "real history" initiates a circular process slipping from history to legend to romance again. Thus "real history" is a fragile construct, a fiction, to which, the narrator of *Waverley* remarks, Ed-ward "was soon called upon to justify his pretensions through reason and philosophy" (p. 371).

If we look carefully at the progress, and the "pretensions" of *Waverley*, we can see it dominated by two interlocking topoi—the kidnapping, and the dream. As, shall we say, one of the first major post-Revelation Epistles of Frye's "Secular Scripture," *Waverley* seems to describe three main actions. It starts with the kidnapping of the romantic, Edward Waverley, by realists, and his exposure to their life. It continues with his recognition of the realists' reality, first through the psychic defense of considering it a dream, then with his participation in the dream. And it concludes with his escape from the dream through exposure to other men's deaths, and his adoption of the dream as reality; that is, his immersion in the field of violent political action and opinion, of history, becomes "real," the real history of his life, because it is, as construct, as pretension (but also, as we shall see, as fait accompli, as fulfilled wish or prophecy) "justified through reason and philosophy."

But if we break down these actions, especially if we consider the actual origins and objects of the kidnappings and the dreams, we will notice a number of curious hitches, catches, and reversals in this apparently smooth passage from romance to real history. Two episodes are especially important in this respect.

The first is the peculiar encounter in chapter 2 between the child

Edward and the uncle who rightly holds the barony of Waverley. This is the first of the novel's kidnappings. Only it is the five-year-old boy who kidnaps the man, or rather, kidnaps the object "he associated with the idea of personal property" (p. 11)—the splendid carved carriage bearing the family shield, three ermines passant. Beholding it, the child "stoutly determined . . . to appropriate the gilded coach-and-six." Although the narrator affects not to know the origin of that recognition/determination/appropriation, he hints at it: perhaps "the boy's nurse had been a Welsh or Scotch woman." The hint is, first, at that fairy-tale figure, the nurse who tells the "changeling" who he really is, and second, perhaps, at the special knowledge the Welsh and Scotch have not only of legend and romance but also of appropriation, a hint at a Welsh and Scotch revenge. In any case, the "round-faced rosy cherub" makes enough noise to bring himself to the baron's attention, and since he is himself the very object to Sir Everard that the coach, mysteriously, is to him, "the very object best calculated to fill up the void in his hopes," the child goes home to his scapegrace father as master of the Waverley carriage, while the baron returns to Waverley with a substitute son in his heart. In his closest brush with death late in the novel, the grown Edward first avoids the sword of, then rescues and then appropriates as his prisoner the Col. Talbot who married the woman whom his uncle loved, and who therefore would have fathered the legitimate heir of Waverley. When Edward first "appropriates" him and later is rescued and aided, re-fathered by him, the novel circles back symbolically to this first action. Edward turns out the legitimate Waverley heir, yes: he is the child Sir Everard, "like a hero of a romance" (p. 9), declined to have by any other woman than the already promised Emily Blandford. He is the child that the otherwise fortunate Talbot and the mysteriously ailing Emily were unable to have, upon whom they now lavish their care. Legitimate he may be in the end, but in the beginning, in a powerful but almost hidden act, Edward Waverley is the appropriator, the kidnapper. The origin, like all origins, like all actions perhaps, was violent and corrupt, like the origin of the Waverley scutcheon itself, first carried, with its lying motto, *sans tache*, by the winners at the battle of Hastings.

On the surface, as persons or nations struggle in and for adulthood, it is as Alexander Welsh proposes in a famous formulation: as a "romance of property" the Waverley novels express the myth that "property devolves upon those who respect the existing arrangements of things" (*The Hero of the Waverley Novels*, p. 150). In the elliptical "pursuit" of the property, the world of the novels paradoxically displays a "premium on *having* and a prejudice against *getting*" which is more than a class prejudice (though it is that too). It is, says Welsh, "as if the romance of property were suspicious of any kind of force or energy" (p. 120).

Suspicious of, but also dependent on it. For it is corrupting force and usurping energy, the novels always reveal, which lies not only behind the revolutionaries and resisters, but also behind the existing arrangements of things, and the preexisting arrangements, and all the arrangements as far back into the haze of passion and legend as one dares to go. There the historian or the balladeer will always find the personal or familial or national or racial or even theological five-year-old snatching the glittering object that is not his.

A key image to parallel this image of the five-year-old Edward Waverley is that of Scotland's adult national hero, Robert the Bruce himself, who killed his rival, John Comyn, the Red Comyn, in a supposed peacemaking meeting in a church in 1306, then had himself crowned at Scone to legitimize his "snatched" authority. Scott alludes to this act twice in the novels, once, as we shall see, in *Redgauntlet*, and once in *Old Mortality*, but I believe it possesses his imagination deeply. *Old Mortality*'s Henry Morton initially finds himself actually unable to judge, to separate himself from, John Balfour's murder of Archbishop Sharpe, so well does he remember "that the way was opened to the `former liberation of Scotland by an act of violence which no man can justify,—the slaughter of Cumming by the hand of Robert Bruce."[10] Well aware of the blood on the hands of the existing arrangements of things, Scott never seeks to chronicle the real origin of Scotland's legitimacy in Bruce's break from England, nor, for perhaps the same reason, does he work directly from Shakespeare's powerful image of the original red-handed king, MacBeth,[11] preferring the subtler usurpations of the Henry plays.

The childhood episode in *Waverley*, little Edward commandeering the Waverley heritage from his uncle, is a kind of hidden foundation for the following chapters, ruefully rational, on Edward's fragmentary education, his castle-building in the air, his day-dreamy solitary wandering, and his supposedly faulty self-guided reading and thinking. But it casts suggestive light on the main actions of the novel too, wherein the self-guiding dreamer is deliberately put under outside guidance, first overt, then increasingly covert, as a means of waking him up and pinning him down to responsible action. The amiably Jacobite young Edward, curious about other lives and lands, in thrall to the dream of "service," lightly accepts his father's order to put himself under command in Col. Gardiner's Hanoverian dragoons, and still more lightly takes command of his own miniature feudal meiny. North of Edinburgh he visits his uncle's proscribed Jacobite friend Bradwardine in a long "leave of absense" as recklessly experimental and self-guided as Prince Hal's with Falstaff. Indeed the early Tully Veolan scenes have more than a passing resemblance to the Tavern scenes of *Henry IV, Part One*: not only does Edward rise sober, like Hal, from the quaffing and feasting which preoccupy his elders there, but he eagerly and curiously, like Hal, moves deeper into the moonlight world of thievery and black-mail, kidnapping and ransom, upon which, perforce, the many feasts of Tully Veolan are dependent. When the Highland caterans "lift" a herd of Bradwardine's cows because the Baron has stopped paying blackmail, and the kidnappers' superior deputs Evan Dhu to ransom the cows and restore the existing corrupt arrangements, Edward is fired with "curi-osity" and accepts an invitation to go along for the ride, or rather walk, into the Highland passes. He goes because he sees behind the life of pas-sive outlawry being lived by Bradwardine and all the Jacobites, in the active outlawry of Donald Bean Lean, that "dream" life of violent faith and loyalty which is his family's past, in fact the "real history" of their lives.

He goes, rashly self-guided, leaving even further behind the com-mand to which and for which he is responsible, but as he passes north from lowlands to highlands, he goes more profoundly under guidance than he has ever gone before. On the banks of the lake guarding Donald Bean Lean's cave he "gave himself up to the full romance of his situa-tion" (p. 100), invoking and provoking the awe and terror of the scene like Wordsworth's nest-hunting or boat-stealing boy in *The Prelude*, and then was "officiously assisted," "moved," and finally "almost carried into the presence" of the chief kidnapper of the region, the man whom he has already pictured to himself as "a second Robin Hood" (p. 100).

Scott's narrator, who likes reversals and contradictions, remarks that the actual cause of this journey, milk-cows, "assorted ill" with the sentimental romance of "wildness" in which young Waverley "wrapt" himself, and from the same impulse assures us that Donald Bean Lean was "the very reverse" of those gigantic banditti figures out of Salvator Rosa for which Waverley had "prepared himself," being thin and sandy and vain, rather than heavy, dark, and proud (p. 103). Still the hidden double-reversal at which Scott *really* excels reveals Donald Bean Lean for the genuinely magical figure he is, the Robin Hood–Puck figure, worker by secret ways, hidden manipulator of actions, the uncontrol-lable element of romance which escapes the political-social apparatus for which the narrative has kidnapped him.

For half the novel Waverley, like the reader, thinks Donald Bean Lean is only a minor tool of Fergus MacIvor, a way station on Waverley's path, self-guided, self-kidnapped, that is, seduced, toward the glitter-ing figure of the Jacobite Chieftan and the access he offers to the still more glittering figure of the Chevalier, Charles Edward Stuart himself.

Yet the truth is that Waverley has been kidnapped by Donald, or rather, and this is the second major kidnapping episode of the novel, the Waverley Seal has been kidnapped off his watch chain. After the unnoticed loss of the Seal, Waverley begins to sense how much longer Scottish hours are, how much further a Scots mile, how much heavier a Scots pound is. Edward misses the Waverley Seal at Glennaquoich, and borrows MacIvor's seal to close his dispatches to Tully Veolan, saying he will be prolonging his leave of absence from there, as well as from the army. Later he will borrow MacIvor's coat and Charles Edward's sword to fight for the Jacobite Cause with: the kidnapping of the Seal initiates that process of disguisings and aliases which will accompany Waverley through his journey to take service with the Jacobites, to fight for them at Preston and Clifton, and hide at Ullswater and sneak into London to initiate the legal action that will free the name of Waverley from its treasonous incarceration, so that Edward can take the name and the Seal and claim the carriage and the scutcheon *sans tache*, legitimately.

For it turns out that Edward did not "loose" his identity on that journey, it was kidnapped; and, manipulated by Donald Bean Lean, has acquired a malign ghostly being which nearly destroys the family. Using the Seal, "the second Robin Hood" carries on treasonous correspondence with Waverley's abandoned feudal troop, seducing some of them to Jacobitism. "Waverley" thus becomes a traitor to his government weeks before Edward does, the ghost identity in fact forcing the real one to change.

White Donald is, of course, a scoundrel and a dastard and a slippery captain to the politician MacIvor. Fergus's rational, definite orders are always transformed by Donald into "a sort of roving commission, which [he] interprets in the way most advantageous to himself" (p. 401), and finally Donald abandons MacIvor entirely and escapes safely into his covering forest. Though there are some social and political "reasons" to account for the independent-minded kidnapper's peculiar use of "Waverley," the man himself remains mysterious, like the first Robin Hood. Deceived about the man he thinks only a simple thief, the shrewd MacIvor remarks that White Donald "couldn't have taken the seal, he would have taken the watch" as well, and later, when he knows Donald did take it, "why he didn't simply plunder or ransom" Edward Waverley "passes my judgment," he says (p. 260).

The truth is that as a kidnapper Donald, unlike Fergus, represents no more stable or social or political idea than pure playful self-expression: the clergyman Morton says he is "renowned through the countryside as a sort of Robin Hood, and the stories that are told of [him] are the common tales of the winter fireside" (p. 219). And as a kind of kidnapee, a bondsman to Fergus MacIvor, Donald has a keen eye for the secret door back into the forest. He took Edward's Waverley Seal, the narrator says, in order to make a big impression on Jacobite minds by single-handedly carrying out the suborning of Waverley's whole troop; but the impression remains that he did so for the general joy of misrule, disguise, assuming and expanding identities. Like Edward, and "Waverley," Donald Bean Lean has an alter-ego too, "a pedlar, called Ruthven, Ruffin, or Rivane, known among the soldiers as Wily Will" (p. 319), who acts as mediator between the troop and the "Waverley" who has gone (who will go) over (gone back) to the Jacobite cause. This peddler makes an arresting appearance, closer to the truth of the white magical figure than the inflated robber-baron of Waverley's "prepared" imagination, in chapter 36, to carry off Edward yet again from the governmental authority which had kidnapped him on his first attempt to return to the lowlands. He holds the Covenanting military leader Gifted Gilfillan in converse while the attack is being prepared, praising the religious leader for his "notable facility in searching and explaining the secret—ay, the secret and obscure and incomprehensible causes of the backslidings of the land," for touching "the root of the matter" (p. 229). But neither this religious theorist nor the political theorist MacIvor, nor the social historian who narrates the novel, really quite reaches that root, which remains, like Wily Will/White Donald himself, secret and obscure and incomprehensible.

In looking for our "realist" kidnapper of the romantic Edward we are on somewhat firmer ground with Fergus MacIvor, whom we first know, from the interpolated sketch of the narrator, as a "perfect politician," a "bold, ambitious, and ardent, yet artful and politic character" of a "mixed and peculiar tone, that could only have been acquired Sixty Years Since" (pp. 121, 118). Fergus knows even better than White Donald what a splendid ransom in prestige and rank the kidnapping of a Waverley to the Jacobite cause would bring, and he lays his trap with great subtlety and baits it, fruit of that mixed and peculiar character, with sincerity. Edward is drawn north and further north, by the color and primitive power of Highland life, and by the beauty and single-heartedness of Flora MacIvor, until a lucky accident, a brush with death at the stag hunt which is a front for a rebel council of war, interferes with that northward movement. Edward stays behind, injured, while the hunting party goes up north to greet the returned Stuart Prince: when he goes back to Glennaquoich and hears that "Waverley" is being sought in England for having done what Edward is only drifting toward doing, he decides to go south to rescue that wayward ghost-identity, to clear his name. This rash and dangerous proposal irritates Fergus for several reasons, but Edward insists, "I must run my hazard," and Fergus responds, "Wilful will do't" (p. 184). But the would-be kidnapper gives Edward his own horse to escape south on, and his own henchman as guide. The horse throws a shoe in Whig country and the guide behaves suspiciously before the natives; both servants of MacIvor, symbolically divining what their master's real wish is, precipitate Edward's capture by the lowland government and his later re-kidnapping by White Donald. And at that, Edward is pushed on his way north again, this time to go the whole way into service with the Prince at the side of MacIvor.

Fergus MacIvor seems essentially a mocker, like Joyce's Malachi Mulligan: he strikes "a theatrical air" and declaims Highland poetry, deliberately breaking the spell of his sister's song in chapter 23. So well does he mock old Bradwardine's chivalric ambition to regain his ancient prerogative of removing the king's boots that Edward thereafter associates that action, and other chivalric/heroic motives and devices, with a "ludicrous idea," a "seamy" as well as a "fair" side, despite his personal attraction to the chivalric (p. 314). Yet despite the politician's character and the realist's distance from the Romance scene that Fergus uses ("The Chieftain . . . had appeared rather to watch the emotions which were excited, than to partake," the narrator remarks [p. 127]), the northerner has, like southern Edward, a sterner ghost-identity which finally pulls him into the action which he, like Edward, had intended only to watch. He is "Vich Ian Vohr," eleventh of that Ilk (p. 118), and when the house-demon, the Bodach Glas, calls him by that name to beware the outcome of the morrow, then, "with a melancholy air, 'my fate is settled,'" says Fergus, "'dead or captive I must be'" (p. 362). Since he must submit, he does; eagerly leading the attack at Clifton he is captured, and eventually put to death. He is the first of a group of kings I want to talk about in the next chapter, who play a dangerous game with the enduring radicals of romance behavior. He has played realist too near the edge of romance for too long, has not meditated sufficiently on the thinness of that line, says Scott's narrator. And he slips over.

With his eyes open. Awake. He spies the Gray Specter in the "clear moonlight," then turns "on the same spot successively to the four points of the compass . . . and the figure was constantly before my eyes" (p. 363). He receives no clemency from his captors because "he came to the field with the fullest light upon the nature of his attempt" (p. 414). "Fergus has taken his measures with his eyes open," Flora emphasizes in warning (p. 168), distinguishing him from Edward, whose eyes are presumably closed as he unpins the Hanoverian cockade from his hat and reaches for "one of a more lively colour" from the Jacobite Flora (p. 167).

Yet the easy connection of open eyes, awakening, with "reality" or "real history," and of closed eyes, "the dream," with romance, breaks down over and over in the novel. War and strife, for instance, are associated with "awakening" in two important songs, one a fragment which Edward wrote after hearing that he had been ordered to service in the Hanoverian army—"distant winds began to wake / And roused the Genius of the Lake / . . . So on the idle dreams of youth, / Breaks the loud trumpet-call of truth" (p. 28). The other is a Highland marshaling song translated by Flora MacIvor—"dark is the sleep of the sons of the Gael / . . . Ye sons of the strong, when that dawning shall break, / Need the harp of the aged remind you to wake?" (p. 140). But the only thing that successfully "wakes" men from the "sleep" of ordinary life is indeed "the harp of the aged," that is, the memory of great deeds, which were originally the daydreams of the castle-building young Edward. In the first part of the novel, in a passage quoted earlier, "it seemed like a dream" to Edward that deeds of violence and treachery should fall "within the common order of things." Once he is acquainted with the Highlands it *is* the common order of things, the notion of a stable rank with a stable government under the patronage of a favored father, had all "passed away like a dream" leaving a new truth, "dishonor . . . disgrace . . . subversion . . . and destruction" (p. 173). And as Evan Dhu proposes, in order to restore amity between MacIvor and Bradwardine, "whether the cloud descended from the hill to the valley, or rose from the valley to the hill . . . no man shall hereafter ask" (p. 95).

Riding through the "desolation" chapter to the usurped manor of Tully Veolan Edward feels, "in internal confidence and mental dignity, a compensation for the gay dreams which, in his case, experience had so rapidly dissolved" (p. 388). Yet all the important experiences had been experienced *as dreams*, his love of Flora ("This, then, is an end of my day-dream" [p. 273]), his identification with Fergus ("Is it of Fergus MacIvor they speak this?" Edward wonders as he hears of a renegade and traitor about to be executed, "or do I dream? of Fergus, the bold, the chivalrous, the free-minded, the lofty chieftain of a tribe?" [p. 423]). Above all, Edward experienced his own chosen participation in political "reality" as a dream. Moving toward the battle of Preston in borrowed dress, among soldiers speaking an unknown language, he suddenly looks down at himself and "wished to awake from what seemed at the moment a dream, strange, horrible, and unnatural" (p. 291).

The truth seems to be in *Waverley* that whatever one is doing or thinking "at the moment" is a dream the next moment, the cloud switching from hill to valley, from valley to hill, as soon as one turns one's eye there. When the cloud, the dream, the gray specter, appears

permanent, at all four points of the compass, when one has lost the sense
of a continual awakening each moment from the dream of the last
moment, then the dream is permanent, and "choice" has been overtaken by "fate." But though the condition of dream, or cloud, may be
achieved permanently, the condition of choice, awakeness, cannot be
permanently achieved in Scott's world, perhaps even should not be
permanently achieved. Edward becomes more and more a figure of fun
as he struggles away from the dream of each moment toward the dream
of the next: "I am the child of caprice" he laments (p. 334); "You are not
celebrated for knowing your own mind very pointedly," grins Fergus
(p. 361). And the whole court, both the real politikers and the passionate
Jacobites, breaks into laughter when, one of the courtiers having
erupted in violent argument and drawn his sword in the conference,
"Waverley lifted his head as if he had just awakened from a dream, and
asked, with great composure, what the matter was" (p. 327).

No, at some level, at some point, it seems necessary to surrender to
the "matter," the cloud, the dream, to cease struggling away, struggling
awake, to choose the permanent fate. Edward's fate, chosen, appropriated, when he was a child, is Waverley-Honour, and in one sense all his
choices, all his awakenings, are a process of gathering into himself all the
deeds (dreams) of his family's past so that appropriation, usurpation,
becomes, in fact, inheritance. This is the slippery surface of the "coming
home" topos: the appropriated thing becomes actual legitimate home
after one has modeled oneself into the master it needs. After all, it is
also at the novel's time some Sixty Years Since the Stuart "home" was
appropriated by the present rulers of Britain. Edward, and the nation at
large, feel irresistibly the legitimizing claim of that house which has
acted kingship for the required two generations, and now *has* kingship.

Yet if we look more closely at the coming home topos, we see it has its
reversal inside itself too. Charles Edward Stuart embodies this side of
the topos most clearly, coming home to a divided and changed nation,
driving south toward London and then forced north again, toward exile,
by his own troops—"like a dog in a string, whether he will or no,"
comments Fergus MacIvor (p. 363). Edward enacts this reversal too, in
a curious, hidden, comic way, for it is part of the "Waverley" identity as
it is of the Stuart. The two ancestral memories that most seriously
shaped him are, first, of a young Waverley heir desperately riding *away*
from home to provide a diversion while the fleeing uncle of the present
fleeing Stuart makes his escape, and dying in that action; and second, of
a Crusader Waverley husband presumed dead and returning "an unnoticed spectre" to find his fiance married and his house taken, yet who
draws his sword to recover his own and then, accepting the inner deeper

level of Waverley fate, "turned away for ever from the house of his ancestors" (p. 21). These two earlier stories will be played out, with some variation, in *Woodstock* and *The Betrothed*, once *Ivanhoe* has released Scott from the nearer, regionalist dream-situation of *Waverley*. In this first novel Edward enacts no such exile. Flora prophesies of him, "You would forever refer to the idea of domestic happiness" (p. 175), and so it seems to prove. Yet it is interesting to note that Edward does not go directly home to Waverley-Honour after he has returned to London from his northern adventures. He goes instead in search of Rose Brad-wardine, to assure for himself and his "home" the fertile mate who was so conspicuously absent from the earlier generation at Waverley, whom his Civil War ancester William died before claiming, whom his Crusad-ing ancestor Willibert lost to another. With the paternal help of his former prisoner, Col. Talbot, who married the mate who was lost to his uncle, he rescues the Bradwardine fortunes and assures himself of Rose before returning to Waverley-Honour in the chapter "Dulce Domum" to await the legal "restoration" of his good name, then journeys away from home to be married. After the marriage Rose and Edward break their journey at the restored lowland mansion of Tully Veolan, Rose's home, which is to be, legally, Waverley's second son's heritage (p. 443). And there, not at home but, at best, on the periphery of home, the novel closes. The occasion is a feast during which, after considerable thought about the hopelessly confused priorities not only between the Presbyte-rian Kirk and the Episcopal Church of Scotland but also between the old and new owners of Tully Veolan, the Baron "requested Mr. Morton, as the stranger, would crave a blessing,—observing, that Mr. Rubrick, who was at *home*, would return thanks" (p. 445). Mr. Rubrick, in Scott's own italics at *home*, is the Episcopal cleric and Bradwardine's chaplain: Mr. Morton, the Presbyterian, Waverley's own representative, is the stranger.[12]

Ivanhoe: Arrows Out of Secret Leaves

"Here is someone either asleep or lying dead at the foot of the cross," the irritated Normans remark as they ride, lost, through the Great Forest that dominates *Ivanhoe*: but it is not the last time they will be mistaken about him. The figure is neither dead nor asleep but thinking, and irritated in his turn: "it is discourteous in you to disturb my thoughts" (p. 20). Brian de Bois Guilbert and Prior Aymer de Mauleverer are foreigners and usurpers in the land; their dress and weapons and ser-vants are Norman, Flemish, Turkish, Saracen, and the "sly voluptuary" is easily visible under the mein and garb of the first, as is the "storm of passion" under the eight-pointed cross of the second. They ride the forest arrogantly as owners, but they are easily misled and might die of the forest's traps except that the disturbed thinker, whose Pilgrim's hat hides his identity like his posture at the crossroads masked his character, knows how to guide them. He is even more emphatically a stranger than they, "but the stranger seemed to know, as if by instinct, the soundest ground and the safest points of passage" (p. 20). For, muffled and muted, "exclaiming in good French" and keeping his Saxon thoughts to himself, the stranger is coming home.

Where is "home"? The castle of Ivanhoe was, it appears, young Wilfrid's inheritance, perhaps his birthplace, but the Norman conquerer took it. Then Wilfrid accepted his own inheritance back as a gift from the Norman King Richard, the first of a series of deeds taking him closer to the usurper and farther from his "fathers." Then Wilfrid and Richard went on Crusade to Palestine, leaving their country but trying to recover their Christian "home," and now both are homeless and countryless, suspended dead or asleep at the crossroads between "home" and home. Richard's younger brother John has retaken the manor Ivanhoe and awarded it to Reginald Front de Boeuf, and is gathering forces at York to formalize his informal usurpation of Richard's throne. Wilfrid is at the crossroads leading toward his father's home, Rotherwood, seat of Cedric the Saxon. At no time does Wilfrid head for, or speak of, Ivanhoe as his home. Lost, hidden, tainted as this home is, the absence of Ivanhoe from the settings of the novel is peculiar. But it is appropriate, and, on still another level, as I mean to argue shortly, it is only an apparent absence. Torquilstone, the neighboring Saxon castle awarded to and taken by the family Front de Boeuf, stands in for Ivanhoe.

Torquilstone is a powerful fortress in the heart of the great forest in which the novel opens. "This extensive wood," where once the Dragon of Wantley "haunted" and once outlaws roamed, and once the main battles of the Wars of the Roses were fought, this forest, says Scott's narrator, is "our chief scene" (p. 1). The settings which seem so cleanly to divide the novel in three—Ashby-de-la-Zouche with its gay tiltyard, Torquilstone with its hotly defended barbicans and its cellar packed full of gunpowder, monkish Templestowe with its hidden cells and its witch-pyre—are surrounded by, or bordered by, can only be reached by going through, the great forest. This forest, glade receding into glade, avenue opening toward avenue, this landscape which in almost Hardyesque fashion is "completed" by "human figures" but in no sense owned or dominated by them, this scene of "intermingling" woods and "discoloured light" in which "the eye delights to lose itself while the imagination considers . . . paths to yet wilder scenes of sylvan solitude" (p. 4), is the real home of the English, says John Fowles. It is, his artist character Daniel Martin says, "the secret place that is also a redoubt"; here the Robin Hood myth "changes from merely symbolizing folk-aspirations in social terms to enshrining a dominant mental characteristic, an essential behavior, an archetypal *movement* (akin to certain major vowel-shifts in the language itself) of the English imagination" (*Daniel Martin*, pp. 288–89).

Coming home to this place, Ivanhoe, asleep at the crossroads, and Richard, the Sluggish Knight, find one already there before them, an active, orderly being secure in the fastness of his intermingling identities and discolored reputation, Locksley, Diccon Bend-the-Bow, Cleave-the-Wand, Robin Hood. In the clever orchestration of the image of "the hero" which Scott has fashioned for his "English" novel, Wilfrid and Locksley, both hooded men, both familiar with the mystery of the forest, occupy in tandem, in palimpsest, the center. Whatever images of untamed energy or Puckish anarchy might have accrued to the pre-*Ivanhoe* Robin Hood, Donald Bean Lean, the linking of Locksley with Wilfrid, rather than with the dark hero Richard, signals the new Robin Hood of *our* civilization. He is an outlaw, yes, but fundamentally he is the manager-king of a hidden but emphatically civil society.

Flashing around Wilfrid and Locksley, splendid, barely recoverable, finally lost, is the "brilliant and rapid meteor" (p. 409) of Richard Coeur de Lion. At the comic-epic periphery of this image, unmoving, unkillable, is the swine-constellation of the Saxon-hero, Athelstane, and at the tragic Gothic periphery, coldly fiery, stable and self-consuming, "separated from life," is the dark star of Norman Brian de Bois Guilbert. These latter two, archetypes of their races, cancel each other out in the end. For Athelstane, the last Saxon Prince, receives an annihilating blow at Torquilstone from the Norman and goes to his grave: though, having earlier eaten enough for two men he rises from the grave "a wiser man than I descended into it" and will now "be king in my own domains and nowhere else" (p. 427). And Bois Guilbert, the Norman self-reduced to pure amoral will, receives only a mild blow at Templestowe from the weakened Saxon Ivanhoe, but dies of it, because he sought death as his fate. And the heroism of Richard is already a national monument to his friends, and as such a subject for respect, and humor, a national resource splendid, and useful, if rightly managed.

For management is the real topos of heroism in *Ivanhoe*, as it was, interestingly, in Shakespeare's history plays—not rule, but management. And in *Ivanhoe*, again, interestingly, as in the Henry plays, the emblem for the kidnapping of rule (romance) by management (realism),

that idea central to our new civilization, is the horse. Henry Bolingbroke
manhandled the second Richard Plantagenet off the throne, but it was
when he kidnapped Richard's horse, and the horse willingly carried him
through the public streets, that London accepted his management too.
Henry's son Hal stays afoot while he is deliberating (or dead, or asleep at
the crossroads), and mocks the romance heroics of the changeling
Harry, who has earned his chivalric sobriquet Hotspur—"He kills himself some six or a dozen Scots before breakfast and then . . . 'give my
roan horse a drench!'" But when the time comes, Hal knows what image
he must appropriate from his antagonist: the soldier Vernon saw him
vault onto his charger "like feathered Mercury" prepared to "witch the
world with noble horsemanship" (*Henry IV, Part One*, p. 124).

Ivanhoe too is coming home afoot, in the manner of a Pilgrim, or of a
Saxon warrior, but he does not (cannot?) move past the crossroads until
he has borrowed a horse, and horsemanship, from his Norman antagonists. Leaving Rotherwood frustrated and by stealth, his identity revealed to the fellow bondsman Gurth, Ivanhoe borrows two mules for
the journey, as appropriate to the Jew he is rescuing from Bois Guilbert's avarice, and to the semi-clerical identity he is temporarily vowed
to. But even Isaac knows his disguise, for he saw "spurs of gold" hidden
in the Palmer's dress, and he guesses the Palmer wants the horse to go
with them. Mounted again, not by deceived Normans but by a reluctant
Jew, Wilfrid makes his appearance as the Disinherited Knight at Ashby,
becoming the central figure at a tournament marked by bizarre feats of
horsemanship.

This late feudal craft, one of the "fantastic arts" Cedric despises his
son for learning at the Norman court, is a major medium for the rivalry of
Ivanhoe and Bois Guilbert too, but not quite in the way that we might
imagine. The horse is the symbol of power, of course, and yet in all the
encounters of the rivals in tournament and battle, the man who wins is
the man who can stabilize, neutralize, even, in one astonishing moment, reverse, this icon of power. Bois Guilbert fares headlong forward,
to frustration, defeat, and finally death, while Ivanhoe displays his
"dexterity" in one scene by "reining back his steed in the same moment"
that he struck (p. 118), in another by reducing "his fiery steed from a
state of violent emotion and high excitation to the stillness of an equestrian statue" (p. 86). In the key image, during the tournament at Ashby,
Ivanhoe "reined his horse backward down the slope which he had
ascended, and compelled him in the same manner to move backward
through the lists, till he reached the northern extremity, where he
remained stationary" (pp. 79–80).

This occasionally absurd, almost magical power of Ivanhoe to reverse his field of power from vulnerable motion to invulnerable motionlessness, to move out from the iconography of the equestrian statue or the legendary pose and then back to that cover, links him again with the Robin Hood–Locksley figure at the center of this novel. For as Bois Guilbert enacts a reversal of Ivanhoe's deeds, moving forward and groundward to his doom as Ivanhoe moves backward and horseward to his success, Locksley enacts Ivanhoe's deeds, for the nonequestrian classes, on the ground, in an archery contest which repeats many of the images of the tournament.

Here, Locksley steps forward to take his bow, telling King John that he is continuing an action begun the day before: "I know not how your grace might relish the winning of a third prize by one who has unwittingly fallen under your displeasure" (p. 126). The first encounter between Norman and Saxon archers, as between Norman and Saxon horsemen, is equal, and interestingly similar. Each horseman hits the other identically and their lances "burst into shivers up to the very grasp" (p. 80), and Locksley duplicates Hubert's shot into the very center of the round target so successfully that his later arrow "split to shivers" the arrow of his antagonist (p. 128).

When Ashby's tournament ends, and the antagonists move north through the forest toward home, or York, which is Isaac's home and the seat both of John's rebellion and, we learn later, of Richard's counter-rebellion, Locksley's yeoman outlaws begin to dominate the novel. Cedric's party and Isaac's, which secretly contains the victorious but wounded Ivanhoe, are captured by outlaws in Lincoln green, actually Normans in outlaw disguise, and taken to Torquilstone Castle, once Saxon, bloodily usurped by Reginald Front de Boeuf's father. The returned King Richard, who has aided Ivanhoe in the tournament while disguised as "The Black Sluggard," travels through the forest to head off the conspiracy at York, meets and befriends Locksley's outlaw friends, and joins them in their attempt to rescue their friends from Torquilstone.

While Ivanhoe lies wounded inside, Locksley outside takes over his function of managing, reining, and protecting the romantic leadership of Richard, the Black Sluggard, the Knight of the Fetterlock. Absolved momentarily of that function, and flat on his back where he can only imagine, not see, the carnage of human war released from the rules of tournament, Ivanhoe undergoes a curious though temporary romantic apotheosis. Kidnapped and a prisoner, he listens to the derring-do outside described by Rebecca and praises it in heated terms both romantic and ghoulish: "The love of battle is the food upon which we live . . . we live not longer than while we are victorious and re-

nowned . . . Glory, maiden,—glory! . . . gilds our sepulchre and embalms our name" (p. 275).[13]

I want to return to this un-Wilfrid-like outburst,this Norman fanaticism, in a moment. For now let it be noticed that it occurs while the
Saxon knight is in a Saxon castle which has been reshaped with Norman
fortifications. Contaminated beyond redemption by the Norman deeds
it has witnessed—murder, usurpation, rape, lust, and greed of all kinds,
and, finally, the crime de la crime for Scott, the one Waverley fears he
has committed when the news of his father's death and his uncle's
imprisonment reaches him, parricide. The Saxon daughter of the house,
Ulrica, had been mistress of Reginald and his father and had caused the
parricide; the quintessence of her revenge, causing the son to kill his
father, repeats itself in her, who destroys her father's house. Torquilstone's daughter, reverted back to the gods of her Scandinavian ancestors, embalms herself in its flames and gathers in its broken stones as her
sepulchre. The escape of Ivanhoe and Cedric is only a side effect to the
orgy of destruction which she hymns from the burning battlements in
imagery disquietingly like the images that the sick Ivanhoe had used:

> Whet the steel . . . thy banquet is prepared. . . .
> The destroyer of forests shall shake his red crest.
> His joy is in the clashing swords and broken bucklers;
> He loves to lick the hissing blood as it bursts warm from
> the wound!
>
> (Pp. 298–99)

With this direct evocation of the destroyer of forests, the novel retreats
back to the forest and the keeper of the forest, the arbiter of its justice,
creator of its alternate world, sender of arrows out of secret leaves—
Robin Hood.[14] Since Ivanhoe is still inactive, rescued by Richard and
sent to a monastery to recover, Locksley retains the hero-manager's
role, settling affairs among all the races and classes of the assembly until
Richard, who can certainly use this lesson, is moved to "expressing his
surprise at . . . so much of civil policy amongst persons cast out" from
law. "Good fruit, Sir Knight," replies the outlaw, stating the necessary
creed for all historians who dare to deal with origins, "will sometimes
grow on a sorry tree" (p. 325).

Nothing shows the centrality, and the mutuality, of Ivanhoe and
Locksley in Scott's narrative so much as their activity in their first
meeting, which does not occur, properly, since they act undercover in
each other's place, in each other's absence, throughout the narrative,
until forty pages from the end. Ivanhoe, still weak from his wounds at
Ashby, pursues the reckless Richard into the forest so he can be with

him to blunt the impact of his Norman entry into Saxon Coningsburgh for Athelstane's "funeral." Locksley, having pressed on Richard the horn he won at Ashby and urged him to call for him at need, rescues the monarch from an assassination attempt minutes before Ivanhoe rides onto the scene. Richard wanted no help and has to overcome "a blaze of hasty resentment" (p. 403) at the rescue. All identities are finally revealed—except, of course, the true name of Robin Hood/Locksley—and the king disappears into the forest for a postadventure revel with the outlaws from which he must be yet again rescued. And here the responsible Wilfrid and the managing Locksley are at one: "I would not that he [Richard] dallied with time which the circumstances of his kingdom may render precious," muses the outlaw, and "It must be by your management, then, gallant yeoman," agrees the knight, "for each hint I have essayed to give him serves only to induce him to prolong [his stay]" (p. 410). Both Richard and the outlaw band, romantics all, are tricked into dispersing after a false "Norman blast" of the horn secretly ordered by Robin Hood, and Richard, forgiving him perforce, links the two managers again: "If I had Ivanhoe, on the one hand, to give grave advice, and recommend it by the sad gravity of his brow, and thee, on the other, to trick me into what thou thinkest my own good, I should have as little the freedom of mine own will as any King in Christendom or Heathenesse" (p. 412).

Commiserating with his brother monarch ("Such a one is my lieutenant Little John, who is even now on an expedition as far as the borders of Scotland" [p. 412]), Locksley guides the knights out of the forest, which Richard promises to liberate from Norman tyranny and make into free national territory, and fades back for good into his "redoubt," the very figure, as John Fowles has said, of free national territory. For as Scott's narrator feels obliged to add, Richard was unable to deliver on his promise, the forest remained interdicted, its fellowship remained exile-outlaws, and its hero, instead of coming forth from the secrets of "Locksley," "Bend the Bow," "Cleave the Wand," and "Robin Hood" and reclaiming/revealing his own secret "good name besides" (p. 321), pulled back his hood over his face and submitted to immortality. And the rest of his career, says the narrator, is "to be found in these black-letter garlands, once sold at the low and easy rate of one half-penny" (p. 412), that career which Carlyle was to describe later, in *Past and Present*, as living under the greenwood tree in some universal suffrage manner.

For all his "civil policy" and good management during his narrative stint as Ivanhoe's alter-ego, his internal Saxon countermyth to his external Norman glory-hound, Robin Hood here remains, as that

"second Robin Hood" Donald Bean Lean did, a secret figure, a magic
figure offering monarch, characters, and readers alike "the hand of a
true Englishman, though an outlaw for the present" (p. 326). And the
present lasts forever. Disappearing into the great forest, Locksley par-
ries Richard's final inquiry after his name: "as I do not pray to be
admitted into your mystery, be not offended that I preserve my own"
(p. 326). But he *is* admitted to everyone's mystery, Richard's, Wilfrid's,
Gurth's, Prior Aymer's—even the most secret hoard of the fanatically
secret Isaac is known to Diccon Bend-the-Bow. By the end of the novel
no mystery remains but his.

Behind the mystery of kingship, behind even the mystery of outlawry which supports it, lies a third mystery, the sacred, whose visible
setting in the novel, corrupt and usurped like Norman Ashby and Saxon
Torquilstone, is the Christian Templestowe, and whose invisible, unre-
capturable setting is Jerusalem. Seeking origins, seeking the sorry tree
on which grow the mixed fruits of western civilization, Scott goes back,
in mind, to the first Act of Chivalry, and supplies as dragon-guards to
this coombe of the sacred, two of the novel's most memorable characters—the unbelieving Jew, Isaac, and the foresworn priest, Bois Guilbert. "I know you Christians," Isaac tells the disguised warrior pilgrim
in as ironic a tone as he dares use, "the noblest of you will take the staff
and sandal in superstitious penance, and walk afoot to visit the graves of
dead men" (p. 58). Trying to make common cause with the Jewess
Rebecca, the Templar says: "Answer me not by urging the difference of
our creeds; within our secret conclaves we hold these nursery tales in
derision"; to him the Holy Sepulchre is only "a barren desert" (p. 220).

It is important to note that Bois Guilbert's sterile skepticism is based,
like Isaac's, upon deracination: like the Jews the Templars are uprooted
from native soil, wanderers on the earth, visibly separated from all
ordinary society by the eight-pointed white cross worn like the Jew's
yellow star on the shoulder or breast. Like the Jew the Christian
Priest-Knight has been, according to Scott's narrative, warped by the
separation: like the Jew the Templar displays poverty outside and hides
his wealth inside. Barred from the normal fruitfulness of land, crop,
family, inheritance, and, most of all, from the fertile responsibilities of
national identity, the Jew and the Priest have developed into separate
centers of power, international, anti-national. But Isaac has at least a
disinherited community to give him stability under all the shifty, half-
conscious roles he plays. Bois Guilbert, despite his talk about an elite
brotherhood within the Templars, has chosen the fate of deracination,
not met it on the way toward a faith or in loyalty to an international ideal.
He chose it when he came home, like Ivanhoe, like Willibert of

Waverley, from chivalric deeds abroad, and found his Rowena, Adelaide de Montemare, married to another: "Since that day I have separated myself from life and its ties" (p. 219). "My manhood must know no domestic home," he continues: his nature is exactly opposite that of Waverley and Ivanhoe. He is building himself an abstract kingdom of power in the single will and needs, he says, "a kindred spirit to share it" (p. 220) and place to display it. Rebecca, whose will matches his and whose dark beauty is of the type he accepted in Palestine when the fair beauty of home rejected him, is in character, though not in values, his kindred spirit. And the proper place of his kingdom, as he sees it (and of hers, as she holily repeats in prayer each night) is Jerusalem. Once Bois Guilbert's ambition reached only so far as the Grand Mastership of the Templars; now, besieging Rebecca at the English Templestowe, he offers her not only his own greater imperial adventure but also the accomplishment of her race's own coming-home myth, the restoration of the original Temple:

> Listen to me, Rebecca. England—Europe—is not the world. There are spheres in which we may act, ample enough even for my ambition. We will go to Palestine. . . .Thou shalt be a queen, Rebecca: in Mount Carmel shall we pitch the throne which my valour will gain for you. (P. 384).

"A dream—an empty vision of the night" is Rebecca's response to the invocation of this myth, as it is her response throughout the novel to every invocation of myth, from Ivanhoe's frantic hymn to chivalric self-immolation at Torquilstone to the vision of interracial love which was her own deepest temptation, the home she could not, waking, see her way home to. The value of healing which she represents is a value for the waking, wounded, world. Mythicized, as everything too easily is at Templestowe, this value becomes witchcraft, black magic, the dark sacred, to those who practice the "fantastic chivalry of the Nazarenes" (p. 276). When the scene shifts from Robin Hood's forest to the monastery of crusading Knights, cells breeding mortal corruptions of the immortal ideals at its origin, there enters, right on cue in a Scott narrative, the figure of the reformer, the cleanser of the Temple, fittingly named Lucas de Beaumanoir. Seeking the origin of the sacred, one finds nothing earlier than a heritage already spoiling, taken over, kidnapped, in need of redemption. And the act of redemption, taking back the temple, requires at Templestowe, as it did in Jerusalem, a death. The death of the innocent Rebecca is planned by Beaumanoir as an appeal to God to restore holiness to the Templars. It is delayed by Ivanhoe, who rides exhausted to this new Jerusalem in accordance with his Nazarene inheritance to substitute himself. The cleansing death is accomplished finally by Bois Guilbert: his complex enactment of his fatal "separation from life and all its ties" and his "vengeance on myself" has, up to now, occurred secondhand in the deaths of others, and now reaches its real target as he lies unmarked on the ground at Templestowe.[15]

The brief recreation of the first Act of Christian Chivalry at home, at Templestowe, recovers the heavenly Jerusalem, momentarily, in a narrative whose lurid background has been the failure of that recovery—even more, the declining of the task of recovery. When those who are under oath to recover the holy city are found purposefully making through the English forest for the house of Cedric the Saxon, says the disguised Ivanhoe at his first meeting with Bois Guilbert, "can you wonder that a peaceful peasant like me should decline the task which they have abandoned?" (p. 21). Something worse than the frustrating compromises which entrapped Richard at Acre, worse than the futility and corruption which left the returning Ivanhoe ill and "asleep or dead" at the foot of the Sunken Cross, has occurred with the Crusaders, however. For Reginald Front de Boeuf had also been in Palestine, licensed by sacred responsibility. And here, "perhaps," Scott's narrator remarks, "he had learnt his lesson of cruelty" (p. 197). Both Front de Boeuf and Bois Guilbert have come back from Palestine with Saracen slaves, mysterious demon presences who undertake the lower acts of cruelty from which chivalry flinches. And while "the Saracen" will acquire other qualities and identities when Scott's narratives encounter them on their own ground in later novels, in *Ivanhoe* they are connected with that dreadful side of Palestine which is not Jerusalem but Askalon, home of the Philistines and their cannibal God Dagon. On their way away from "home" but "home" to Jerusalem, the European Crusaders were stopped in just the wrong place for learning lessons. Prince John argues that he may legitimately seize the English possessions of those who, like his brother and Ivanhoe, "have wandered to foreign countries and can neither render homage nor service when called upon." But his priest advisor, Prior Aymer, adds a clerkly qualification:

> The Blessed Jerusalem could not indeed be termed a foreign country. She was *communis mater*—the mother of all Christians. . . . But . . . the crusaders under Richard never proceeded much farther than Askalon, which, as all the world knew, was a town of the Philistines, and entitled to none of the privileges of the Holy City. (P. 123)

The privilege of the Holy City is to make a home for the sacred, and to defend that home. The Jerusalem that Scott respects is the Jerusalem that repels; the Jerusalem that fights to defend itself is the only setting where fighting is, perhaps, legitimate. But that legitimacy is long lost: "I am . . . sprung from a race whose courage was distinguished in the defense of their own land," says its last representative, a woman, a healer, a mourner, "but the sound of the trumpet wakes Judah no longer" (p. 276). Ivanhoe, impatient, but shifty, as a chivalric hero must be, mocks the Jewess's uncertainity about the "fantastic chivalry of the Nazarenes": "Thou art no Christian, Rebecca; and to thee are unknown those high feelings" (p. 276). Yet the psychoracial turmoil in Western Christendom that raised to such heights the fantasy of the defense of the land of sacred origin is clear to the meditative historian of Scott's narrative. If Jerusalem is *communis mater* to Christians and is in the hands of usurpers, then to defend her requires to attack her, to preserve her is to destroy her, to recover her is to lose her. Such is, on the national level, the case dramatized at Saxon Torquilstone in the stones of the building and in the mother figure of Ulrica, de-Saxonized, even de-Christianized in the task of recovering her home. Such too is the case on the level of the sacred: the intolerable psychosis of attacking and destroying the Holy Place in order to defend and recover it properly yields stalemate, abandonment of the task. This is preferable, but only just, to self-destruction.

This we see in the two final scenes of the novel, king facing king, queen facing queen, right facing right—poignant stalemate, and then abandonment. As the quarrel between Ivanhoe and Bois Guilbert at Templestowe, right facing clear wrong, is cathartically settled, Richard and his civil forces ride in to challenge Beaumanoir and his defenders of the sacred. For some moments the two lines of spears, each defending a right, confront each other: Scott's narrator giving dignity and some nobility to the "formidable and experienced" body of knight-priests who resist, as they must, the "doom" of encroaching secular monarchy (p. 44). The crisis passes in stalemate, the Templars departing in state to refer "our quarrel" to the Pope and Princes of "Christendom"—that high kingdom of fantasy of which "chivalry" is the cement—and Richard paying them tribute: "By the splendours of Our Lady's brow! It is pity of their lives that these Templars are not so trusty as they are disciplined and valiant" (pp. 441–42).

An interestingly similar scene closes the novel. Rebecca of York visits Rowena on the second morning after she has become the wife of Ivanhoe. There has of course never been a real quarrel between Rebecca and Rowena: their rivalry for the crown of the Queen of Love and Beauty at Ashby was strictly the creation of the men around them. But they do represent not only two kinds of beauty but two kinds of fortitude, and of love. Rebecca's special qualities, both lovely and dangerous, arise from suffering; her mind is realistic and her soul mystic. Rowena's special qualities, both lovely and dangerous, arise from security; her mind is romantic but her soul domestic. Both characters are "right"; Rebecca's right like the Templars'—dark, mystic, and connected with the origins of things—is unmistakably receding back to its coombe, its secret leaves, its unrecoverable Jerusalem, where Rowena's "right"—sunny, domestic, and connected with achieved things—is covering the other right. Yet there is a curious moment of confrontation between the two women. Rebecca has come not only to say farewell and to pass on to Rowena the diamond necklace and eardrops which once at Ashby drew men's eyes to her uncovered bosom, but to ask the Christian woman to unveil. Rowena, "expecting the same from my visitant," complies (p. 448). Both women color deeply, uncovered, and then recognize in each other the competing principle which animates each: Rebecca eyeing "the world's pride" in the wife, and Rowena recognizing the sacred in the face which is headed for the Jewish equivalent of convent life. Each knows herself and her opposite, and accepts her proper "home"; yet "an involuntary tremor" from Rebecca and "anxious inquiries" from Rowena suggest that in each heart the opposition has not been reconciled so much as stalemated, and the fight declined (pp. 449–50). And as for the crusader Wilfrid, who has hung stalemated between a divided home and a divided Jerusalem for most of his life, and who retains both the "bonds of early affection" for Rowena and the "deep impression" left by Rebecca, "it would be inquiring too curiously to ask" (p. 450), says the narrator, how much of his national, social, religious, personal, and sexual conflict is reconciled and how much is simply abandoned.

A Destiny of Choice: *Rob Roy* and *Quentin Durward*

"I am, under the king, in some authority here."
"Under which king, Besonian?"

Be it better, be it worse,
Be ruled by him that has the purse.[1]

Though there are monarchs in the early verse narratives, and royalty dicing with men's lives at the edges of the first Scots novels, the author of Waverley was not fundamentally interested in kings until *Ivanhoe* allowed him to be so. The novels immediately thereafter—*The Monastery, The Abbot, Kenilworth, The Fortunes of Nigel, Peveril of the Peak, Quentin Durward (The Pirate* is an odd exception, of which more later)—rely to a greater or lesser extent on the charismatic presence of the source of authority, the king. Even *Redgauntlet*, the post-*Ivanhoe* novel most like *Waverley*, manages to make the climactic entrance of an older Charles Edward Stuart into his and the novel's "domain" a much more narratively significant action than young Charlie's stay in the final pages of *Waverley*.

No, as the author first conceived his narratives and borrowed the iconic demand of Shakespeare's Pistol to set on the frontispiece of the series, it was the dilemma of the captains, not the kings, which interested him—how to find the favoring service, how to submit to the most personally fertile authority, "Under which king, Besonian?" may one freely sit down to one's destiny, having first made the choice which is the mark of manhood. Under which king may one's double-sided desire to be "in some authority," that is, to submit to authority so that one may exercise it, be satisfied?[2] For all the young squires of all the divided houses—and there are only divided houses now that "home"

49

has receded into the fastness of the forest of legend, subject to its multiple interpreters—the question surfaces in consciousness as the third phase of a process which always starts as an intuitive flight from the destined service, authority, king, head of the house, chief of the name, the father. Dreamingly eluding him/it, the squire, son, heir, captain, puts himself, half willingly, in the way to be kidnapped, freed, reinterpreted, by other royalties, rights, fictions, until the question rises to consciousness and forces the choice. Since it is a choice, it becomes a destiny. Since it is a choice constructed by the author of Waverley, it is, somehow, at some level, always partly the original service, the eluded destiny, that is chosen at the end.

The romance-structure of the choice never changes in the Waverley novels—we have first the flight, then the quest, the risk, the error, the recovery, the commitment. But the object of the choice—the specific authority, service, destiny—is in each novel's case a real thing, a historical thing. Paradoxically, but truly, as Lukacs admired Scott for seeing, kings and destinies come and go, changing, revealing the "real history" of the world in the nature of their changes. But captains-choosing, the figure who in each age, divided between loyalty to the old and a dim perception of the new, must "waver," register the old dream and the new reality, and then stabilize his identity in real history—this figure is always the same. Since this figure, this element, this function in the tale, as the structuralists might call it, always remains the same, it constitutes functionally the "romance" of the Waverley novels. Paradoxically but again truly, it is the king and his changes, object, never protagonist, of the romantic choices, who contributes, functionally, the realism. And this obtains whether the choosing youth has the *emotionally* "realistic" temperament and the chosen king the "romantic," as in *Ivanhoe*, or the choosing youth has the emotionally "romantic" temperament and the chosen authority the "realistic," as in *Rob Roy*, as in *Quentin Durward*.

These two novels, even more different in construction, setting, and tone, than *Waverley* and *Ivanhoe*, still yield similar dividends, I think, when considered as repetition, extension, confirmation of essentially the same act of imagination—in this case the penetration of the mystery of authority. Here too Scott makes use of his Shakespearean source, offering his form of *Hamlet* in *Rob Roy* and the Henry plays in *Quentin Durward*. As in the first chapter, I should like to propose a general argument for treating this mystery through these two novels, and then look at important workings-out of it in each.

Like *Ivanhoe*, *Quentin Durward* seemed to mark another major departure from Scott's "destined" patrimony; where in *Ivanhoe* the author of Waverley stepped over the provincial border into national mythmaking, in *Quentin Durward*, his first novel off British soil, he moved into international mythmaking. But then, in *Waverley*, even in *Ivanhoe*, the king had always come from his exile "over the water," or been summoned thence to his "home" on the island. As Quentin Durward hesitates in the first pages at the edge of the French stream on whose far bank the king sits waiting, we can begin to see some of the reasons why this "medieval" novel too is less a departure for Scott than an arrival.[3]

It arrives, in its first chapter, in the domain from which the protagonist of *Rob Roy* fled at the opening of that book, and to which he returned toward the end, to the service of the new international authority, icon of its capitalist myth, the merchant-prince. In his first chapter Frank Osbaldistone comes back to Britain from his father's branch counting-house in France, having learned there a love of "literature and manly exercises" rather than of duties, debentures, and mercantile processes. Moreover "I had lived long enough in the territories of the *Grand Monarque* to contract a hearty aversion to arbitrary exertion of authority" (p. 11). When the elder Osbaldistone offers him, in a brusque and arbitrary way which partly conceals a desperate love, the heir's responsibility in his banking house, Frank resists this destiny in lofty terms borrowed from that romantic France of literature and manly exercises—"I will never sell my liberty for gold" (p. 18). Fleeing the arbitrary, or even rational, or even loving, hand of authority— "Perhaps—for who can judge of their own heart?—I felt it unmanly to yield on the first summons, and expected farther solicitation" (p. 20), Frank accepts his father's punishment, enforced rustication at his uncle's Northumberland estate, intending to finish his translation of (what else?) *Orlando Furioso* while awaiting his father's capitulation to the destiny of all fathers.

Fathers are bound to rely on their sons for the continuation of their house, their immortal/earthly "body": "what would become of the world of schemes which he had formed unless his son were moulded into a commercial Hercules, fit to sustain the weight when relinquished by falling Atlas?" (p. 7). And of course what would become of the patriarchal scheme of the world did Hercules refuse to sustain Atlas who sustains all? Frank feels so confident that Atlas needs him that even when the older man, like a stronger Henry IV, actually arranges to exchange his "Harry" for one more fit and willing to sustain his commercial empire, his brother's son Rashleigh, the younger man begins detailing in his imagination "the articles of our supposed treaty," especially those "on which I would make a firm stand" (p. 23).[4] But this firm stand is and will be compromised by that flaw in the destiny of all sons. They have no

money, no property, no "right" of their own. Only "labour in getting
and care in augmenting, can make a right of property," says the older
man (p. 17), describing the rite of loss, labor, and gain with which each
new generation must establish that right. Disdaining commercial labor,
its rite and its right, Frank yet expected Atlas to support him, expected
an "independence," a "competence" (those two delicious Anglicisms for
cash money) as a gift. His freedom is thus, embarrassingly, tied in his
father's purse; therefore, says the father wryly of the son's plan to make a
profession of literature and manly exercises, "you wish to lean on my
arm, and yet to walk your own way? That can hardly be" (pp. 20–21). But
it can be, Frank thinks, if an older "right" be invoked, one not made by
labor but bound in the blood, the right of the son to the patrimony.

William Osbaldistone, however, is a new kind of man, "making"
right, making money as he does; perhaps he can, not like Atlas but like
Zeus, bestow it where he wishes, away from the son. Taking the great
north road out of London, "lord of my person" and of an ample purse,
Frank still feels a chill at the ease with which his father had apparently
"slipt a knot, usually esteemed the strongest which binds society
together" (p. 22). But of course Frank had "slipt" the knot first. Now, on
the loose, a kind of outlaw, he rides to the outlawed north, playfully
discoursing about, and pretending to his fellow travelers to be, a highwayman. And he is properly taken, retaken, not exactly mistaken, for
such. Exploring, fleeing, being pushed further north, he will meet the
avatars and business partners of his father at every stage, lean on them
while trying to walk his own way, until at the apogee of his flight from
service he finds himself in league with the mysterious king-merchant-
thief Rob Roy, who serves in his crooked way both the House of
Osbaldistone and the king over the water. And of the many flaws of that
service one of the most significant, in 1715, is that the money belongs to
the Osbaldistone, not to the Stuart. The aptly named Andrew Fairser-
vice, who attached himself to Frank, willy-nilly, through some mysterious premonition of his master's final "choice" of his own house, acts out
in advance the proverbial wisdom of his mother about the new world:

> Be it better, be it worse
> Be ruled by him that has the purse.
>
>   (P. 259)

But how new is the new world? As Scott looks back in his post-
Ivanhoe novels, to the time when a king was a king, when authority
paternal or monarchical existed pure, grounded firmly in the psychodrama of chivalry, he finds no such time, no such white shield, no such
king, Besonian. The kingship of John, and even of Richard the

Lionheart, is compromised, and of course fertilized, by the international protocommerce of the Jewish bankers, a commerce whose binding agent, in a distinction I will return to later, is "credit," not that "honor" which united Feudal Christendom. And when Quentin Durward swims the stream to the seat of authority in France, the France of the 1460s which is just about to become the great national power which the Osbaldistones know, he finds it occupied by a man in merchant's garb, a king disguised, or rather, undisguised, as a buyer and seller. And by his side, alarming and inevitable tool and "gossip" of the new authority, sits the hangman.

These two opening actions of the novels, Frank's rather sly and petulant flight from service, Quentin's merry and strong-thewed swim toward service, form that significant kind of opposition which serves ultimately as comparison. The two are brothers in many ways, active, self-directed, "fearlessly frank" as Quentin is,[5] passive and pushed and guarded as Frank is. Each, for instance, is cut off from "home" and self-criminalized by an act of robbery, though both robberies are "fictions." Quentin had actually arranged with the Abbot who educated him to steal the Abbot's falcon as a way of protecting the monks from the anger of clan Ogilvy, which had forced him to become a monk in order to end the house of Durward. And Frank had only playacted the preliminaries of robbery before his shadow-Osbaldistone, his cousin Rashleigh, made good the play and fully criminalized his rival. Frank's story ends with the destruction of all the male members of his uncle's family, whose inheritance he takes in combination with his father's; Quentin's story begins with the destruction of all the males of his family except one uncle, and ends, in a provocative sideways Oedipal snatch, with his appropriation of that uncle's prize-won bride. Thus in him, as in Frank, a split house, ruthlessly pruned, becomes one again. Frank and his bride, Quentin and his bride, move to their appointed places, both men owning to a guilty feeling of being "usurpers." As always in the Waverley novels their job is building domestic lives which keep the borders between north and south, chivalry and commerce, honor and credit; the one in Northumbria between Scotland and London, the other in Flanders between Burgundy and France.

Above all, both young men associate authority, to which manhood owes service, with that high blood—in both senses of the word—which is the carrier of "honor." Quentin, a wandering soldier of fortune, seeks a captaincy under the Prince whose service carries the most honor; he is drawn to Charles the Bold, Duke of Burgundy, by reports of the "honour to be won under his banner" (p. 48), and hesitates about the higher-blooded King of France, Louis XI, because he "gains his victories by his ambassadors' tongues" (p. 48), or even worse, by purchase or bribery. Frank, a self-exiled wandering poet and gentleman, rejects the mathematics and money, the conveyancing and deal-making, of his father's house, for the greater honor, not to say pleasure, of a scholar's or a soldier's life. And though Frank, every inch the modern man stricken with the burden of the past, wishes to evade the life of action, wishes not to "play the conspicuous part in society" (p. 16) which the head of the firm of Osbaldistone and Tresham would play, and Quentin, the Renaissance man stricken with the urgency of the future, must seek the life "where a brave deed . . . might work me a name" (p. 49), both recoil from the new alliance of authority and money.

Each has an elder counselor in the family to draw him back toward the new, or eternal, reality of authority. "You speak like a foolish boy," says Ludovic Lesly, "Le Balafre," to the reluctant Quentin:

> and yet . . . when I came hither I was nearly as simple: I could never think of a king but what I supposed him either sitting under the high dais . . . with a great gold crown upon his head, or else charging at the head of his troops like Charlemagne in the romaunts, or like Robert Bruce or William Wallace in our own true histories . . . Hark in thine ear, man—it is all moonshine in the water. Policy—policy does it all. (Pp. 48–49).

And to Frank, fascinated by the legendary Highlander "whose fate was doomed to have influence over, and connexion with my own" (p. 227), and entranced by the discovery of an utterly new, and as he imagines, romantic and feudal world in the glens north of merchant Glasgow, Baillie Nicol Jarvie must make the same disclaimer. Rob Roy MacGregor Campbell is "nane o' your great grandees o' chiefs, as they ca' them," but of a lower status, "weel born . . . and of gude gentle Hieland blude, though he may think weel that I care little about that nonsense—it's a' moonshine in water—waste threads and thrums, as we say" (p. 243).

Indeed the "documents and evidents" which testify to the relationship between the Glasgow man and Rob Roy, who is nevertheless the significant authority in the Highlands, are "amaist a' about borrowed siller" (p. 243). And it is kingly authority which has borrowed the money, turned its honor, quite literally, into credit.

This is an alarming development for the partisans of honor. But it has its defender in Baillie Nicol Jarvie, who responds to Frank's wish for advice on "the best way to act for my father's advantage and my own honor" with a warning which French Louis, in his more corrupt and violent way, will give to Quentin too:

> I maun hear naething about honour—we ken naething here but about credit. Honour is a homicide and a bloodspiller, that gangs about making frays in the street; but credit is a decent honest man, that sits at home and makes the pat play.[6] (P. 238)

Baillie Jarvie's conceit indicates an awareness that a change not merely material but psychic also is in process, from an economy of honor to an economy of credit. Now, the material consequences of the transition or negotiation between an economy of honor and one of credit are evident all through both novels, where the gold and silver crowns/coins of kings give way to the deeper magic of "policy," of paper, of credit. The plot of *Rob Roy* concerns a son's efforts first to evade that new economy and then to rescue it in the form of negotiable bonds or credits which had been stolen from his father's counting-house and transported north to the glens. There, primitive honor has already become a creditor of the London banking houses, who have bought the very trees off the hills. Frank must lay hands on that magic money, money only in the sense that it is backed by the credit of the House of Osbaldistone, or the House itself, its debtors and creditors, from the rascally Glasgow firm of MacVittie and Company to the Highland lairds and King Charles across the water himself, will collapse. Quentin Durward's honor jibbed at accepting a half cupful of coins from the mysterious but "liberal and authoritative" merchant who, not for the first time, "has found the true way to make gentlefolks serve at his beck" (p. 38). But the young man nevertheless finds himself in service to a monarch who has "bought thee, body and soul" (p. 125) with a paper commission in the Scots Guard of Archers.

He is astonished to be reminded by his uncle and fellow archer that in fact it is *only* a merchant-king like Louis who can provide service opportunities for soldiers of fortune like themselves, who would like to consider themselves knights-errant but who are actually mercenaries. And Louis, Le Balafre boasts, is so clever a merchant that he knows how to "fight with other men's swords and to wage his soldiers out of other men's purses" (p. 49). Fight and pay, in other words, on credit. Indeed it is finally Quentin's rescue of the king's credit that climaxes the story. Possessed of all but documentary proof of Louis's double-game with him, and with the Duke of Burgundy's rebellious burghers of Liege and his escaped vassal Countess of Croye, Quentin nevertheless testifies before the honorable, if homicidal, Charles the Bold, only to the evidence of the words of the king, backed by his psychic credit as king, and thus preserves that useful fiction, to the end of preventing war between the two nations.

This material fiction, called credit, allows the building of much larger material structures, nations, empires, than the golden crowns/coins of honor. But it also makes those structures more vulnerable to the rash deeds of honorable men or the careful undermining of manipulative men. The very fact that Credit sits at home rather than going about in the streets makes him twice as vulnerable to the frays of homicidal Honor when he does go out. King Louis was an honorable man, and a warrior, before he learned better, and now sits at home as much as possible in the "blind" (p. 20) castle, which offends the chivalric soul of young Quentin. He augments this inevitable blindness of Credit, however, by wandering the streets in the dress of a merchant, Maitre Pierre. But he nearly loses credit and life when he ventures out, in his crown, to meet the Duke of Burgundy in *his* castle. The senior Osbaldi-stone is robbed by his manipulating nephew when he leaves his House in London for a trip to the Continent, and the Baillie himself, reluctantly sallying north from Glasgow with Frank to recover the Osbaldistone-Jarvie credit, is, in a comic episode of considerable symbolic impact, hung by his skirts between air and water as he vainly retreats from the homicidal fray of dishonored MacGregors and the law at the Pass of Aberfoil. Yet old Osbaldistone, returning, arms himself with vouchers of credit from his house and recovers the missing moiety of it at last, through the joint efforts of Diana Vernon and Frank.

And more interesting still, Baillie Jarvie recovers from Rob Roy the borrowed thousand pounds he had never expected to see again. Freebooter, merchant, outlaw, soldier, the hidden Robin Hood of this epic, Rob Roy possesses the money from across the water in payment for future services in the Jacobite cause. Suspecting this, Credit, decent man as he is, resists at first accepting the coin of rebellion. But Rob Roy reconciles him—"you came by the gowd . . . in payment of a just debt"—and in the same breath recognizes the transfer of power from Honor to the new brokers of authority, Credit: "it came from the old king, you may gie it to the other, if ye like; and it will just serve for a weakening of the enemy, and in the point where puir King James is weakest, too, for, God knows, he has hands and hearts enough, but I doubt he wants the siller" (p. 342).

Thus material structures grow both larger and more vulnerable, yet finally do hold stable in Scott's picture of the transition from the bloody coins and crowns of honor to the domestic paper and policy of credit. The same is true of psychic structures. In that primitive psychic econ-omy of honor called chivalry, as Scott dramatizes it, superego, ego, and libido knit together in a hot tight structure which expressed itself harmoniously if violently in religion, family pride, and war (with war's attendant dimension of rape, for the commonalty, and love, for the gentlefolk). Charles the Bold is this sort of harmonious man, whom Louis likens to a wild bull; so is William de la Marck, who calls himself the Boar of Ardennes. In Louis, the bull-baiter, and to some extent Quentin, the Boar-slayer, the transition to a new psychology is underway. Its signs are a loosening of the harmony between ego and superego. The resulting conflict is expressed in an ambivalent attraction/repulsion to parricide, and in the breakdown of religion into superstition. And, interestingly, in the shrinking, or numbing, of libido, of pleasure. Quentin in the beginning of the novel makes hearty meals and responds viscerally to music, color, pageantry, but Louis is suspicious of, and hence indifferent to, food and clothing, sound and form. By the climactic battle at the end, the harmonic and open-acting Quentin has changed a bit; under Louis's direction has undertaken many an act of indirection and guile, if not of outright dissimulation. Caught in between the two psychologies, he is diverted at the instant of establishing his credit and killing the man whose death will bring him wife and fortune, by the call of pure selfless honor, the cry of a young woman in danger of rape. He goes, but it is not the harmonious response that characterized him earlier; "like an unwilling spirit who obeys a talisman which he cannot resist," he is drawn by Gertrude Pavillon's cry, "For the sake of your mother's honour . . . as you are a gentleman, protect me . . ." (p. 428).

The psychology of Hotspur gives way to that of Hal in the early Renaissance setting of *Henry IV*, of *Quentin Durward*. And with *Rob Roy*, in the only narrative fashioned as the first-person monologue of its shifty and alienated young protagonist, we have arrived, I think, at the psychology of *Hamlet*, where every internal structure, from filial and national and religious bonds to the deepest constructs of identity, sensuality, and sanity, must be held, lost, redeemed, purely on credit.

It is the old king, Louis XI, who displays the psychology of Hal in *Quentin Durward*, who goes among his people with his kingly glory disguised and degraded, but who uses with calculation the "general ceremony" of legendary kingship to achieve the mercantile-national ends he seeks. "Fond of low-life" (p. 4) like Hal, Louis had been "an ungrateful and rebellious son," though he went to much greater lengths than Shakespeare's hero, not simply taking the crown before his father's death but actually levying war against him (as Richard the Lionheart did against his father). Yet Scott depicts a man not unlike Shakespeare's protagonist who is still half bound to the codes which he is now abandoning, or manipulating, an emphatically self-made and self-remaking king who is nevertheless in constant ludicrously genuine negotiation with those two authorities, the Deity and the father, whose ghosts haunt Louis's mind.

In Louis Scott makes quite real, as Shakespeare does in Prince Hal, the contradictions of a man ready to "pay the debt I never promised," that is, mediate the responsibilities of authority with the private needs of a complex and guarded and powerful ego, by enacting public "reformations" that would be sheer blasphemy if they did not have that odd streak of real spiritual dread mixed in with the calculation. Scott's remarkable picture of Louis at prayer, promising Our Lady of Clery the revenues of the county of Champagne for her forgiveness of his debts of sin—"I promised thee this once before, but this time I will keep my word" (pp. 329–30)—is of course much less subtle than young Hal's godlike "imitation of the sun" in arranging to send a sudden "reformation glittering o'er my fault," or than the older King Hal's plea to the "God of battles" to bring him and his men victoriously through at Agincourt without thinking on "the fault my father made in compassing the crown." But the psychology is similar: these are men committed, because they are kings (they tell themselves) to life-strategies of acting, role-playing, alter-egoing. And neither quite knows what their creators know, that the strategy evolved to deal with the world has become their way of dealing with themselves too.[7]

Thus it is as an actor that Scott has Louis first mention the historical figure who haunts his own imagination, "that terror of France, Henry V of England," who was defeated only by the patched-together alliance of France and Burgundy depicted at the end of *Henry V* which Louis is laboring cannily to preserve. After he invokes this threatening figure to calm the wrath of Burgundy's envoy, the Count de Crevecoeur, Quentin sees Louis change, and droop, exhibiting "all the fatigue of a celebrated actor, when he has finished the exhausting representation of some favorite character, in which, while upon the stage, he had displayed the utmost vivacity" (p. 122).[8] In his next appearance on that stage that same "character" is evoked and represented less directly as Louis faces, and baits, and tames, the bull himself, Charles the Bold, with an echo of the words Shakespeare's king used when courting "France" herself. "I love France so well that I will not part with a village of her," said the actor king of England to the princess, and "I see that you are so good a friend to France, that you are unwilling to part with aught that belongs to her," says the actor king of France to the Duke of Burgundy. France's king is thinking of England's king during this novel, and Scott is clearly thinking of Shakespeare's.[9]

He is thinking about Shakespeare's *Hamlet* while writing *Rob Roy*, and of how unpredictable that psychology of self-enacting credit is in an emergency. Arrived in Glasgow to try to rescue his father's credits, Frank discovers his father's associate Owen has been imprisoned for the older Osbaldistone's imagined debts, and can only soliloquize, not for the first or last time in the novel, "what was to be done?"(p. 204). Baillie Nicol Jarvie, who knows the answers to such questions, arrives to the rescue, is introduced to Frank, and taunts him with the curious rumor-identity which, along with that of highwayman, symbolizes his real psychic state. "O, I have heard of tha smaik," says the merchant contemptuously:

> It is he whom your principal, like an obstinate auld fule, wad make a merchant o', wad he or wad he no, and the lad turned a strolling stage-player, in pure dislike to the labour an honest man should live by.—Weel, sir, what say you to your handi-ward? Will Hamlet the Dane, or Hamlet's ghost, be good security for Mr. Owen, sir? (Pp. 212–13)

Frank has been playing poet, highwayman, estate-manager, lover, without much success, and indeed without much enthusiasm, at his uncle's house before this; his wooing, his business, his mock-robbery were as easily abandoned unfinished as his translation of *Orlando Furioso*. Young and handsome, accomplished and facile, Frank is the envy of his sly cousin Rashleigh: "you are a happy man, Frank—you go and come, as the wind bloweth where it listeth" (p. 105). He himself tells us that he had always a mind curious to explore every pathway of human and social behavior: "I was born a citizen of the world, and my inclination led me into all scenes where my knowledge of mankind could be enlarged" (p. 29). Yet world citizenship is even in the early eighteenth century scarcely distinguishable from deracination, as Scott pictures it. And no one is so easily led as a "free agent," no wind so easily harnessed as that which blows without a direction. No mind is less secure, less of a "security" for its friends, than one given to explore every pathway, considering too curiously, like Hamlet, all its options, roles, conflicts. Frank's Hamletian recoil from, then tardy pursuit of, his father's task, his father's credit, shows a guarded ego at war with the principle of authority, a "blunted purpose" which is alternately egged on and imprisoned or thwarted by the more simply organized ego-powers around him. It shows a mind's eye constantly led in and in, to the mystery of the "utter darkness" at the farthest point of the "labyrinth," the "vacuity of vaults," (p. 186), which material reality continually offers to the body's eye in this novel, whether in the perspective of the pillars at Glasgow Cathedral or that of the wooded Highland Glens.

Frank Osbaldistone, like Hamlet the Dane, obtains little security in these echoing vaults, and gives little: it is Baillie Nicol Jarvie who "redeems" Owen and travels with Frank into the Highlands to further redeem the Osbaldistone credits. Yet we will see that Scott allows Frank to help accomplish that redemption, rather like Hamlet accomplishes his task, by accident. In a sequence opening with Scott's habitual dream/wake imagery:

> Hitherto I had been as it were a mere spectator, though far from an uninterested one, of the singular scene which had passed. But now I heard a voice suddenly exclaim, "Where is the English stranger?" . . . "Cleave the pock-pudding to the chafts!" cried one voice. . . . I was immediately awakened to the sense of my situation. (Pp. 323–24)

Frank is accosted by Diana Vernon and an "authoritative" stranger, given the missing credits, and bidden farewell "for ever." Like Hamlet, Frank scarcely notices that he has succeeded in his task, come to the end of his road. For the object attained, never quite the point anyway, fades, and the endless vaulted labyrinth of mind opens on still another aching perspective. Gazing after the mysterious Diana, "eyes glazed . . . by the exertion of straining after what was no longer to be seen," he suffers a complex rush of feeling, a "hysterica passio," and sheds the "first and most bitter tears . . . since childhood" (p. 329).

In one of his few solitary moments then, Frank makes the passage to manhood which for Edward Waverley involved abandoning romance for the "real history of his life." For Quentin Durward, "left alone" to think after Le Balafre's description of the mercantile monarch they both serve, the same passage occurs: his earlier hopes had been "a chapter of romance, and his uncle's conversation had opened to him a page of the real history of life" (p. 52). For both Frank and Quentin, the act of reaching the king, completing the quest, putting oneself in authority, involves a kind of death of feeling, or abandonment of hope. What they have in exchange, Quentin, disturbed, with his half cup of silver coins, and Frank, "motionless with the packet in my hands" (p. 329), is success, dry, paralyzing, disorienting. Quentin has almost the entirety of his novel to recover from this enigmatic moment of success, and Frank a hastily finished quarter of a novel. Both moments are echoes of Scott's truest picture of this achievement, this success, this choice of life rather than death, a choice which always presents itself momentarily as a blight, a blow, a drying up. That picture we shall consider in the next chapter; it is the tableau that ends *Old Mortality*.

Rob Roy: Proper Names

Like Hamlet, and to a lesser extent Hal, Frank and Quentin are surrounded in their narratives by doubles, foils, or as Scott calls it in *Quentin Durward*, "wraiths." These are alter-egos playing out the positive or negative aspects of the protagonists' hidden desires or fears. As external characters expanding or clarifying the inner debate of the choosing youth, they are closely allied with the "romance" *function* of the plot, though the number and fine-tuned quality of them attest also to the psychic fragility and disharmony of man in the "modern" age, forced to rely on, or credit, fictions of the self. Some are youths like themselves. One of the wraiths is the woman each youth comes to love, and they are part of the romance emotion of the plot as well. Others in each novel belong to the previous generation; they send or lead the youth into the legendary "woods" of self-discovery; they are teachers, authorities, destinies, futures whom the young heroes must evade as destiny, watchfully distance as teacher or magus, and finally choose as self-authorizing choice. In *Quentin Durward*, as we shall see, this process is carried on by a number of shadowy symbolic figures like those in a tarot game—the hanged man, Le Balafre (the Scar), the Boar of Ardennes, the Lady of the Turret, and Quentin himself, the Varlet with the Velvet Pouch. In *Rob Roy* the figures wear the harsher realer magic of the Christian and family names which mark them, from "Frank" and "Rashleigh," contenders for the Osbaldistone name, to the curious resonance of "Die" Vernon, to the quadrupled power of "Rob Roy MacGregor Campbell" himself.

We are reminded at the start of *Rob Roy* by "the Editor of the following volumes" that except for those of the title character all the names of the characters in this autobiography have been "new written" by him as part of his editorial responsibility to the "unknown and nameless correspondent" who sent him the "Outlines of this narrative" (pp. v, vi). The author of Waverley, for the first and last time, formed the narrative as an autobiography and chose for his narrator the wonderfully duplicitous name of Frank.[10] Frank begins his life story with his return to England from the land of the Franks, expecting his father to frank him in the poetic or military enterprises he has closest to heart, which are the subject of his father's contempt. His father had himself been exiled from the long line of Osbaldistones who had distinguished themselves militarily.

Making a virtue of his punishment and a punishment of his lost inheritance, he had gone on to repudiate (but also to express) "that most

contemptible species of vanity . . . family pride," by investing all his
hopes and energies in the founding of a new name—also Osbaldistone.
He would not be William the fifteenth Osbaldistone of that Ilk, he
would be William Osbaldistone the first, of the new Ilk, "William
Osbaldistone, the first, at least one of the first, merchants on Change"
(p. 31). When his son refuses to become Osbaldistone the second the
elder man, rashly as his son thinks, but really out of policy, chooses a
new son from the Osbaldistones of the old Ilk, by name, Rashleigh.

Rashleigh is one of Frank's wraiths in the narrative, dark where
Frank is fair, mentally and bodily crooked where Frank is straight,
addicted to management as Frank is to drifting freedom. They know
each other's characters to be opposite: Frank recognizes that Rashleigh
needs to "calculate the degree of candour which it is necessary to use"
(p. 105) with each of his fellowmen, in which mathematics Rashleigh is
excellent, and the cousin recognizes in Frank, sardonically, someone
who "makes a point of following the banner of the good knight Sincerity" (p. 107). Rashleigh is, as the youngest Osbaldistone of the old Ilk,
destined for the priesthood as surely as Frank is destined for the
counting-house, but he is "in no hurry to take orders" (p. 43) anymore
than Frank is. He aspired to the person of Diana Vernon, as Frank does;
he will, reluctantly, he says, give up his own dreams of eminence in a
gentleman's field, the clergy, for the place in the new House of Osbaldistone which Frank vacated because he refused to forego his gentle-
man-poet aspirations.

But more than the priest-merchant versus poet-merchant choice for
the future links Frank and Rashleigh. For on the great north road one
thief called another "Osbaldistone" in the hearing of a witness, one
traitor-papist-Jacobite answered to that name (p. 75). This outlaw identity, like that constructed for Waverley by Donald Bean Lean through
the use of the stolen Waverley Seal, both repels and intrigues Frank.
The odd experience of being taken in public for the criminal he played at
being, while rejecting his father, paralyzes him at Osbaldistone Hall;
while Rashleigh takes his cousin's place and role in the counting-house,
Frank takes Rashleigh's place as his uncle's factor and manager, and
becomes as well the sneaking, half reluctant lover of Diana Vernon, a
threat, like Rashleigh, to her father, her freedom, and her moral ascendancy.

Frank still makes no move out of his criminal surrender to Rashleigh's identity until news arrives that that wraith has himself come
north with bills of credit to coin into money which, if removed from the
House of Osbaldistone and Tresham, will cause it to collapse. Drawn
north ostensibly to confront but actually to absorb this criminal "Os-

baldistone" identity, Frank almost kills Rashleigh in cathartic swordplay at Glasgow, but his odyssey, and criminality, is prolonged by the interference of Rob Roy, whose Jacobite purposes require Rashleigh, and the criminal Osbaldistone identity, to live.

The dance between the two wraith contenders for the Osbaldistone name continues through the unsuccessful Jacobite rising of 1715 and ends, with a neat and typically Scott-like twist of reverse symmetry, when the treasonous enterprise has failed and Rashleigh, having turned his coat, and Frank, having rejoined his father, are contending for the legitimate Osbaldistone patrimony, then Rob Roy kills Rashleigh, and retreats, like Robin Hood after Torquilstone, into his woods.

It is interesting that when Frank descends on Osbaldistone Hall at the end of the novel in full manhood at last, a military hero, a manager in the counting-house, and possessor of all legal title as well, he nevertheless "felt myself an usurper" (p. 377). As so often in the Waverley novels full legitimacy, final expunging of the criminal wraith-self, the outlaw hero-self, requires not only the choice to be, finally, one's father's son, not only the achievement of male adulthood, but also domesticity, the taking of the destined/chosen wife.

For Scott has, in one of those apparently simple but actually subtle conceits, prepared two documents of Osbaldistone legitimacy for Frank, in both of which his name is substituted at the last minute for someone else's. One was the will of his father's brother, which "cut" Rashleigh out of the Osbaldistone patrimony and settled it, if none of the five elder sons survived, on Frank. But the more telling document has lain all along in the Osbaldistone house waiting for the name of the inheritor to be written in, a blank space waiting, like the maiden shield of Ivanhoe, on the writing tablet of the author of Waverley. This was the wedding contract signed long ago which commits Diana Vernon "to marry *Blank* Osbaldistone, Esq. . . . and it only remains to pitch upon the happy man whose name shall fill the gap in the manuscript" (pp. 109–10).

In the two life-and-death encounters which the rival cousins have, Rashleigh speaks with chilling rage of the way Frank has continually "crossed" him. And though we have in mind, certainly, the many times Frank has, mostly by accident, physically stood in his path or his place, crossed his trail or his planned track, the word seems even more appropriate as a description of the competing, sometimes overlapping inscriptions of their names on the documents of Osbaldistone. Rashleigh and Frank are in fact the only men at Osbaldistone Hall who can sign their names, can read and write expertly. But Rashleigh is by trade and temperament a forger; he clearly forged his uncle's signature on the documents of credit he was able to turn into cash, and he used his position as Diana Vernon's reading and writing teacher to try and seduce her so that he might eventually trace his name in the blank of the Vernon-Osbaldistone marriage contract. Frank is a would-be poet, but, interestingly, not an originator, rather a translator, of Ariosto, Dante, and others. Rashleigh, as a forger, must actively change and hide, cross out or pervert language, especially names, to bend the world to his desires. Frank's translator's touch is much more sensitive, is less energetic and creative; but in the end his is the pen that inscribes the gap in the manuscript, his the intelligence that translates "blank" into "Frank."

Given these two contending scribes for lovers, one a villain, the other a drifting sulky poet, it is little wonder that Diana Vernon would rather keep the name opposite hers in the marriage contract forever a blank. She is the true "frank" of the novel, "over-frank" as the protagonist thinks. She seems the very type of freedom when he first meets her, a huntress in male attire on the hills off the great north road, "impetuous" as her horse, black hair "streaming on the breeze," having "escaped from the ribbon that bound it," free of bonds and bounds, free of fear, free even of gender (p. 40). Yet it is not as "Diana" that she really knows herself, or that her friends know her, but rather as "Die" Vernon, and we soon become aware how suitable are the two meanings of that name for her. Her keenness of spirit comes from a life lived at the edge of a kind of dying; her apparent ability to "take the readiest means to gratify any wish of the moment" (p. 61) and her apparent capacity to run free of any bridle (p. 65) arise from the knowledge that the dice determining her fate—enclosure in a convent or marriage to a brutal cousin—are still in the air, and from the compulsion to enjoy "the freedom of wild heath" (p. 126) before the dice hit the board. In her recognized fear of enclosure she offers another parallel with the less self-aware Frank, whose "largely unconscious fear of jails" is, as Welsh proposes, the dominant, if not the intended, source of unity in the plot (*The Hero of the Waverley Novels*, pp. 183–84). "Whoop, dead, dead!" announces the end of the hunt as Die and Frank begin to speak on meeting, and almost immediately her own bitter metaphor describes the true dark nature of her freedom and its destined end: "'I shall be . . . that is,' said she, correcting herself, 'I should be rather like the wild hawk, who, barred the free exercise of his soar through heaven, will dash himself to pieces against the bars of his cage'" (pp. 40–43).

Hawk Diana Vernon may be, "merciless" and "ruthless" and a "termagant" not only in her monitoring of the arch compliments and sulky moods of Frank but in her unsparing satire of all the men around her.

But her freedom carries death in it, that is, the caging which causes death, from any or all of the three causes for which she admits to Frank that she is worthy of pity. First, "because I am a girl, and not a young fellow, and would be shut up in a mad-house, if I did half the things that I have a mind to"; second, because she is a Catholic and a Jacobite she can be politically imprisoned at any moment; and third, because "fate has involved me in such a series of nets, and toils, and entanglements, that I dare hardly speak a word for fear of consequences" (pp. 89, 90). Not only her movements but her speech, overfree as they seem, are actually sealed enclosures to Die Vernon, death to the wild hawk. The nets and entanglements are not only the "coif and pinners" (p. 89) of gender, the Jacobite intrigues of her father's family, but also, as we learn shortly after, the words of the marriage contract. When it is enforced by her choosing/speaking/writing the one missing word for Blank Osbaldistone, the contract will enclose her more miserably than ever as the mistress of "Stun Hall," as the servant appropriately miscalls the Osbaldistone patrimony.

It is clear that the first enclosure, the mad-house, seems very near to Diana Vernon; much of the neighborhood thinks her wildness is madness. She herself intends to choose "the fatal veil" when she must choose between alternate enclosures, and her bitter consciousness in this matter reminds us not only of that old Gothic identity between the convent and the mad-house which Scott and later Charlotte Bronte were to make part of the mainstream of English fiction, but also of the more recent feminist analysis of nineteenth-century fiction's characterization of womanhood split between the vital madwoman in the attic and the "stunned" angel in the hall. Of this more in Chapter 4. Her growing, prickly affection for Frank, which increases, Scott makes clear, as her perception of the nets and entanglements that beset even his envied male freedom grows, almost precipitates her into the second deadly enclosure, the political prison. For it is because she is pursuing Frank's business of the lost documents of credit that when she comes north with the mysterious authority who is her father, and Frank's "rival," she delays almost long enough to fall into the government traps set for the Jacobites.

For all her apparent activity, so different from, annoying to, humbling to, Frank, Diana has, like him, been living in a willed Eden of free inaction: to take an action—she to try to save Frank, he to try to save his father's credits—precipitates each into the real world of compulsions, drives each "under authority." Diana can easily evade the authority of the magistrates of the town, of her uncle and "the ourang-outangs, my cousins" (p. 91). But Sir Frederick Vernon has the authority of a father, and Rashleigh has entangled himself in that authority because he holds so many of the older Vernon's secrets. As for Frank, a sensitive listener to her woes, a sensitive translator of his own similar entrapments— "well, it is very seducing to be pitied, after all," Die admits (p. 88), and even more seducing to pity. There grows up between this high-mettled, easily offended pair, neither fully approving of the other's character, an "intimacy without confidence," a "love without hope or purpose" (p. 148), an affection which expresses itself almost entirely in mental "observation" or silent attempts at "penetration," and which discourses by "signals of correspondence" (p. 91), while the surface conversation "evaporates in repartee" (p. 148). Yet this "agitation of the passions" over the whole range, from embarrassment, displeasure, and irritation to pity, fear, and fellow feeling, only increases the attachment. He is an Orlando Furioso, loving a lady surrounded by mysteries "as with an enchanter's spell" (p. 153); she identifies passionately with a youth caught in the toils of the Osbaldistone who once almost seduced her, that Rashleigh who "bears a charmed life" (p. 125).

It is their lack of resemblance to the conventional of their sex that attracts Diana and Frank to each other, but the attraction communicates itself on the conscious level as "displeasure" rather than pleasure, and in the end each must enter the conventional state of their gender if they are to wed. Diana virtually orders Frank into male action. He obeys her, and his heart, and enters that series of activities in the north which ends with him in authority under the king as a captain, putting down the Jacobite uprising, in authority under his father over the affairs of the counting-house and of Osbaldistone Hall. As Frank leaves for the north the dice hit the board for Die Vernon; her father carries her north with him to engage the Highlanders in the uprising, and "she's under lawfu' authority now; and full time" (p. 333), comments Rob Roy. Frank sorrows at this news, for he thinks her "authority" is another lover, but he is relieved too, like everyone else, that she has passed into the protective convention of her gender, which requires passivity, as he has passed into the active convention of his gender. This, it seems, is the necessary condition for their marriage, for though the "gulf of absolute perdition" that separated them just before the uprising had specifically to do with the various promises and contracts to which they had bound themselves, it had more subtly to do with the peculiar nature of the "friendship"—"any other union is as far out of our reach as if I were man, or you were woman" (p. 161)—which is Diana's deepest wish. The wish, I think, is that she and Frank might be men together, or women together, evading that third enclosure, the marriage contract with Blank Osbaldistone, which she knows will be the death of her.[11]

And so, interestingly, it may be. Though both their "authorities," her father and his, finally leave them free of contracts, to choose each other as husband and wife, though her final term as a "femme couverte" (p. 87) in a convent and his as a male overt at war have fashioned them into marriageable people and they do marry, though doubtless Scott's "hurried" ending makes the exact weight we should place on final events uncertain—still, in all his hurry, Scott manages to have his living narrator specify that Diana, having been "seduced" by pity and married, has died. Frank had a vivid dream before they married, when he feared "fanaticism" would keep them apart, that Diana and he were held prisoner by Helen MacGregor, to be thrown together from a rock into the sea at the firing of a canon signal by Diana's father. In the dream "the deadly signal exploded" and repeated itself in the thunder of Rashleigh's final attack on Osbaldistone Hall, as this Waverley hero once again "awoke from fancied horror to real apprehension" (p. 387). Rashleigh triumphs this time and takes the two prisoners, but they are freed and he is killed by the final decisive intervention of Rob Roy. His wraith removed, Frank settles down firmly on the rock of his patrimony, his identity, and eventually his domesticity. But on Diana's behalf it is difficult not to hear the dream's deadly signal repeating itself in the wedding bell that ended "Die" Vernon.

This intervention of Rob Roy marks the fourth time that the "Robin Hood of Scotland" (pp. 395–96) has exercised the legendary authority of his hidden and alternative kingdom, to the better management of the outside world. He gave evidence for Frank before the Northumberland justice; he persuaded Frank away from the arrest warrants waiting for him in Glasgow and stopped the deadly battle between him and Rashleigh in the same city; his henchman Dougal saved Frank from Helen MacGregor's wrath, and he himself shepherded Frank and Baillie Nicol Jarvie out of the way of the contending armies in the Highlands and put them on the road south again, toward the law. Rob Roy is at hand to show that what the "secret leaves" of Sherwood Forest are to England the glens beyond the Highland line are to Scotland. They are the heart of its mystery, the seat of its outlaw justice, an enclosure of dark and bright passions which is, as Rashleigh Osbaldistone magniloquently describes it, barricaded within the "concentric bulwarks" of patriotism, clan, family: "within these circles a Scotchman's heart throbs, each pulsation being fainter and fainter, till beyond the widest boundary, it is almost unfelt" (pp. 98–99). Diana protests, and she's correct, that the "widest boundaries" are wider than Rashleigh pretends. Still the identification of this familiar magical figure in Scott, the outlaw king, the kidnapper savior, as a secret hid within concentric bulwarks or covers, is peculiarly appropriate for the many-named, or covered, title figure, Rob Roy MacGregor Campbell. Like Donald Bean Lean Wily Will "Waverley," like Robin Locksley Bend-the-Bow, this outlaw chief has "in his time played many parts" (p. 355), and the roles, or covers, are embodied in his names.

Campbell is, so to speak, his daylight name, his working name; since his clan-name of MacGregor has been outlawed and wiped out because of the violent deeds of his ancestors, he has filled in that blank with the clanname of the powerful Duke of Argyll. In Scotland, however, he bears a name which, "whispered in this lonely street would make the stones themselves rise up to apprehend him," a name which "creates . . . a deep feeling of terror" (pp. 196–97), which opens prison doors as well as invites the hangman's noose, a name which is a growl— "Gregarach"—MacGregor. The man who first utters this, his deeper identity (and cover) at the Glasgow tollbooth, seems practically a different being from the witty and socially self-possessed Campbell Frank knows, whose "cool and condescending politeness" once seemed to "sink everyone strangely under this authority" (p. 34). Now he is a powerful physical totem, "the idol of his tribe" (p. 199), whose long "half-goblin" arms make him seem "wild, irregular, and, as it were, unearthly," "like one of the "old Picts" (p. 214). This primitive being invites Frank north to the lawless glens of his clan where all the passions of the novel, the avaricious and revengeful ones of Rashleigh, the loving ones of Diana, the political ones of Jacobite spy and government soldier, are being drawn as if by the action of a lodestone. There at the Clachan of Aberfoil Frank meets the pure MacGregor, Rob's wife Helen, before whose savage Druidical nobility the life of the coward Morris is sacrificed. Like *Ivanhoe's* Ulrica she seems a Christian princess reverted under stress to a pagan deity. Helen has locked into the proscribed MacGregor identity, but Rob Roy, though he demands the information about Morris's death with a tribal roar—"Speak out, sir, and do not Maister or Cambell me—my foot is on my native heath, and my name is MacGregor!" (p. 334)—regrets the deed, like the canny monarch he is, as bad policy.

As "Campbell," the title figure can move easily in the daylight world of politics and commerce; as "MacGregor" he is sure of a helping hand in the night world of violence and outlawry. Yet, Frank notices that the chief is even at this moment playing a kind of role: "I could plainly see, that . . . by the enumeration of his wrongs he was lashing himself into a rage, in order to justify in his own eyes the errors they had led him into" (p. 346). No, like "Campbell," "MacGregor" is a coat he must put himself into: his deeper identity lies in the double meaning of his nickname. Roy he is, the red MacGregor, as Frank first understands when he sees him for the first time in his native Highland dress, redheaded, redshanked like a "red-coloured Highland bull," caught red-handed at rebellion by the government and under heavy guard, yet now, in his "real and formidable character," still a third kind of man: "I could scarce recognize him to be the same person" (p. 317). This person "Roy" is also, of course, a king, the red outlaw king of revolution, fire, and blood, and as he takes Frank and Baillie Jarvie to their farthest point north, beyond Aberfoil to Lock Lomond so they can take a boat south to Glasgow, he becomes more and more monarchical, though Rob Roy's court is one whose "hands were red" (p. 355).

The title figure makes one more appearance as the red-handed king, leading his Highlanders to the rescue of Frank and the Vernons, and himself killing Rashleigh. But this is not how we last hear of him. For after the failure of the Jacobite king to whom he was allied, Rob Roy MacGregor Campbell returned safely to his glens and to the "equivocal profession" (p. 396) which gave him his first name, "Rob." The Robin Hood of Scotland, "self-elected Protector . . . dread of the wealthy, but the friend of the poor" (p. 396), maintains his authority through levying blackmail and manages thereby to suggest that all authority has a similar basis. Indeed the first time Frank "had heard the Scottish accent," in the inn on the great north road, Rob Roy spoke "in a strong deep voice behind him" of the explicit connection between the in-law king's authority and his own outlaw profession, though he has not yet so identified himself to Frank: "Your English gaugers and supervisors, that you have sent down benorth the Tweed, have taen up the trade of thievery over the heads of the native professors" (p. 30). Rob Roy's first act in the novel is to rob King George's courier Morris to pay King James's soldiers, and his penultimate act is to turn over money intended to pay King James's soldiers to Baillie Jarvie instead, in the knowledge that it will go eventually in taxes or as loans to pay King George's soldiers.

Thus in the deepest sense the "robber" is the mover, the shaker, the changer of the world and its bases of authority. On one level the hard headed MacGregor-Campbell knows that the revolution he is helping to brew is a "cockatrice" and a futile waste. But more deeply, Rob Roy knows his job: "Let it come, now, let it come . . . if the world is turned upside down, why, honest men have the better chance to get bread out of it" (p. 352). To follow the travels of the money in the novel is to see that robbery, blackmail, the forcible lifting and scattering and gathering of money, is the very ground of authority, a ground that shifts with the shaking of Robin Hood from court to court, and finally, from courts to the counting-house. This is the truth of western capitalism, in law or out of it. There is that legendary alternative ground, of course, in the hidden glens, the secret leaves, of the "native professors" of robbery. But, crucially, the native professors are in this novel literally giving away that ground, selling off the timber that was their "cover," in a half-mythic and tragic transaction brokered happily by, among others, the House of Osbaldistone and Tresham. Early in the novel its king, William the first merchant on Change, is the subject of Frank's gentle raillery for his immersion in financial matters, for thinking that "the exact effect which the depreciation of the louis d'or had produced on the negotiation of bills of exchange 'the most remarkable national occurance of my time'" (p. 10). And yet this was a man who had seen the Revolution (of 1688), marvels the widely educated Frank, naively ignorant that the depreciation of "louis" and the appreciation of "William" *was* the Revolution.

Quentin Durward: The Authority of Revolution

Scott too had seen the Revolution (of 1789–93), and there seems little doubt that all his history, like the rest of the century's, was in part an attempt to fathom this most remarkable international occurrence of his time. After so shattering a change, so fundamental a turning of the world upside down, the imagination immediately seeks to restore normality to the great intrusion of the French Revolution, to have anticipated it, to construct the history of revolutions to which Lukacs would say it belongs. In a peculiarly English way, as Lukacs hints, this means Scott is in a good position, conservative that he is, distanced as he is by time and Scottishness from the English civil war, to establish the *authority* of revolutions. It is no accident that the historical novel as the continuation of the tradition of the eighteenth-century *realistic* novel made its first appearance in England, says Lukacs. "The fact that England had fought out its bourgeois revolution in the seventeenth century and had from then on experienced a peaceful, upward development, lasting over centuries" made the English example an ideal to continental politicians who were combating the Restoration in France of another Louis, the wrong "louis," in the name of the historically (in England) established ideal of progress. It also "awoke in England, too, the feeling for history, the awareness of historical development," since that awareness could rest comfortably on a generations-long memory of stable development (*The Historical Novel*, p. 32).[12] David Brown feels that Lukacs overemphasized the role of the French Revolution in producing the new idea of phased history necessary to the historical novel, reminding us, as scholars of Scott's intellectual history like Duncan Forbes and Peter Garside have earlier, that Adam Smith's lectures in the 1750s responded

to the great intrusion of "the 45" by an analysis of history as "stages."
Scott's own teachers in the 1880s and 1890s, Dugald Steward and David
Hume, reinforced this analysis, offering a specifically British-Scottish
ground for his historicism (*Walter Scott and the Historical Imagination*,
pp. 197–99). An important new study of *Revolution as Tragedy* by John
P. Farrell deepens our understanding of Scott's achievement, and his
limitation. It argues that the British example of revolution did indeed
offer that ground for optimism about progress which Scott's novels state
on the surface, but that the French Revolution, imperfectly assimilated
by Scott, accounted for an underlying tragic note in the novels which
"derives more basically from apprehensiveness than from regret." For
Farrell the new revolutions, "the French Revolution and the coeval
Industrial Revolution, made an indissoluble link between the political
question and the social question, between the hunger for freedom and
rudimentary, biological hunger."[13] Blind to the magnitude of the second
hunger, vaguely aware of the link, Scott averted his eyes from the
profound rent this was causing in the "social affections," the classless
community of the household tribe. The hunger for freedom could be
psychically accommodated through "moderation"; not so the hunger for
bread. From the violence that resulted when the emotion of the second
hunger passed into the first, broken communities might not easily
reknit.

When Scott comes to write a novel about the French Revolution he
appears, like William Osbaldistone, to have his eye on the wrong time
and place, the wrong "louis." Yet according to Scott's sly narrative
conceit the author of Waverley uncovers and reconstructs the manuscript of *Quentin Durward* in the ruins of a chateau dispersed and
leveled "by popular fury" in 1790. And though the author's comic-
pathetic accountings for the origins of his stories often bear suggestively
on the stories themselves, in no other novel does the setting and detail of
narrative origin cast so intriguing a light on what follows (narratively),
that is, what came before (chronologically).

In the first place, the author affects to have come to inexpensive
France because he has "had losses" in the credit market in expensive
Britain. Prices for his beasts and corn have "shrunk" and so must he for
the time, so he goes to the appropriate "diminished" land whose
prosperity his new custom increases while its loss diminishes the merchants at home (p. xx). This comic picture of the monetary interdepen-
dence of the two nations receives another flourish when he makes the
acquaintance of the "reduced" descendent of Quentin Durward, the
Marquis de Hautlieu, whose blasted grounds remind him of the sudden
new taste for stripped-down landscaping in his own country, where

"fickleness of fashion has accomplished the [same] change which dev-
astation and popular fury have produced in the French pleasure-
grounds" (p. xxvi). The old Marquis himself, cut off and reduced from
his past, "wanders about the halls of our fathers, rather like ghosts of
their deceased proprietors, than like living men restored to their own
possessions" (p. xxxv). This, because the Revolution, that unnatural
Improver of the civil landscape, rendered down people and even events
into the likeness of itself, "the naked tameness of a large house, placed
by itself in the midst of a lawn, where it looks as much unconnected with
all around, as if it had walked out of town upon an airing" (p. xxvi).

It is the business of anything thus diminished, reduced, rendered
naked and isolated, to connect itself again with "all around." It is the
business of the author of Waverley, reading and taking notes amid the
"wrecks," or rather "the precious relics" (p. xxxviii) of the Marquis's
library, to begin that work by reconstructing the imaginative terrain
linking the present Marquis and his naked house with the young and
energetic founder whose ghost he is. This also links the present Revolution with the earlier uprising out of which the House was founded,
connects the territory of Scotland from which the author of Waverley
comes to France in 1821 with the process by which the founder came
from the Highland line to the borders of Burgundy and France, and, not
least, connects his own past works, which the Marquis has imperfectly
absorbed as "The Bridle of Lammermoor" and "Miladi Lac," with this
new work. That very linking terrain and the book themselves make an
appearance at the Marquis's dinner table as "an immense assiettee of
spinage . . . swelling into hills and declining into vales" (p. xxxiv) on
which the characters from *The Lady of the Lake* repeat their actions. But
the author is forced to recognize that the landscape and characters
turned out to look more French than Scottish, since "the spinage" has a
will of its own.

The hero of the spinach, Quentin Durward, comes into French
territory from an Angusshire home which has been totally leveled,
stone, tree, and human being. His hope is to take service with an
authority who will help him rebuild the house of the Durwards, and he
arrives at a crucial place and time in a slow-building Revolution which is
not only an analogue to the one which reduced his descendent the
Marquis but the very condition of Quentin's own rise to aristocracy.

The time is 1468, during the passage from feudalism to nationhood in
France; the place is a ford in a dangerous river north of the royal castle of
Plessis le Tours. The central figure in this scene, and this revolutionary
passage, is the king himself. Louis XI has come out to the ford disguised
as a merchant, Maitre Pierre, in whose coat he is taken for a "substantial

burgher . . . a money-broker" (p. 12) by the ingenuous Quentin. The king is amused at how right he is, for Louis, by this and other still less reputable ways, is attempting to associate himself privately with, and to co-opt, the revolution being planned by the commercial classes of the city of Liege. And though he, and especially Quentin, are on the surface defenders of feudal royalism, he, and especially Quentin, will at mid-novel be "taken for" defenders of the commercial and urban revolution. The city will rise for its rights at this false—and yet true—signal of support, calling to its aid the anarchic power of William de la Marck, the Wild Boar of Ardennes, and Quentin and the king will ride against it and him and put down the revolution, striking off the head of the boar in a highly contemporary symbolic act. At the end we sense that the city, defeated—and yet vindicated oddly—will pass, with the country itself, from the feudal Charles of Burgundy to mercantile Louis, while the newly Franked Quentin Durward marries the Burgundian Countess of Croye and builds a House to "ward" the borders of these countries.[14]

Crucial for its "mistaken" recognition of the world's new king as a money-broker, then, the opening scene of the novel is even more remarkable for the king's mistaking of his captain-to-be. Or rather it is his inseparable companion, the hangman's, mistake. For Louis/Maitre Pierre and Tristram L'Hermite, the broker and the butcher, have come out to the ford to watch for two persons this day. One of them is "the Bohemian," a spy they have employed to foment revolution in Burgundy. Him the Machiavellian Louis must probe for information, and then have killed, because he has become, inevitable, a double-agent. The other person is a figure that the superstitiously feudal Louis has seen in a dream; he is a magic hero, a "lucky" youth who will "escape the sword, the cord, the river, and . . . bring good fortune to the side which he should espouse" (p. 144).

Striding to the river with a "half-smile . . . of animal spirits," like one "entering on life with no apprehension of the evils with which it is beset" (p. 9), Quentin might be either of these figures, for he is dressed like the first, in the blue cap and gray cloak that mark him immediately as an alien, and he walks like the second, a hero-huntsman, a Parsifal, a Tristram, before his agon. Quentin calls across the river for information as to its depth and danger. The hangman recognizes him as the Bohemian and desires him as his lawful prey, and the king would test part of his dream. Both men have in mind the "old saw" that a man born to be hanged cannot be drowned, so they keep silent about the danger of the river and Quentin enters, to reach, if not immediately espouse, "the side" the king sits on. He survives the risk of the river, and Louis learns he has already survived the Ogilvy sword which cut down the rest of his house. This leaves the test of the cord to be taken before he can fully take on the adventure to which, says the schizophrenic king, he is called "by destiny and a monarch" (p. 155), that is, by Louis's dream and by Louis's policy. And this test involves Quentin with the first and most significant of his "wraiths," his alter-egos, the man born to be hanged, the double-agent bound and free, the alien, the Bohemian.

Quentin first sees "the hanged man" outside the prison-like palace, bare and grimly warded by walls, not trees or gardens, of Louis XI, the king whose service he is contemplating entering. Dismayed by the nakedness of this house,[15] contemptuous of the fear and suspicion its design bespeaks, Quentin is even more alienated when he sees what "acorn" the single oak before the castle bears—"on that oak hangs a man in a grey jerkin, such as this which I wear" (p. 23). It is this vision no doubt which causes him to remark, after "Maitre Pierre" has described the moral ambiguity of all the authorities whose service Quentin might choose, "if that be the case, I begin to think . . . that a choice among them is but like choosing a tree to be hung upon" (p. 31). His uncle, Le Balafre, "the scar," tells him the same thing, and urges him to choose the service of Louis, who pays for service in coin, though not always in honor. But Quentin hesitates, until his second meeting with his totem, "the hanged man," forced him to choose Louis's tree to be hanged upon, symbolically, in order to escape being literally hanged upon it. Still pondering his choice, Quentin has seen another man, also dressed in clothes similar to his own, "convulsed by the last agony, suspended on one of the branches" of a tree bearing the "talismanic scratches" (p. 57) which mark it as the king's oak, and the hanged man as the "king's acorn" (p. 23).[16] Attempting to restore the man to life, Quentin is first attacked by the dead man's friends and then taken for one of the dead man's kinsmen by the king's soldiers, and bound and strung up to the same branch by the "king's hangman. A Scottish Archer intervenes, and, Quentin reluctantly agreeing, the about-to-be-hanged man is inducted into that service, whose privileges include freedom from the authority of the king's hangman, though not from that of the king.

Thus Quentin escapes "the cord" and "the destiny" of the man born to be hanged by choosing the golden noose of the service of the king of France, joining "the scar" who had once recommended that noose to him, shaking his own golden chain "with complacent triumph" (p. 48). In that service his first act is to kill a wild boar at the royal hunt, his second to let the king take credit for the act—a reminder of the expropriating source of the king's "credit."

The adventure which "destiny and a monarch" have in hand for Quentin is essentially to take the place of the hanged man, that is, to promote revolution in the dominions of Burgundy by giving aid, or signals of aid, to the escaping Countess of Croye and to the burghers of Liege. And his guide in this enterprise is the hanged man in the flesh, Hayraddin Maugrabin, brother to the man Quentin had tried to save, a member like Quentin of an alien race in a service, like him, which he knows to be, at bottom, a dishonorable, if golden, noose. The very password by which the two recognize each other refers to Quentin's equivocal act of service to the king: "The page slew the boar, the peer had the gloire." "A true token," Quentin admits, of the chain he has chosen (p. 177), though as we shall see he will undergo a reversal of that action, and that dishonor, at the end of the novel.

Meanwhile he must make his passage through the figure and territory of the man born to be hanged. Hayraddin, a Bohemian, Zingaro, a "Gypsy," is a wanderer with no country, no religion, no property, no law, no family, no home, a proudly given testimony of negatives which reminds Quentin of his own bareness before he took service. Appalled, the Scot asks, "What is it that remains to you, deprived of government, domestic happiness, and religion?" to which the Bohemian responds with a doomed passion like that of Die Vernon, "I have liberty." The advocate of reason reminds the passionate advocate of freedom that such liberty invariably ends up in prison or on the king's oak. And nowhere in the novels is Scott's romantic technique of putting the deepest truths in the mouths of outlaws headed for death or madness more evident than in Hayraddin's reply. His freedom is in his thoughts, he says,

> which no chains can bind; while yours, even when your limbs are free, remain fettered by your laws and your superstitions, your dreams of local attachment, and your fantastic visions of civil policy . . . I can always die, and death is the most perfect freedom of all. (pp. 179–80)

In his admirably logical understanding of the "end" of perfect freedom (he knows his "end" in both senses of the word, but, interestingly, he refuses to reveal his "origin") Hayraddin joins the parade of "dark" heroes in Scott and Byron and the Gothic novel proper.[17] Since his nature is to serve no authority, god or king, not even "the Father of our Tribe," the opportunity to cancel out his mission for Louis by collaborating with William de La Marck is irresistible. Here as elsewhere Quentin recoils from, and foils, treachery and betrayal when he has a choice. But at the end of the novel, when Quentin and Heyraddin, like Frank and Rashleigh, exchange places for good, the choice is much cloudier. Hayraddin, betrayer of every loyalty, slipper of every noose, is finally caught and hanged, leaving Quentin free to use the last secret the Bohemian gives him, the secret of de La Marck's intention to trap Charles of Burgundy in a night raid during the upcoming siege of Liege by pretending to be in league with Louis's French. Quentin can sell the secret to either of the authorities, to save one and destroy the other, or he might keep silence, as Hayraddin says he would have, and let the three armies, Charles the Bull, William the Boar, Louis the Fox, destroy each other in confusion and suspicion.

Louis's willingness to betray Quentin himself in the service of his policies has alienated the young chooser, as has Charles's "honor," seen from afar as splendid, now revealed as homicidal. He can take no "side" here. On the other hand, as Hayraddin cruelly snickered, he is still bound by the "fantastic vision of civil policy," he is uncomfortable without a service. His "choice" therefore is to watch for an opportunity to tell his secret to both princes at once, thus serving the phantasm of civil policy by serving both princes—that is, as Louis irritably understands, neither prince.

Corrupt and equivocal as all these public services are, Quentin would willingly absent himself from the novel's final battle, or butchery. Yet he is there, and active, and victorious finally, in an oblique way, as the boar-killer. For he is in possession of another secret, and serving in a private service, which satisfies all his honorable desires, that is, rivets all the golden fetters of his mind, at once. The secret is that the Boar will be disguised as Dunois, the newly hopeful suitor of his loved Countess of Croye, and the service is the domestic one of that countess, Quentin's Lady of the Turret, whose hand in marriage is to go to the one who kills the Boar of Ardennes. Thus the final battle, or butchery, is elevated in his mind to the status of a tournament. And this game Quentin can play.

Quentin's hope of putting himself "in authority" under this Queen, rather than in service to either of the kings, surfaces after he has recognized that his first authority, Louis, not only depends upon the hangman but is not above alliance with the Boar. Tired of being chivied from prince to prince, from the violence of Charles to the policy of Louis, the Countess and Quentin have "jested" about setting up an independent authority, a domestic authority, at Croye, with Quentin as Seneschal, "fortifying her strong castle against all assailants whatever" (p. 196). (This jest harks back, as we will see in the next chapter, to Scott's handling of Mary Stuart in *The Abbot*, a key figure in the Renaissance corruption of the feudal idea of the purer authority of the Prince as Queen.) It is also, for Quentin, a serious form of that attraction which he had expressed early in the novel to "Maitre Pierre" to the service, or rather to the position, of the Constable of France, who was wise and powerful enough to "make his place good" as a balancing pivot or solid fulcrum between Louis and Charles, "between the two lodestones . . . like the boy who stands on the midst of a plank, while two others are swinging on opposite ends" (p. 31).

This attraction, sufficient to counter that of the two powerful male lodestones, underlies the magical similarity, the "sort of mysterious connection beginning to exist between them" (p. 128), which makes Isabelle de Croye another wraith or foil for Quentin. For she was tricked into Louis's service as Quentin was. Situated by him as "the Lady of the Turret" she reminds Quentin, dimly, after their first meeting in the inn prearranged by "Maitre Pierre," of himself: "If, as he shrewdly suspected, there was a beautiful dark-tressed damsel inhabitant of the one turret, he could not but be conscious that a handsome, young, roving, bright-locked gallant, a cavalier of fortune, was the tenant of the other" (p. 41). And though this first recognition of mutuality and identity is couched in erotic romantic language—"two persons, who, though far different in rank and fortune, strongly resembled each other in youth, beauty, and the romantic tenderness of an affectionate disposition"—the deeper psychic bond between the two wanderers, the two inhabitants of turrets, becomes clearer, like that between Diana Vernon and Frank Osbaldistone, as the supposedly freer male understands just how bound he is. For while it is Isabelle who is constantly being enclosed—even in freedom at Liege she lodges in the Dauphin's tower, causing Quentin to notice that she "seemed still destined, wherever she made her abode, to be the Lady of the Turret" (p. 225)—and Quentin who constantly acts to free her from jeopardy, yet all his frenzied activity as her guide and protector serves at best only to keep them both poised perilously at the center of that frail plank gripped at both ends by the competing powers of those two "lodestones." Essentially her plight is Quentin's too: "The little world within me is like a garrison besieged by a thousand foes, whom nothing but the most determined resolution can keep from storming it on every hand, and at every moment" (p. 263). She understands, as King Louis understood, surrounding his castle with bare walls, that self-defense implies self-imprisonment. Like Diana she has accepted this, with some bitterness, as the lot of women, and as the novel began she was headed for a convent, loath to be the marriage prize either of a boar or of a boar-killer.

Freedom is not for women, no, but like Diana she knows that freedom is not for men either, really. Her most important conversation with Quentin begins with an apparent conventional gender distinction on this issue: Quentin sings, "Ah, freedom is a noble thing, Freedom makes man to have liking," and Isabelle replies, "Freedom is for man alone—woman must ever seek a protector." But she introduces the subject only so that Quentin may admit in the end that there is *no* corner of the world, not France or Burgundy or even the lost Edenic home, Scotland, where a man may even guarantee himself free to protect his woman, let alone where a woman may live freely without a protector. This "little world" of domesticity between the two lodestones may stand for a while, when there are two lovers to garrison it, but the realities of political history are stronger than the garrison, and from this double dream of erotic and civil service to the Lady of the Turret independent of princes, Quentin must be, like all the Waverley heroes, shocked awake to the realities of power by "a well-meaning friend, though he shake thee something roughly by the shoulders to awake thee" (p. 282).[18]

Yet as Alexander Welsh has cautioned us to note, so fluid and dream-like is "reality," is "history," as Scott sees it, and makes it, that the exigencies of policy itself bring about in the end the dream love and valor have had firmly to renounce. Not only erotic and domestic reward, independent service and "new attachments," and the new "name" he has been seeking, but even the "gloire" which he once won and another took, comes to Quentin, won by another and given to him. For the "secret information" that Louis has about Isabelle's love for Quentin allows him to concede, for political ends, to Charles's demand that the Countess of Croye wed the Duke of Orleans, knowing that the Countess will refuse the Duke. This leaves intact Louis's near-fratricidal policy of cutting off short Orleans's "house" from heirship to the crown of France by marrying him to his own lame daughter, a woman Orleans loathes and will clearly not father children with. Enraged at this development, Charles reverts to his most primitive and fantastic chivalric behavior, and offers the hand and lands of the Countess of Croye, his feudal dependent, to the man who kills the Boar of Ardennes in the coming battle. Quentin enters this "tournament," expecting to kill William de La Marck in his own private battle, for his erotic domestic "little world," the hand of Isabelle, but is called away at the very moment of victory (and homicide) to rescue another woman, and de La Marck is killed by Quentin's uncle, Le Balafre.

"The Scar," however, is physically unable to withdraw from his bachelor life in "the field" of war to take up the domestic prize he has won, and Le Balafre's king, Louis, owes Quentin a "gloire," or "credit," anyway. So, as the novel ends, the king confirms Le Balafre's "gift" of the hand and lands to Quentin.

Separating the act from the "credit" here is a nice and characteristic touch on Scott's part. For Le Balafre has already been portrayed as the anti-domestic and infertile branch of Durward's house: where Quentin's father was, amid all his derring-do, "no man to live without a wife" (p. 45), his uncle is a purely mechanical-instinctual being along the whole range of his activities from sex to politics. Brooding on his uncle's indifference to the destruction of his family, Quentin early in the novel wondered if the battle-slash across Le Balafre's face has bled out of his nature not only the comeliness that attracts wives but also the "gentle blood" that seeks wives, and "order," and the building of "houses." And indeed the uncle's scar seems the physical emblem of the bar-sinister that cancels out Dunois, the Bastard of Orleans, from the dangerous yet life-bearing field of domesticity whose political and economic expression is dynasty, the House. If Le Balafre is in fact to make the fortune of his house by marriage, as prophesied in Scotland (p. 78), it will have to be by a thrust which another man must, so to speak, consummate. He can kill the boar, but he cannot wive the lady, or the lands. Quentin, who can do both, and bide his time for the fruition, or the credit, of his acts, is the man.[19]

There is, clearly, a fabulous element in the figure of Quentin: for the ruined house of Durward he is the fertile corn king, for the half-superstitious Louis he is the lucky youth promised by St. Julien, even for the choleric chivalric Burgundians he is, they irritatedly recognize, the favorite of "her humorsome Ladyship," Fortune. But the core of his character and the source of his success is a quality that will increasingly command the authority, under the world's new kind of king, a quality distinguished moodily by the maternal uncle who used to be at the center of things because of his instinctual response to authority, and is now, dimly aware, at the periphery. "I never could give a reason for anything I have ever done in my life [except that] the Captain commanded me. I know no other reason!" reasons the Scar; as for Quentin, "the silly boy . . . hath an answer or a reason ready to be rendered to everyone. I wonder whence he hath caught the gift" (p. 112).

The gift, if it is a gift, of elaborating reasons, is clearly "caught" up out of the wreckage of the old system of pure reason almost wordlessly linking the feudal commander's will and the knight's action. The interpolation of reasons between the desiring and the doing puts a heavy burden on language, and on the psyche constructing the discourse of reasons. The language that sustains that burden is the subject of the next chapter.

3 The Language of Carnal Reason: *Old Mortality*, *The Monastery*, *The Abbot*

"Speak or Die" (*Henry IV, Part II*)

"Hush, Ephraim!" said Burley, "remember he is but as a babe in swaddling clothes." "Listen to me, Morton. I will speak to thee in the worldly language of that carnal reason, which is for the present, thy blind and imperfect guide. What is the object for which thou are content to draw thy sword!"[1]

The novelist is a deployer of languages as well as a recounter of deeds. The historical novelist has an especially wide field of choices to play with in this respect; the more different his language is from his characters', the more inevitably will that difference become a dramatic presence in the novel. The more conscious he is of this difference, the more likely it is that he has embedded some fable of difference, some drama of linguistic change, in the narrative. For the poet and light journalist Walter Scott, turning to the historical novel was at some fundamental level the wish to play with the recognition that language has a history. Language, like other actions, has its dialectical process; languages, like other characters, have their dramas of competition and mating.

Scott set himself to show all this, and more, I think, to show, dimly as he, or we, feel this, that at some deeper level the principle of language itself has a history. And this history Scott presented, hazily, in the dialects of his time, as a rising up of the new "language of carnal reason" out of the ancient fountain of verbal "enthusiasm." That, Scott answers the query of Le Balafre, and other bulls, boars and bears of *Quentin Durward*, is where men like Quentin "have got the gift." In novel after novel we see this history laid bare in the speech of Scott's characters. "Enthusiasm" is the fundamental, the natural, language; more, it is enacting, enabling language, performative, magic, ultimately divine, always creatively breaking out from feeling toward doing. Reason is the strenuously made artificial language; more, it is instructing language, informative, tensely restraining, indeed almost disabling language, always breaking (things, itself) down. The Enthusiast Burley may well scorn the restrained young Morton of *Old Mortality* for requiring an object, a proper command, the right word, to put hand to sword. In the adult state of his natural language, Burley's word and sword, action and object, are one. In the infant state of his artificial language, wrapped in swaddling clothes, stunned by the unvanquishable distance, the fell disjunction, between subject and object, sword and word, Morton talks like a man building a careful bridge of words over the abyss. His words are more often sticks than swords: "I am willing to contribute to everything within my limited power to effect the emancipation of my country. But do not mistake me . . . I desire you to understand, that I join a cause supported by men engaged in open war, which it is proposed to carry on according to the rules of civilized nations, without, in any respect, approving of the act of violence which gave immediate rise to it" (pp. 198, 200).

"Fiddlesticks," Virginia Woolf's Mr. Ramsey calls the young lovers of *The Antiquary* because of this kind of language. Woolf herself, amplifying in *The Common Reader*, tells us that "we" don't "care a straw" about the hero and heroine because Edward Lovel, asked by Isabella to clarify and restrain his feelings for her, replies, not "I love you, goddammit," or "a man's a man for a' that," but rather, "Do not add to the severity of my repelling my sentiments the rigour of obliging me to disavow them."[2] Language which can neither approve nor disavow the act of origin and so is tentative in every step of its grammar, language from a split mind splinted humbly with qualifications and conditions, dialogue-language which gives the impression of assembling, rather than communicating, the private character—this is the language of carnal reason. It sounds funny. It irritates readers, character-auditors, its own speakers. But it has the central role in the dramas of language, the primary place in the history of language, the dominant tone in the medley, or is it chord, of languages that is the Waverley novels.

Readers of any novel of Scott are aware of this medley. Conventional criticism likes to distinguish two fundamental languages. "Living" Scots is richly metaphoric, rhythmic, inflected, "popular," and "natural"; and "wooden" or artificial English, guardedly "produced" rather than genially flowing, is a code of reason, and reasons, shared by the narrator and his protagonists. Closer scrutiny has distinguished a third basic language, one founded upon a book, the Englished Bible, yet paradoxically, for reasons firmly grounded in history, one "enthusiastic," "popular," and "natural." And as the author of Waverley crossed the great divide of *Ivanhoe* a fourth language added its codes, a language also derived from popular books, though this language, paradoxically, has seemed to many the most artificial and inanimate of Scott's "tongues." This is the language of medieval chivalry, "high" or "low," that "tushery" of which Robert Louis Stevenson complained, an echo chamber of Spenser and Chaucer and old balladeers and, loudest of all, Shakespeare's histories and comedies.[3]

Each of Scott's four languages is involved in the continuing interpenetration and usurpation of speech by text, and of action or behavior by language, which has been of major interest to nineteenth- and twentieth- century students of language. And this drama underlies and often dominates issues of plot and character in the novels. For "Scots" is, in the novels and in Scott's own time, an oral-poetic language under racial and political-economic siege, and is compromising itself into text to preserve its existence. Walter Scott the antiquarian and poet was an agent and victim of this process. The author of Waverley was an agent, an observer and dramatist of it, especially in the speech of Scots characters like Lady Margaret Bellenden and Jonathan Oldbuck and Baillie Nicol Jarvie who are, because of their class or professions, living on the interface of that compromise. "Scripture" too is in the novels an oral-poetic language, but one that has broken loose from its Script to wield swords against the rational state, and the novels show it literally being forced back into its grounding, confining text. As for Spenser and Shakespeare and the balladeers of Robin Hood and the translators of Ariosto and Roland and Amadis, they were the first teachers of independent speech and private dreams to the young romantic protagonists of the Waverley novels for whom life is a constant negotiation between this corrupt but crucial personal language and the impersonal "destiny" or "fate" which familial or national history has, in Scott's continuing metaphor, "inscribed" or "written" in their stars.

"English," the language of carnal reason, is the tool of all these negotiations; no wonder it sounds so constructed, so "built," so almost "written" even at the moment of its speaking. Its power is actually linked with its textuality, as Scott imagines it in a remarkable conceit in *The Monastery*. The violent-spoken hasty-acting protagonist of that novel suffers a typical Waverley change to manhood as a reaching out for the holy book, the "awful volume"[4] kept hidden by the magic "White Lady" of Avenel, and recognizes it specifically as a change in the nature and power of his language: "I came hither a boy," says Halbert Glendinning, "I will return a man—a man, such as may converse not only with

his own kind but with whatever God permits to be visible to him"
(p. 98). And the change is immediate, as book in hand, Halbert returns
home "in contemplative walk" from a journey he took originally in
deer-like bounds, to speak with equanimity before a party of high-
ranking visitors an excuse for his late arrival "calculated so justly betwixt
the submission due . . . and the natural feeling of dignity" as to excite
"universal satisfaction" (p. 126). More poignant still, his changed language changes others, so that his Scots tenant Martin, whose speech
previously ran to laments like "where to go, I'm sure I ken nae mair than
eny tup I ever herded" (p. 16) now marvels, "surely even now, while I
speak with you, I feel sensible that my language is more refined than it is
my wont to use, and that—though I know not the reason—the rude
northern dialect, so familiar to my tongue, has given place to a more
town-bred speech" (p. 152).

This change, while historical, is not, of course, very "real"—*The
Monastery*, with its sequel *The Abbot*, is not so much a novel as a fable of
changes, where differences in language are linked to differences in
character and in political systems, all grounded in changes of religion.
Old Mortality, the other subject of this chapter, is both historical and
densely real, as a fiction, in its study of those achieved changes of the
sixteenth century under assault in the seventeenth. *The Monastery/The
Abbot* is Scott's first story after the immensely popular *Ivanhoe* opened
new fictional territory to the author of Waverley: it traces the fortunes of
two Border houses, one of poor gentry, the other of nobility, during the
mid-sixteenth-century political and religious reformation. *Old Mortality* was Scott's fifth novel on his Scottish territory; written just before
Rob Roy it follows its repressed and guarded hero, Henry Morton, from
the post-Protestant Cameronian reformation to the Glorious Revolution
of 1688. Critics felt, and many still feel, that *The Monastery* was the
author's first failure, largely because he introduced two alien languages
into it, the Gothic Verse of the White Lady and the Euphuism of the
"southern" Sir Piercie Shafton, and Scott dropped both of these from
The Abbot.

Critics felt, and some including myself still feel, that *Old Mortality*
is the finest of Scott's novels, largely because of its skillful marshaling
of its several languages—Cameronian Scripture, Scots peasant, royalist-
chivalric, the language of carnal reason itself—as indices to character
and as codes of action, and inaction. Yet again, different as they are,
these pre-*Ivanhoe* and post-*Ivanhoe* Waverley novels yield fascinating
evidence of Scott's continuing effort to dramatize his intuition that,
somehow, language is the trigger of character and action, and show how
philosophical, even theological principle, is the source of language.

For, moderate, tolerant, "ethical" rather than "theological" as his religious sense appeared to be, the author of Waverly heads every time for the zone of theological conflict, where reason emerges, battered and divided and oddly guilty and fragile, but victorious, from the fires of fatal but divine enthusiasm.[5] In *Old Mortality* Reason, with its special language, beats down that challenge at last and remains in its fundamental nature a Protestant achievement. In *The Monastery/The Abbot* Reason frees itself from the fires of Catholic faith and the ice of rigid doctrine and clerkly sloth, but as the careful textual language of private religious judgment replaces the performative significations of communal myth we see Scott recognize, uneasily, that reason is a Protestant problem as well as a Protestant victory.

The three protagonists of these novels are quite different men; yet from the angle we are approaching them Henry Morton, Halbert Glendinning, and Roland Avenel can be seen to represent the Waverley hero in three connected phases of his language. Halbert begins as the almost preverbal prelinguistic signifier of the natural glen, and he rises in stature, power, and even·class as he lays hold of the text—with interleaved commentary—that is crucial—of the English bible, the language of spiritualized carnal reason. Roland, who as an infant appears virtually out of his father's and mother's dying bodies into Halbert's hands on the battlefield, which sees the Monastery pass from sacred to secular hands, begins as the most delightful and ridiculous of self-called child-knights. "I will kiss no hand save yours, lady," he flames out,[6] and "Heard mortal ears the like of this . . . he speaks as if he were the son of an earl or of a belted knight the least penny!" mocks his fellow servant (p. 48). Raised by and for and under women, he talks the glorious "tushery" of linguistic childhood as long as he can: "Sordid slave! dost thou think I would have accepted a boon from one who was giving me over a prey to detraction and to ruin . . . ?" (p. 59). Finally, tossed from the tyrannic service of competing lady to lady, witch to mother to Queen, humiliated in a grim parody of that fundamental medieval-chivalric desire, he too comes to the language of carnal reason: "I know not what you expect of me, or fear from me . . . I neither avow nor disclaim the doctrines of the reformed church . . . sooth to speak, it would require some bribe to make me embrace, with firm and desperate resolution, either one side or the other" (pp. 263–64). Henry Morton has lived his whole life under the time-serving neutrality of a miser uncle and of the political and religious compromises of the Restoration: so embedded is he already in his heritage of reason that language itself is in danger of extinction in him, so dangerous an action does it seem. *Old Mortality* opens with a display of marksmanship, horsemanship, valor, and generosity on Mor-

ton's part which announces him immediately as the romantic hero, yet
the very condition of these feats, the materials of this heroism, are
precision, control, self-forgetfulness, and silence. His first recorded
words under his own name, as Whig and Tory meet in the alehouse to
celebrate his victory, and partisan language heats up around him, are
words calculated to cool down, or even extinguish, language: "Come
gentlemen . . . we have a right to expect we shall not be troubled with
this sort of discussion" (p. 31). The partisans recognize that all language,
especially nonpartisan, is partisan, but Morton's marksmanship at the
day's games has won him the prophetic comic title of Captain of the
Popinjay, military chief of the town, for the day, so he is obeyed—for the
day. "I shall not disturb your reign," says one of the contending Enthu-
siasts, "I reckon it will be out by twelve at night" (p. 31).

The reign of the language of carnal reason is never quite "out" in a
narrative, especially one by the author of Waverley. Yet challenges to
this new king of language are constant, and so too are the tests and trials
of loyalty to him or his rivals. Often "muffled," "disguised," or even
mute, the spirit of this reign stands beside the rival spirits, often
"shining," "fiery," or highly colored, in each text of each novel. To him,
occasionally her, someone points over and over, and challenges the
protagonist—under which king, besonian? speak, or die. And we remember that the very language of the very character created by
Shakespeare to phrase the challenge which stands on the title page of
the whole Waverley series, a character theatrical, ancient, fateful, is
anti-reason. To make a choice couched in these terms (yet what other
terms does "choice" have?), even a choice for reason, is to let go reason.
To speak is to die.[7]

To see how this works, and to confront once again Scott's habit of
raising an issue in a novel on his Scots territory and then elaborating or
exploring its origins in a later novel set in earlier historical time, I want
to take up an incident of language trial or test from each of the three
novels under discussion here, before going on to examine in greater
detail the drama of language, character, and action in *Old Mortality* and
in *The Monastery/The Abbot*. God and Mammon in *Old Mortality*, the
White Lady and St. Mary in *The Monastery*, the Abbot of Reason and
the Abbot of Unreason in *The Abbot*, challenge the allegiance of all
tongues, call for a contract of service in speech and often in text. And
adept users of language, interpreters of signs, always recognize that
when the dense milieu of signification which is human life is offered,
suddenly stripped down to this duality, any duality, the issue is already
mortal, whatever the choice.

The early chapters of *Old Mortality* are a carefully organized series of tests where the field of possibilities, first multiple, swiftly narrows to two, and then one. It is the role of the Waverley hero, in action and in language, to hold off this remorseless narrowing, to keep the bridge open between choices, to try to add width and depth, memory and posterity, condition and qualification, to the stripped-down dualities which are always presenting themselves as "reality" to him. He is, in more ways than religiously, a latitudinarian. Henry Morton is, moreover, a "sick" young man at the beginning of the novel, "sick of my country, of myself, of my dependent situation, of my repressed feelings, of these woods, of that river, of that house, of all but Edith, and she can never be mine!" (p. 50). His sickness is the condition of living between irreconcilable opposites. Presbyterians and Royalists claim his country; an ignorant idolatry of his dead Presbyterian soldier-father and the dutiful dependence on his miser uncle make up his situation; the woods, the river, and the house are his/not his; and so is Edith Bellenden, whose walks he "haunts" when the ghost of his repressed manhood, his active marrying, soldiering self, is uppermost. His language is fundamentally interrogative, and spirals down and down to nonconclusion and impasse, whether in soliloquy, as above, or in response to external questioners. To his own questions—"Shall I do well to remain inactive, or to take the part of an oppressive government, if there should appear any rational prospect of redressing the insufferable wrongs to which my miserable countrymen are subjects?"—he replies with a contending question—"And yet, who shall warrant me that these people, rendered wild by persecution, would not, in the hour of victory, be as cruel and as intolerant as those by whom they are now hunted down?" (pp. 40–41). And in the careful placing of his subordinate clauses lies the recognition of the man of true, and fragile, reason, that inaction is an act of oppression and that action has *no* warrant outside the fictions of the self.[8] No wonder, in the single most poignant and typical gesture of all the protagonists in all the Waverley novels, Morton comes home from his truant activism, his captaincy, at the revels, to knock on the door of home with "a sort of hesitating tap, which carried an acknowledgement of transgression in its very sound, and seemed rather to solicit, than command attention" (p. 40).

Morton begins the novel by winning a marksmanship contest and the title, or kingship, of "Captain of the Popinjay," a prospect which so discomforts him that he has the last shot between himself and a young royalist, who is also a rival for Edith Bellenden, restaged. Contests, tests, irresistibly seek closure, victory, that self-assertion which seems somehow a "transgression," and Morton immediately seeks to merge his singularity as "Captain," as "the green chasseur" (p. 20), with the community in the festivities which follow his victory at Niel Blane's alehouse. Here the second test, specifically a linguistic one, occurs.

Francis Bothwell, a royalist soldier, deliberately offers the health of the Episcopalian Primate to a covenanting-looking stranger, in language which parodies the rapturous Scriptural dialect which covenanters affect. The stranger returns the toast in a parody of Loyalist prose, and Bothwell, dimly noting the parody, complains, "I don't understand what the devil the crop-eared Whig means." Unwilling to end the contest the soldier abandons language and offers, parodying Scripture, to wrestle a fall with the stranger, who, accepting the move from language to action, we later understand, partly to avoid getting the watching Henry Morton mixed up prematurely in his quarrel, replies, in the strong cadences of "Scripture": "Then, as my trust is in them that can help . . . I will forthwith make thee an example to all such railing Rabshakehs" (pp. 30–32). The wielder of the primary force, both of language and action, wins the contest and departs with Morton, and when a document comes to the tavern moments later describing the murder of the Archbishop of St. Andrews by a band of Whigs led by one fitting the description of the stranger, Bothwell shouts, frustrated, "the test, the test, and the qualification! I know the meaning now" (p. 34). He pursues the guilty Scripturist, John Balfour of Burley, who has asked guidance down the dark road from, who is himself darkly guiding, the repressed and neutral Morton.

On the road Burley keeps his secret but betrays his nature in his language: "Your uncle is one . . . that could willingly bend down to the golden calf of Bethel, and would have fished for the dust thereof when it was ground to powder and cast upon the waters. Thy father was a different stamp of man" (p. 36). Morton, displaying his fundamental nature in his language, had earlier cautioned the Scripturist that he was "unnecessarily using dangerous language in the presence of a mere stranger, and that the times do not render it safe for me to listen to it" (p. 35), and he is shocked to find that Burley knew his secret identity. The encounter begins Morton's supreme test, as Burley presents himself virtually as the ghost of Morton's soldier-father and calls him, Hamlet-like, to join the grinders of the golden-calf of Bethel in oppositon to the mean-minded moderation and pusillanimous political equivocation of his uncle and the government in power. "Now, make thy choice, young man" (p. 34) says the voice of doom, and after "a thousand recollections" of the idolized but ghostly father, and prolonged temptation to God-sanctioned murderous revenge from the devil in the father-shape beside him, Morton constructs his answer in the very diction of carnal reason, the answer that would have made *Hamlet* a novel instead of a tragic drama: "These are subjects, Mr. Balfour, on which I am ill qualified to converse with you . . . but I own I should strongly doubt the origin of any inspiration which seemed to dictate a line of conduct contrary to those feelings of natural humanity, which Heaven has assigned to us as the general law of our conduct" (p. 45).

Yet Burley's invitation, withstood in this refusal-to-converse, does trigger a choice in Morton, for it directly provokes the "I am sick" soliloquy rather as the ghost's challenge deepens Hamlet's perception of the earth and its works as a "foul and pestilent congregation of vapours." And the solution, for both men, to the withdrawal from language and the resulting impasse of thought, is action. "I will take an irrevocable step," thinks Morton in desperation, an action which cannot be erased by vocables (p. 50), and returns home after hiding Burley from the pursuing troopers. Ironically, though the act he has in mind is to leave the country, the inaction, the refusal to turn Burley in to the authorities, was already the irrevocable step. And it is as this perception is borne in upon him that Morton confronts the test that will finally defeat his language, the language of carnal reason.

He shot the parrot, silently, and drank the health of the king, according to the general laws Heaven has laid down for our conduct. But at home he is confronted by Bothwell seeking Covenanters and their sympathizers by means of a test-document. The narrative thrust into Morton's hands at Milnwood describes the murder of the Archbishop in the most intemperate language: for this very reason, says Bothwell, "it's a new touchstone we have got for trying people's metal" (p. 72). When old Milnwood had been asked his opinion, he had servilely spoken back the touchstone-text's own language, hastily "gleaning" its "strongest expressions" with the aid of "their being printed in italics": "I think it a—bloody and execrable—murder and parricide—devised by hellish and implacable cruelty—utterly abominable, and a scandal to the land" (p. 71). When old, deaf, comic Mause Headrigg, a peasant-Whig who is seeking asylum at Milnwood because her intransigent speaking of "Scripture" had caused her to be thrown out of her cottage on the Bellenden manor, finally understands what she is being asked about, she replies in language rich with the texture of both "Scots" and "Scripture":

> "And div ye think to come here, wi' your soul-killing, saint-seducing, conscience-confounding oaths and tests, and bands—your snares and your traps and your gins?—Surely it is in vain that a net is spread in the sight of any bird? . . . Eh, sires, ower weel may the sorrowing land ken what ye are. Malignant adher-

ants ye are to the prelates, foul props to a feeble and filthy cause, bloody beasts of prey, and burdens to the earth. . . ." (P. 75)

Morton, acting the irrevocable, grasps the touchstone-text and reveals his metal: "I have no hesitation to say, that the perpetrators of this assassination have committed, in my opinion, a rash and wicked action, which I regret the more, as I foresee it will be made the cause of proceedings against many who are both innocent of the deed, and as far from approving it as myself" (p. 72). And Bothwell, who delights in the old miser's time-serving language, and in the old woman's robust Scripture ("Here's a Whig miracle, egad!" [p. 75]), recognizes, by the precision and rational duplicity of his language ("the test, the test! and the qualification"), the strange young man of the alehouse, who came in with the Popinjay and departed with the murderer. That he came home having resisted but not repudiated the murderer is apparent in his language, which holds on even as it holds off, which remembers and foresees the reason for the oppressed sect's violence even as it disavows the deed.

So he is taken prisoner by Bothwell, to undergo throughout the novel that series of kidnappings and counterkidnappings constructed by romantic novels, by which the external world responds to a reasonable man's unreasonable desire to inhabit both sides of every bridge, fight both sides of every battle, speak both sides of every question. Moved under guard to the loyalist household of the Bellendens, silenced by internal constraints and external commands, Morton hears his rival, Lord Evandale, speak for his life, and "a singular and instantaneous revolution in his character" (p. 128) occurs. "I now lay my commands on you to be silent," orders the loyalist General, Claverhouse, and "I will not," responds Morton, his new clipped language, says the narrator, "electrifying" all around him.[9] Only the general, interestingly, is not surprised at the new performative speech. For, drawing upon that secret knowledge which an antagonist always has of the protagonist in a romance, and on the memory of the soldier-father of the "diffident," "reserved," and "muffled" young man before him, "your language corresponds with all I have heard of you," Claverhouse confirms (p. 129), and condemns him to die for the actions of treason and conspiracy performed in his speech.

The instantaneous revolution in character that signifies itself in the adoption of a new form of speech against the touchstone of a text ocurs in more explicit and fabulous form early in *The Monastery* against a similar background of preliminary tests and repressed feelings. Here, however, it is the wholly performative language, the almost beastlike wholeness of

sound and deed, that Halbert Glendinning must mute into the language
of carnal reason: it is not the language of his soldier-father but that of his
beloved's mother which comes forth in the revolution. Old Simon
Glendinning, a tenant of the Monastery of St. Mary's, has died in the
battle of Pinkie, where many of that race whose "headlong and impatient courage" (p. 10) harmoniously suited rash deed to fiery word "bit
the dust" (p. 11), as Scott says. In the fairy-tale opening of the novel, the
nine-year-old Halbert is offered a tiny cross of St. George by the
conquering English soldier and throws it down, "his eyes shooting fire
through tears," because St. George is a "southern" saint. The younger
brother Edward saves the cross "because it is the common sign of
salvation" but refuses like his brother to join the genial Englishman
because he is a "heretic" (p. 11). The incident, built symmetrically
around the novel's fundamental sign, the cross, displays the seamless
simplicity of Halbert's language and the greater density and hesitation
of Edward's:

> "Mother," said the elder boy, "I will not say
> "amen" to a prayer for a Southern."
> "Mother," said the younger, more reverentially,
> "is it right to pray for a heretic?"

And it offers in Elspeth Glendinning the first of the novel's many
mothers, whose role is to remind men of the deadly import of words if
regarded as contiguous with deeds: "The God to whom I pray only
knows," answered poor Elspeth. "But these two words, southern and
heretic, have already cost Scotland ten thousand of her best and
bravest . . . and, whether blessing or banning, I never wish to hear
them more" (p. 13).

Disfathered in the guerrilla warfare that followed the battle of
Pinkie, the child Mary Avenel had come to live with the Glendinnings,
guided by her mother and by a mysterious White Lady who signals but
does not speak, and whom the people of the countryside superstitiously
half believe in, but ward off by not speaking of her and her race. Mary's
mother reads from and writes in a mysterious black book which is
discovered after her death to be the Bible, rendered into English; and,
even more interesting, it is seen to be interleaved with meditative
commentary by its reader. It is for his own slothfully doctrinaire purposes, of course, that the woman's confessor, Father Phillip, warns the
Glendinning household that the book is dangerous—"*The Word
slayeth*—that is, the text alone" (p. 35). Yet the author of Waverley
clearly dramatizes the truth of this, in *Old Mortality* as well as in *The
Monastery*: for Catholic or Protestant the word kills, the pure language

of Scripture in the mouth enacts death, and even safely confined in text is "the book they most dreaded" (p. 36). Which minister should do the rational, sanitizing, dis-enacting interleaving—monk or mother, church or family—is the question, isn't it? between Catholic and Protestant. But that the interleaving of the languages is necessary, Scott never doubts.

Father Phillip takes the dangerous Avenel book, a theft which brings him a visitation from the tutelary Avenel spirit, the White Lady. In this, her first full appearance, she responds with "inarticulate sounds" to the "signs, the common language of all nations" (p. 40), by which the monk offers to take her across the river to Saint Mary's Monastery. Once abroad, however, she speaks, ominously-merrily, to him in her own language, the sinister-genial metric ballad stanza which is the most ancient and Gothic form of "tushery":

> Merrily swim we, the moon shines bright,
> Downward we drift through shadow and light,
> . . . The Kelpie has risen from the fathomless pool,
> He has lighted his candle of death and of dool . . .
>
> (Pp. 40–41)

Only the accidental touching of the stolen black book saves the foolish monk from a watery grave—"Landed—landed! the black book hath won" (p. 42)—and when he returns to the monastery it is seen that the White Lady has virtually commandeered the tongue of St. Mary's man: "Swim we merrily—I shall sing it at the very mass—woe is me! I shall sing all the remainder of my life, and yet never be able to change the tune!" (p. 54). The cleverest monk, Father Eustace, in a phrase which marks all Scott's dealings with texts, reasons against the obvious Scriptural interpretation of this mysterious visitation: Father Phillip doesn't really look much like holy Job set upon by Satan under God's ruling hand, and in any case, says Father Eustace comfortably, "for every text there is a paraphrase" (pp. 51–52). The monks of Saint Mary's are sure, with fifteen centuries of tradition behind them, that the text is theirs alone to paraphrase, so much so that when the black book reappears without human agency at the Glendinnings, Father Eustace goes back again to fetch it "home." Returning, he too sustains a visit from the White Lady, and the same usurpation of tongue—"how my thoughts should arrange themselves into rhymes which I despise . . . baffles my comprehension" (p. 73)—before the book disappears again. This time it remains hidden until the passionate hunter Halbert, unconsciously in love with Mary Avenel and jealous of the bond which the study of ordinary books makes between Mary and his brother Edward, flees angrily from the schoolroom: "to the fiend, I bequeath all books, and the dreamers that make them!" (p. 92).

Halbert had fearlessly received the book from the White Lady before Father Eustace had taken it away again and had learned then how to call her back. Now he does call on her, to give him the black book and its interleavings and its powers, promising that he will change from the passionate but contradictory and ineffectual boy he has been to a disciplined and thoughtful man if he is given the book. The White Lady shows him the text-talisman, lying "not only unconsummed but untouched" on the rising and falling breast of a pulsating fountain of fire. "Desperately desirous of showing the courage he had boasted," "trusting to the rapidity of his motion" (p. 100), Halbert makes an uncouth snatch at the text and misses, sustaining a burn as his sleeve catches fire. Better instructed by the rhymes into which his thoughts have arranged themselves, he bares his arm and reaches again. When he removes the text the flame which had seemed to support the book extinguishes itself after one final flare, celebratory, or elegiac.

If the Lady's mute and glorious flame was the source of language, its rhymes and songs the mother of texts and their reasoning paraphrases, then the release, or separation, of the child is the death of the mother. A conundrum to ponder; and as its climax a further conundrum. For though the White Lady is mistress of the fire and the water which guard the text, she cannot read it: inhuman as Ariel, a citizen of the prerational world, she is an already "finished" being in both senses of the word.[10] Only those whom the text can, in "Scripture's" fashion, enact into fully human beings, can "trace . . . these holy characters" (p. 102), says the Lady. The half-humanized Halbert, shuddering like Bunyan's pilgrim at his encounter with the forces under, and in, the Book, returns changed from the cave of fire, "slowly pacing forth his course, with the air of a pilgrim rather than of a deer-hunter" (p. 103), to begin, like the changed Henry Morton, the forced travels out from home which will teach him to read the texts of his changed character, the characters of his changed text, and their Protestant paraphrases.

A half-generation later in the sequel novel, *The Abbot*, when the interleaved self-constructed Protestant text has become the sign under which both politicians and populace have destroyed Saint Mary's Monastery, when the spell-binding White Lady whose day is ending has realized herself as Mary Queen of Scots, the black book has been restored to Halbert Glendinning and Mary Avenel, who have married and changed from Catholic to Protestant. Significantly enough, no child has emerged from the marriage of these mutated beings, and into the household, after an accident on the lake around Castle Avenel, comes the mysterious child Roland Graeme. He is really the Avenel heir, secret son of the atheist Julian Avenel, Mary's uncle, and grandson of Magdalen Graeme of Heathergill, the demonic Scripturist of this novel, witch-Catholic to Burley's devil-Cameronian. Loved by the Lady of Avenel, cherished fiercely in secret by the Catholic Lady of Heathergill whose Catholic minister in secret is that Edward Glendinning who is now Father Ambrose of the ruined Saint Mary's Monastery, Roland Graeme/Avenel grows up a divided soul. His heritage and temperament, like Halbert's, is action: his environment, like Morton's, has been one long catastrophe of repression. But this has not bred reason and Hamletian reflection in him, as it did with the man of the later age; rather, this last child of the chivalric tradition feels a wild desire for escape from the emotionally gratifying but smothering and somehow futile service of womanhood. This desire is, however, at odds with that deepest desire of chivalric youth, and of the Waverley hero, the desire to derive one's honor from the service of womanhood, the desire for domesticity. No wonder he suffers, as Alexander Welsh remarks, from a peculiar "compulsion to stab people" (*The Hero of the Waverley Novels*, p. 48). The Lady of Avenel wants to duplicate her husband's rise from lower to upper class with the progress of her foster son into the new Protestant gentry: Magdalen Graeme wants to use him to restore the defeated Catholic cause. And Roland, "devoured with the desire of independence and free agency" (p. 82), stuck between a blacked-out past identity and an all too competitively plotted future, moves in sheer desperation slowly out of the chivalric poetry of his early life toward the language of carnal reason: "I will be no reclaimed sparrow-hawk, who is carried hooded on a woman's wrist, and has his quarry only shown to him when his eyes are uncovered for his flight. I will know her purpose ere it is proposed to me to aid it" (p. 75).

In this frame of mind he sustains his test, in a remarkable scene set by the author of Waverley in the ruined monastery as a debate between the newly elected Abbot, who is Halbert's brother and Roland's secret teacher, Edward Glendinning, now Father Ambrose, and the leader of the destroying, merrymaking civilian Protestant mob whose title is the Abbot of Unreason, and who connects this narrative with the secret leaves of the generating Robin Hood myth.

The meeting of the Abbot and the anti-Abbot first occurs on the level of language: "the official hymns of the Convent" are challenged and then erased by the "Babel of sounds" (p. 117) from the mob, and the authority of the Right Reverend Abbot is barely vested in the person of Edward Glendinning before it is challenged by the authority of the Right Reverend Abbot of Unreason shouting "we will try titles with you" (p. 119).

Physical and spiritual violence rides just underneath this drama of language and titles; excommunication is a real threat to the mob in its sober moments, and death is a real possibility for the monks. Moving the confrontation to the level of language and dramatic comedy actually allows each leader to evade these violences. The scene offers a fable akin to Michel Foucault's analysis of "madness" as a double-sided intermirroring of reason and delirium.[11] The Abbot of Unreason is Adam Woodcock, Roland's friend and Halbert's falconer, who got himself "elected" king madman so he could moderate the crowd, and the Abbot of Reason is, of course, the Catholic leader committed to the discourse of mysticism. In the encounter, speech and counterspeech enable each other, provoking genuine reflection but also offering a glimpse of the hidden delirium of language that powers Reason as well as Unreason:

> "My children—" said Ambrose.
> "My children, too,—and happy children they are!" said his burlesque counterpart; "many a wise child knows not his own father, and it is well they have two to choose betwixt." (P. 124)

Scott, narrating straightfaced the discourse of Unreason, tells us that when Ambrose spoke in return of the peace-loving nature of the monks to the costumed mob, "the bear could not restrain his sobs, and a huge fox was observed to wipe his eyes with his tail" (p. 126).

Edward's rational spirituality is shattered, however, by the melodious performative language of Scripture—"Scoffers, men of Belial, Blasphemous heretics and truculent tyrants!" (p. 127)—unleashed by his supporter, Magdalen Graeme. The crowd, released, shouts "a doom! a doom!" and the watching Roland, consciously serving his lady despite his anger at the "visionary schemes of women," feeling his compulsion invited forth, stabs to the heart the Abbot of Unreason, who falls lifeless on the pavement at the end of the chapter (p. 128).

It is of the essence of Scott's master fable, however, that Unreason, shouting "A doom" and drawing the same upon itself, returns as Reason, "calling aloud 'A miracle'" at the beginning of the next chapter (p. 128). Roland's knife had gone astray in the straw which padded the anti-Abbot's belly, but Adam Woodcock had seen the language of unreason gain a moment's ascendancy in the act it caused, so he directs his followers, with dispatch and cunning, to isolate and guard the flammable elements of the scene, Roland and Magdalen, while diverting the "spirit of demolition" in the mob away from persons and toward the remaining stones and statues of Saint Mary's (p. 132). Immediately after, the arrival of Sir Halbert Glendinning forces a general unmasking and reorganizing, and Roland, whose act has given him his ambiguous manhood, passes into the service, almost the custody, of the Knight of

Avenel. In custody he goes out from home, like Morton and Halbert himself in the earlier novel, to serve, or be kidnapped or tricked into serving, both sides of the national Unreason, until a final choice can be made, until the language of carnal reason may venture beyond its ordinary negatives—I neither avow nor disavow the doctrines of the Reformed church—to the most chivalric of positives—"I am determined to take the adventure" (p. 332).

Support the Catholic cause of Mary Stuart, restore to authority a queen who may have connived at the murder of her husband, Roland at the end cannot. Yet reason offers a cavil at the dishonest conduct of the Earl of Murray to his sister, now imprisoned at Lochleven castle: "One thing is clear, that in this captivity she hath wrong" (p. 332). Reason in its hot youth may try to stab Unreason to death, but this is unreasonable. Freeing a captive is another matter entirely. To hold off death from the enthusiastic speaker who courts it; to keep at large as long as possible the "other side" of a controversy, a duality, is the fundamental act, the outlaw adventure even, of adult reason. Steadfastly neither avowing nor disavowing, Roland nevertheless takes Reason's adventure and aids Mary's escape. In the world of carnal reason, authority, that will-o'-the-wisp of history, will pass from force to force, side to side, blowing, like the spirit, where it listeth. But captivity, even for the force that authority has deserted, is always "wrong."

Roland, of course, was not to know that Mary, with his help, escaped only into a new confinement in England. But the author of Waverley did. "Contaminated" himself with the language of carnal reason, the author of Waverley surrendered to its genial paradox and contributes to what Foucault understands to be its cruel conspiracy. First among the artists of his time, Scott kept alive, kept at large, let escape, all the languages that Reason had bested—the high "tushery" of Roland Graeme and the everlasting high tushery of Mary Queen of Scots and her sister, the magic White Lady of Avenel, the low tushery of Adam Woodcock, the doom-dealing Scripture of Magdalen Graeme and John Burley, the magnetic and flexible Scots of the Milnwoods and the Glendinnings, their servants and tenants. Set these all free into the confinement of that giant magpie genre, that merciless discourse of nonmadness, the epic of the language of carnal reason—the English novel. That was *his* adventure.

Old Mortality: The Muffled Man at the Bridge

At the climax of *The Abbot* young George Douglas, betraying the whole political, religious, and familial stance of his fathers and his house, rides on an errand connected with the escape of Mary Queen of Scots from prison: "the night will be dark," he notes hardily, "and suits a muffled man" (p. 366). Scott calls attention to the iconic nature of this figure in a note: "generally" a man disguised in some way but "originally," says the antiquarian, a man who muffles his mouth with cloak or mantle to conceal his identity and his voice. That this muffled-and-masked man is connected in Scott's mind with the outlaw figure who dominates his imagination is further suggested by the note: "I have on an ancient piece of iron the representation of a robber thus accoutered, endeavoring to make his way into a house. . . . It is part of a fire-grate said to have belonged to Archbishop Sharp" (pp. 438–39).

Four years before *The Abbot*, of course, in *Old Mortality*, the author of Waverley had established the irony of that artifact: the outlaw had gotten in, the fire had broken out, Archbishop Sharpe had been murdered by rebel Cameronians, and the document describing the deed became the touchstone for dividing the outlaw from the in-law. Before he read the description Henry Morton had heard it muffled from the lips of the robber himself. Rising from a dream of Edith Bellenden in danger, in which he himself had struggled, mute and impotent to help, Morton had gone to wake John Balfour of Burley, whom for his father's sake he had hidden from his pursuers, and heard the man, dreaming, repeat the murder scene in "abortive" gestures and "broken words:" "Thou art taken, Judas—thou art taken—Cling not to my knees—cling not to my knees—hew him down!"(p. 48). When, as we have seen, Morton attempts to repudiate the murder while muffling his information about the hiding place of Burley, he is recognized by those who know him as his father's son, the old ally of Burley, and taken from home in Royalist custody. He has made his "irrevocable step," not quite in the direction he had intended, and almost immediately, learning that the cortege intends a stop at the royalist stronghold of Tillietudlum Castle where Edith resides, he invokes in grief and resentment his fated identity: "Let me be muffled up for the time in one of your soldiers' cloaks" (p. 83).

When the women discover the muffled soldier is in fact Morton, Edith "muffled herself" (p. 92) so completely in her plaid that her identity too is obscured. And when the muffled man and woman confront each other in the castle's prison, both stand paralyzed, "without having either the power to speak or to advance" (p. 96) until the maid deliberately "breaks the ice" with her own lament. Each has taken the "irrevocable step" out from the cover of their conventional characters and into their true identities as muffled or outlaw figures, Morton by his sympathy for the oppressed Covenanter who ambiguously represents his father, and Edith by her repressed love for the forbidden Morton, a love which sent her to aid in his rescue despite "a fear that she had degraded herself in the eyes of Morton by a step which might appear precipitate and unfeminine" (p. 96).

Though the sudden appearance of Trooper Tam Halliday aborts Jenny's plan to muffle Morton in her cloak and escape that way, the "precipitate" step of Edith, which has revealed her own heart to her as Morton's irrevocable step did his to him, involves her too in a "speak or die" dilemma, a peculiarly female one. The arrival of "Bloody" Claverhouse at Tillietudlum ("You are lost," Edith warns Morton. "Root and branchwork is the mildest of his expressions," [p. 98]) means that she must speak up for Morton: the arrival of Morton's rival-wraith in love, sport, and politics, Lord Evandale ("who now entered in complete uniform," p. 117) means she must speak to him, whose advice Claverhouse will certainly take. Yet she knows that "the advantage which a beautiful young woman gives to a young man when she permits him to lay her under an obligation" (p. 115) will add the final confirming word to "the voice of the gossips" which has Edith already engaged to the eligible Evandale. Her own words are politically powerless, but he will speak for Morton if she speaks that confirming word for him; more, says Evandale enthusiastically, and prophetically, "By heaven! he shall not die, if I should die in his place!" As Edith assembles, in the qualifying language of carnal reason, her answer: "There is no friend I esteem more highly, or to whom I would more readily grand every mark of regard— providing . . . ," Morton is brought in and overhears all but the last negating word. His distress and reproach throw her into "confusion," the "exception with which she meant to close the sentence" is never "framed," and so both young men misunderstand Edith's feelings (p. 121). Without the spoken exception ("the test! the test! and the qualification") Edith's speech virtually engages her to marry Evandale eventually, and Evandale's speech engages him to die eventually in Morton's place, if necessary. The absence of the exception, the qualification, makes even these hesitatingly reasonable people's language performative, a situation which Morton, trying to goad himself into the rebellious anger that suits his forced-on (or is it forced-out?) outlaw identity, tells himself is a punishment to his private self for "being dead to public wrongs" (p. 127). It is as though private speech as well as private relationship has been invaded, but also, of course, released, by the enacting impulse let loose by the speakers of Scripture, and returned in full measure by the government whose "mildest expression" is "root and branchwork."

"Waking up," then, to public wrongs, Morton rides out a prisoner but a soldier from Tillietudlum, experiencing privately "that blank and

waste of the heart which follows the hurricane of passion" (p. 135). He
crosses a similar external wasteland,

> a wide and waste country . . . without grandeur, without even
> the dignity of mountain wildness, yet striking, from the huge
> proportion which it seemed to bear to such more favoured spots
> of the country as were adapted to cultivation, and fitted for the
> support of man; and thereby impressing irresistibly the mind of
> the spectator with a sense of the omnipotence of nature, and the
> comparative inefficacy of the boasted means of amelioration
> which man is capable of opposing. (P. 144)

And his heart allies itself, irresistibly and now actively, this former
"indulged" government supporter now a condemned Whig rebel, with
the denizens of the waste regions, who have at least in their language
and bearing "the dignity of wildness." "Surely," said Morton to himself,
"a handful of resolute men may defend any defile in these mountains
against such a small force as this is" (p. 145).

Morton's fundamental cast of mind is defensive, a cast adapted to
preserving and opening at least two, preferably three, sides to every
issue. Syntactically, as we have seen, this means keeping the frame of
the sentence open for the qualification, the condition, the provision;
tactically it means defending, preserving, defiles, causeways, passages,
and, above all, bridges. Now that the word is the sword, and the private
speakers of reason are detached from home and committed to enactment, the novel moves to the battlefield and to the bridges on these
battlefields which separate, that is, join, the antagonists.

Old Mortality's battles are peculiar; the narrative, following Morton
and his cast of mind, always finds itself on the losing side, or, more
precisely, always positions itself where it can observe the defense and
explore the reasons for defeat. The issue between the Covenanters and
the government is publicly joined four times between the opening
murder of Archbishop Sharpe and the closing tableau of deaths, first in
the wastelands above Tillietudlum, at the battle of Loudon-hill, where
the Covenanters defend their position and win, then almost simultaneously at the Royalist strongholds of Tillietudlum and Glasgow,
where the government defends its centers and wins, finally at Bothwell
Brigg, where the Covenanters, more numerous than at Loudon-hill but
more divided in counsel, refuse to come forth to defend the crucial
bridge, and are decisively defeated.

Morton experiences the defeat and ignoble retreat and scattering of
the government troops at Loudon-hill as a prisoner, and speaks to save
the life of the stricken Evandale from the victors, risking death in his

place. He joins the rebels, speaking his futile conditions and exceptions whenever he can get his sentences closed, and shares in the defeat of the besieging Whigs at Tillietudlum.

Burley, who understands perfectly that Morton's purpose, even in his committed rebellion, is to make disputed ground neutral rather than Whig (or government), to maintain cultivation rather than extend the wasteland, to ameliorate rather than vindicate, orders him away from Tillietudlum to the assault on Glasgow, telling him, his adopted language of carnal reason slipping revealingly for a moment into "Scripture": "Thou art unwise, Henry Morton, to desire to sacrifice this holy cause to thy friendship for an uncircumcised Phillistine, or thy lust for a Moabitish woman." "I neither understand your meaning, Mr. Balfour, nor relish your allusions, and I know no reason you have to bring so gross a charge, or to use such uncivilized language," returns Morton, "indignantly," Scott's narrator tells us, so we can be sure to hear the duplicity beneath Morton's own reasonable syntax (p. 239). "Confess, however, the truth," demands Balfour, but only to put further guilty pressure on the younger man's tried soul, for which Burley is "travailing," since the last thing Burley wants to hear is the lengthy sentence of qualifications which constitutes the truth about Morton's wraith-identity with Evandale and his love for Edith. Doubling the pressure a moment later, restoring the language of carnal reason, Burley argues, "At Loudon-hill thou wert a captive and at [Tillietudlum] it was thy part to fight under cover . . . shouldst thou now remain before these walls when there is active service elsewhere, men will say that the son of Silas Morton hath fallen away from the paths of his fathers." This allusion to the ghost-father effectively shuts Morton's mouth: "as a gentleman and soldier he could offer no suitable reply," and "hastily acquiesced in the proposed arrangement" (p. 241).

At the attack on Glasgow, briefly narrated in the novel, Morton faces Claverhouse himself and sustains an inconclusive defeat in the narrow streets, since the defensive position in such a tactical situation is so strong. Heroic, like the archetypal hero of epics, in "maintaining order in the retreat" (p. 242), Morton experiences for the first time the refusal of many of his men to follow him to, or through, the narrow passageway, the vulnerable bridge between—a refusal based as he knows on their recognition that he is in fact fighting to keep passages open, fighting not to destroy the enemy but to establish conditions with them. The conditioning language he speaks has thus robbed him of the "authority" (p. 243) he must try to exercise as general of the Whig army; the troops literally cannot understand his commands.

The only one who can is his wraith-rival, the royalist Evandale,

whose Morton-like moderation during the continuing siege of Tillietudlum has earned him a death sentence when he is finally captured by
Burley. Retreating from Glasgow back to the castle, Morton frees
Evandale to deliver a petition to the government on behalf of the
"moderate party" of the rebels, saving his life a second time. The two
young moderates understand each other's language so thoroughly that
Evandale agrees without hesitation to be the mouthpiece for Morton's
text, though both recognize that the retreat from weapons back to words
via the conciliatory document of demands Evandale carries will not be
accomplished until the deeds that "Scripture" has unloosed have been
played out to the end. And readers who have been keeping track of the
score of lives risked and saved, Morton's two to Evandale's one, sense
instinctively what the novel's final deed must be.

In the end the Babel of languages on the field of battle defeats the
Covenanters. In the scenes leading up to the first major battle the
mutually muffled trio of Morton, Evandale, and Edith have dramatized
the fragile hopes pinned on the language of carnal reason, the King's
English, as Scripture raises its competing guns and Scots, already much
tried by the enveloping language of English, further weakens itself
by dividing alliance between the two contending languages. The dramatic vehicles for this language-action are two wonderful old women,
Lady Margaret Bellenden, whose royalist English tends to break down
into pithy Scots when she is angry or frightened, and Mause Headrigg, whose Scots rises to eloquent and Fury-like Scripture in her passion.

In the first battle at Loudon-hill, marshaled as defenders of high
ground behind a morass spanned by a single "bridge" of solid footing,
the rebels had communicated orders seamlessly to each other in that
prerational language which issues, briefly, in Scripture, and then, immediately, in action. So the author of Waverley constructs his marvel-
ous set piece of the generation of the authority of rebellion. "Shrill cries"
from the women following the army raise an answering "wild halloo"
from the men, which gives way to the "summons" of "trumpets and
kettledrums"; this releases, "in answer," a psalm sung by "a thousand
voices"(pp. 148–49). And while the royalist army, from whose tail
Morton watches, a prisoner, debates whether to attack, negotiate, or
withdraw, the chief singer moves forward with his rifle. The royalists
send an envoy to speak to the Presbyterians. But he speaks the language
of carnal reason, with its qualifications: "I proclaim full and free pardon
to all, excepting—" (p. 155). And the singer, partly because he is Burley
the carnal reasoner, who knows that he is the exception who will not be
pardoned, but more because he is Burley the Scripturist, for whom the

word spoken means the deed is already done, fires the "mortal" shot and engages the battle (p. 155).

It is as if rebellion's authority, finding itself in a single song-deed, needed no counsels or commands, as if, indeed, such authority is negated by such modes of operation. After the victory the Presbyterians, now with the rescued and reasoning Morton among them, take counsel. Half-a-dozen languages compete in council, Morton's reason, issuing from his heart, Burley's false-hearted but expert "translations" of his reason to the others, and several carefully calibrated dialects of Scripture ranging from the genuine performative eloquence of Ephraim McBriar to the schizophrenic ravings of Habbakuk Mucklewrath ("I am made a terror unto myself—I heard it—What heard I! The voice that cried, Slay, slay—smite—slay utterly" (p. 207). The room becomes a genuine Babel, a "discord wild, and loud uproar . . . " which supplied "an evil augury" (p. 201) from the beginning of the "council's" existence. And it is in this Babel condition that the Covenanting army draws itself up to meet the strengthened forces of the government in the last third of the novel, having before them, instead of a morass with a land "bridge," the River Clyde itself, "which is passable by a long and narrow bridge, near the castle and village of Bothwell" (p. 246).

While Morton rides to the royalist side to make a last try at negotiation, the camp settles its agenda among the preachers-for-the-day, striving to create again that seamless unity between sound, word, and deed which first won the day. But the text of Scripture can no longer sustain the pressures of the wordless cry seeking the bloody deed: the agenda's moderate preacher is pushed aside by the psychotic Habbakuk Mucklewrath, who "applied to Morton by name" (p. 288)—not by implication or metaphoric comparison—the treason of all the shirkers and slackers of the Old Testament. The camp splits into half-a-dozen factions; the opening psalm of battle betrays "a quaver of consternation" instead of the "bold strain which had resounded along the wild heath of Loudon-hill" (p. 29); and the command of Morton to defend the bridge, coming as it does from the mouth of "Gallio" or "Achan," from the "Laodicean" and "Erastian," is misunderstood, lost, and squandered, and with it the "the moment was lost in which the advance might have been useful" (p. 295), the moment, the bridge, the battle, and the cause.

It is this multi-named figure from Scripture, the pretended ally who shrinks in his heart, the bold attacker whose natural place is in the defensive cover to which he retreats before the final stroke, whom in Morton the Covenanters want to kill when the last "precious remnants" of the rebels take shelter in a wretched hut after the defeat at Bothwell Brigg. To them he is the murderer of their cause, the muffled robber stealing into the house to plunder its only treasure, unreasoning passion: "lo! the very head of the offense is delivered into our hand. He hath burst in like a thief through the window; he is a ram caught in the thicket" (p. 301). Burley would have made Morton Isaac; to the "remnant" he is no longer the mythic savior-sacrifice son but the Judas. Since sacrifice may not be done on the Sabbath, both Morton and his executioners settle into a trance, watching the clock until mortality ends, a trance during which Morton feels his body shrink and his mind literally "waver" among all the identities which have been thrust upon him, or pulled out of him, while the figures around him, huge with the authority and simplicity of the identity they have made for themselves out of Scripture, grow larger and more grotesque, like "a band of demons" (p. 304). He instinctively lays hold of the Book of Common Prayer, and the demon priests, enraged, try to turn the clock forward to the moment that will authorize his death.

But death does not, at this moment, confirm him as that Laodicean Erastian prelatist. Nor does his rescue and re-imprisonment immediately thereafter by his original royalist captors confirm him as that dangerous Presbyterian red-cross knight, "modest, quiet and unassuming in manner, but in his heart peculiarly bold and intractable," who is described in Claverhouse's three-year-old notebook of potential troublemakers, his name marked by "three red crosses, which signify triply dangerous" (p. 315). For his heart is more than ever that "blank and waste" which succeeds "the hurricane of passion." Though he has, since he was last "in custody," enacted as far as he was able that righting of public wrongs which he has all but consciously substituted for the paralysis of his private life, his public activity has only separated him the more decisively from the fundamentally domestic places of his identity. Tillietudlum, that mythically situated fortress astride the passage between the northern waste and southern "cultivation," between fierce northern duality and southern "amelioration," lies empty of Edith, threatened, soon to be in ruins, while Milnwood, his home, has always been a place of cramped cold exile. After his rescue, following his closest brush with old mortality, Morton slept so deeply that, wakening, "he hardly knew where he was" (p. 312), and as for who he was, "he was now . . . like a rider who has flung his reins on his horse's neck" (p. 317). From this emotional distance, his scattered self anesthetized, he watches the government execute upon the captured Whigs the martyrdom toward which Scripture yearns, which triumphantly confirmed *their* identity. He accepts, with "an astounded and confused look" (p. 328), the banishment that Evandale, intervening to even the life/death balance between them again, procures for him, and sails for

Holland with the other man's clothes and recommendations supplying a new identity, while "the land of his nativity" becomes "indistinguishable in the distance" (p. 330).

The ship he sailed on went down and "a 'body perished . . . neither man nor mouse was ever heard o' mair" (p. 337). So says the voice of Scots rumor, and it does not exactly lie, for the man who returns to Scotland ten years later as Major General Melville, supporter of the Prince of Orange and the Glorious Revolution, and possessor of its rationalist rewards, is a stranger to the Henry Morton who leaped safely from the sinking ship and found his way to Holland. He is a stranger especially in this respect: the Henry Morton who struggled to accommodate the homicidal identity of Enthusiast offered on behalf of his father Silas by Silas's old compatriot John Burley now knows that Silas was not the rebel and destroyer whom Burley represented him to be. Silas Morton was a bridge builder, occupier of both sides of an argument, carnal reasoner; for him honor and religious Enthusiasm counted, yes, but it was life that mattered supremely, the lives of enemies as well as allies, so that he was a soldier in arms only to end war. At this discovery, significantly, Morton took the public name of his mother's family, Melville, but anchored his identity on the rock of this secret paternal heritage. So the "resolution" which makes the lineaments of his face almost unrecognizable when he returns, even to his friend Cuddie Headrigg, marks a resolution of one of his most intense private dilemmas in the way Scott's protagonists almost always must—unmuffled at last, he is his father's son.

In a crucial visit to Milnwood, between paroxysms, Melville enters the parlor, noting how all the grand objects that were not his own and that earlier made "home" a place to be entered only after a hesitating tap, as if he were somehow guilty, have now "lost much of their influence over his mind." All but two, that is: "the counterfeit presentment of two brothers . . . dissimilar as those described by Hamlet" (p. 371). One figure is in armor, the other in velvet and brocade. Now he knows that the armor did not fully, or even fundamentally, express his father's reasoning, husbanding soul anymore than the finery expressed the real truth about his wealthy but miserly and joyless uncle. That is why there is now no paroxysm connected with "home." He has begun to square the triangle linking himself, his father, and Burley; the portrait of his uncle gives him his purchase on the problem.

In simplest terms, the difference between the two brothers, the true and the false father, is the same as that between Quentin Durward's father and his bachelor uncle, Le Balafre, "the scar." Silas Morton took a wife, a human act, a commitment to life—and to mortality—which is unthinkable either to his materially parsimonious brother or to his immortality-obsessed counterpart, Burley. "God gives every spark of life," says Morton in a much quoted response to all who would play God on behalf of political principle, "and those who destroy His work recklessly or causelessly must answer" (p. 313).[12]

The triangle linking Morton, Evandale, and Edith Bellenden, however, is, to use a word much repeated in the closing pages of the novel, paroxysm to the end, the strangest, perhaps the most important, end in all the Waverley novels. Morton-Melville's task as his father's son and his author's protagonist is to take a wife. After the interval of years abroad he still loves Edith; she, glimpsing as he rides away in paroxysm what she thinks, correctly on several levels, is the ghost of Morton, finally admits to herself that she loves him, despite her word of engagement to another. Between them, in their domain, stands Morton's double, his rival Evandale, loving Morton himself, sensitive to Edith's feelings, but determined not to give her up in bodiless marriage to a figment of her imagination, willing, as he said at the accidental enacting of that engagement, to die in Morton's place, but not to die and leave the place empty.

The exchanges of identity between Morton and Evandale complete themselves in the final pages of the book. With the fall of the Stuarts it is now Evandale who faces and embraces outlaw status reluctantly but with hidden elan: with Morton's ghost claiming his affianced bride it is now he whose feelings of private resentment must be repressed, to issue in a wild commitment to political violence. As the pages of *Old Mortality* dwindle in this impasse the forces of evil which once aimed at the irresolute Morton converge upon Evandale. The time-serving, money-grabbing, shabby evil Milnwood returns in the person of Basil Oliphaunt; the time-mastering death-eating charismatic evil Burley returns in his own person. Evandale, irresolute now, in his own paroxysm, rides out from Fairy-Knowe against them and is shot down. Morton-Melville, arriving just too late, that is, just on time, presses the hand of the man who kept *his* appointment with old mortality, and the place of the husband, the cultivator, is filled, though Edith, sinking numbly into her place, her eyes on the dying man, remains still and mute, "nor was she aware that Fate, who was removing one faithful lover, had restored another as if from the grave" (p. 406).

Evandale restores their presence to each other by joining their hands "and expired in the next moment." But what sort of domesticity this sign encoded, what sort of future was worked out in the extinction of splendid personalities so that a third more normal could survive[13]—this the author of Waverley, in his alarm, or charity, or guilt, refused to guess at.

For he ended the novel in that phrase of expiration. Speechless, Evandale died; mute, Edith and Morton live, handfasted. And when, as the narrator imagined in a sly conclusion, the "common reader" insisted on knowing how everything turned out, he made an ending to her specifications ("a glimpse of sunshine in the last chapter . . . is quite essential," p. 40) and then seized his hat and ran, he admits, lest "the Demon of Criticism" (p. 410) pass his guard to complain of the uncertain and traumatized future which the novel's real "last chapter" offered.

The Monastery/The Abbot:
The World Upside Down

The Monastery/The Abbot is the only novel-with-sequel the author of Waverley ever wrote: among the curious causes and consequences of this single essay in the double form is the fact that the author could not seize his hat and escape as the engaged pair of *The Monastery* melted back into "ordinary" life. In *The Monastery's* Halbert as in *Old Mortality's* Henry we see the desperate construction of a fragile identity out of fears, repressions, deaths, an identity which seeks closure in marriage: in *The Abbot*, unprecedented, we see the nature of the marriage.

We see it is sterile.

In fables no event signifies more sternly than this one. If it ends the story it is a sign of sin coming "home"; if it begins the story it is the sign of a coming necessary change or transfer of power. Scott needs two stories, with the sterile marriage at their pivot, to make it signify both. For the sterile hero of *The Monastery* and the promiscuous knight who fathers the hero of *The Abbot*, different as they are, are "they that turn the world upside down" (p. 47), and though the alliance between them is inevitable, and the change, on the whole, desirable, the sin is there and requires punishment.

We have met this phrase before, examining *Rob Roy*. One of those Waverley outlaw-kings whom the protagonist seeks and shares identity with, at least for a time, Rob Roy commented about the upheaval of "the '15" "let it come . . . if the world is turned upside down, why, honest men have the better chance to get bread out of it" (*Rob Roy*, p. 352). In this image he had combined the elan of the outlaw-artist who loves simply to change the picture, and the bitter sarcasm of the dispossessed Highland aristocrat for whom the current situation, not the planned counterrevolution, is the upside down one. For the author of Waverley, drawn partly as a historian but more as a romancer to the scene of great dislocations, the unusually broad canvas of *The Monastery/The Abbot* represents his attempt to confront more fully the upside-downing, and the downside-upping of western Christendom in one of its most enigmatic figures, Queen Mary Stuart.

In the complicated and sometimes half-buried fables of that double novel he imagined four linked and dangerous reversals in language, class, religion, and gender: these together upended the world. Forever now "underneath" are "naturally" creative song and performative speech, the mystic and sensuous half-pagan Roman Catholic Church, the old founding national "houses," and, iconically representing all of these, representing Chivalry itself, "the Lady." Uneasily on top now, characterizing the modern world, are constructed commentating text and the language of carnal reason, the rational ameliorating Protestant Church, the new bastard houses of national political accommodation, and, iconically representing all these, Reason itself, the self-made man.

I have already described the tableau of fire and female witchery through which *The Monastery's* Halbert Glendinning passes, obtaining his manhood, his new mode of speech, and the black book which is the key to his future. It will be his teacher of Protestant religion, his prebridal gift to Mary Avenel; and Protestanism and bride together will win him possession of the barony and power of the old House of Avenel. This tableau, which bears some gentler affinity with the holy fire of destruction presided over in *Ivanhoe* by Ulrica, is the work of the White Lady of Avenel, guardian spirit of the old House. As with Ulrica, her speech is a rhymed distillation of the best in old "tushery," beautiful, terrible, and morally ambiguous. She and her fire exist as an ordeal for the hero, as with Ulrica and Ivanhoe; after the fire frees the hero from his old captivities the fire and the enchantress fade together. In *Ivanhoe*, as later in *The Pirate*, the "supernatural" enchantress had "realistic," if sketchy, ground, in an old woman's psychotic accommodation of her young tragedies of loss and guilt. But the maiden White Lady of *The Monastery* has no human ground. She is, as the author of Waverley conceded later to hostile critics, "machinery" interpolated into the real (created) territory of the narrative for fun, as his fellow Gothic novelists were interpolating theirs for terror. She is, he comments more seriously, of the imagined race of Shakespeare's Ariel (p. xiii), who are pranksters and world-upenders at heart, whose interlude of service to man, temporary and testy, is to reveal or remind us, rather offhand, what final steps we must take to become "human," if that's what we want to be.

Deepest of all, I would say, is her affinity with the Elf Queen who offers the world of art and Unreason to the minstrel Thomas Rhymer—in exchange for full control of his "tongue."[14] "True Thomas" of Ercildowne, the minstrel figure with whom Scott undoubtedly identified, at first mistook the Lady for the Queen of Heaven: set straight, he went with her anyway, to the land of the unsayable origin and end of all things on this earth. "My tongue is my own," doughty Thomas insists, and returns with his songs, but the wonderful old ballad hints nevertheless that the only tongue which cannot lie about that land of ultimates is the mute tongue. If we posit this affinity, then, we must note that the text Scott's protagonist brings back from this non-Heavenly Queen, Christendom's holy book of life's origins and ends, solves nothing for anybody, only generates lies, and accusations of lying. Confronted with the text's warrant for believing that the Devil specially torments God's chosen priests, the Catholic debater of the novel, Father Eustace, evades—"for every text there is a paraphrase" (pp. 51–52). Confronted with the text's warrant for the establishment of a mediating priesthood upon the Rock of Peter, the Protestant debater, Henry Warden, contends eagerly, "it is a perversion of the text . . . grounded on a vain play upon words" (p. 314).

Perversions, "plays," paraphrases are inseparable from text, and even from language itself, it seems; language carries its upside down deconstructing element inside it. In *The Monastery* the author of Waverley creates his pagan White Lady to mirror and linguistically reverse and undo Saint Mary and her monks, breaking down Masses into verses on the unfortunate Father Phillip's tongue. In *The Abbot* the service of election is countered and dismantled by the Babel of the elected Abbot of Unreason. That these two pagan anti-Catholic forces should appear in the end to be Protestants in disguise, the White Lady protecting the Englished Bible, the anti-Abbot a retainer of Protestant Sir Halbert, offers evidence for a deep confusion or anxiety in Scott about the Protestant right-side upping of the Christian religion which he championed. In line with much Episcopal orthodoxy Scott argues in *The Monastery/The Abbot* that it was Rome's inner alliance with paganism that turned primitive Christianity on its head and perverted its texts, that made of Saint Mary and Satan characters undistinguishable in superstitious glamor from fairies and hobgoblins, and of the disciples of Christ that Rock which, in its cathedrals and monasteries and cells, had to be smashed. The Abbot of Unreason himself, after superintending that destruction, assures Roland Graeme in *The Abbot* that the tales told by monks of the early encounters of Sir Halbert with the White Lady were made "to gull us simple laymen withal: they knew that fairies and hobgoblins brought aves and paternosters into repute" (p. 151). So? In order to free their tongues for aves and paternosters the Christians had first to accept, or even create, the verses of the fairies, which forever after threaten to derange the paternosters? To escape that waiting derangement the Protestants will speak only the words in the holy text?

The anti-Abbot, escorting Roland through the de-mythicized glen of the White Lady a generation after Halbert's ordeal, assures the half-fearing half-longing youth that "now we have given up worship of images in wood and stone, me thinks it were no time to be afraid of bubbles in the water, or shadows in the air." Roland, secretly educated a Catholic, half-heartedly defends the besieged religion—to which Unreason (or Reason?) answers robustly, "Pshaw! they told us another story . . ." when they wanted money for relics or monuments (p. 151). Another story, another version, another paraphrase; the shadow and its emblems. Is Christianity really free of its subversive fairies and hobgoblins when its reformers inhabit the old emblems and then affect to throw off the mystic emblems to become mere carnal "morality," as the Covenanter John Burley scornfully called Morton's "indulged" Episcopalo-Presbyterianism? Is it still Christianity? Is it even still "religion"?

The fate of this religion is worked out in the fate of the figure to whom Roland rides in the second half of the novel, moving from the monastery destroyed by its anti-Abbot in the spirit of Protestant reason into the apparently rationalized and politicized secular world. But his destination is the lake of Lochleven, real icon of the mythic "Limbolake" to which an old song has it that all the elves, fairies, and magic of the vanishing feudal world have been banished.[15] There the White Lady herself, Queen Mary Stuart, waits out the processes of a conspiracy to restore the emblematic religion, to turn the downed world right side up again (or, every text has its paraphrase, to turn the righted world upside down again). And to this conspiracy, pushed by complex psychic desires and pulled by outside agents, painfully articulating his qualifications and conditions like Henry Morton, Roland Graeme goes in service.

Halbert Glendinning and Roland Graeme, two generations of protagonists who turn the chivalric Catholic world upside down, were born Catholic and become Protestant. But their change is less a conversion than an accommodation to rational, or bourgeois, politics. Psychically unequipped to challange any man's chosen religion,[16] anxious about the "heroism" of any character who abandons a deeply felt principle, the author of Waverley evaded this issue by making both young men merely "dutiful," almost amoral, Catholics. Insofar as they change religiously at all, what they admit into their hearts as religion is not "Protestantism" so much as doubt of romanized, paganized Catholicism with its Unrational, faith-grounded certainties. And since the "new" religion emphasizes the private world between the Scriptural text and its individual reader, a text inscribed by the reader between its leaves with the commentary of his own paraphrases, Protestantism makes a place for the doubt, or, more strictly, the humility in the face of God, that the Waverley protagonist experiences as his primary religious feeling.[17]

No, the more fundamental and lasting upending that links the two young men is of class: both are servants who become masters. *The Monastery*'s Halbert is the son of a very minor gentlemen; his fate is clearly to be a tenant farmer or huntsman supplying the tables of the lord of the neighborhood, Avenel, or its "Lady," St. Mary's Monastery. His rise to be lord of Avenel and knight "protector" of St. Mary's is as "realistic" a story of a strong character attracting the loosened powers of an upended world as Scott could contrive; this, paradoxically, because of the parahuman "machinery" of the White Lady, not in spite of it. Roland, on the other hand, is the son of Julian Avenel and Catherine of Newport, the legitimate blood heir of the barony which Halbert holds through merit and hard work and the political patronage of the Protestant Earl of Murray, with only fragile legitimacy conferred by his wife's Avenel blood. This blood legitimacy actually makes the progress of Roland, the chronologically later protagonist, more "fabulous," more chivalric, than Halbert's, this despite the apparently greater psychic consistency of the portrait of the page who became an earl, and despite the absence of fairies from his world. What does Roland need a fairy godmother for if he really is, within and behind, what he wishes to become? And how but magically can one explain Halbert's desire to construct what there never was, a Glendinning knighted and belted and owning no master? This desire, backed by a phantom and crowned ambiguously with power and sterility, is what makes Halbert "modern" and, I would argue, the more poignant and interesting of the two protagonists, humorless as his "tushery" often makes him, attractive and spirited and witty as is his invading "son" and eventual supplanter, Roland Graeme.

It is Halbert's second visit to the Lady in her ghostly glen that enlightens us, and him, about the mysterious desire that drives him. It arises out of his contact with a figure who is, however comic to the reader, a mysteriously intolerable scourge to Halbert, as much his wraith-rival as Evandale is Morton's, a body who occupies his very place. This is Sir Piercie Shafton, a beribboned gallant from Elizabeth's court who comes north speaking a Euphuistic dialect of sonneteering "tushery." He is quartered, like all the loose powers in the shaken world, upon the hapless widow Glendinning in her hidden decayed tower, until the politico-religious quarrel which had made southern Scotland dangerous ground for this self-proclaimed intimate and agent of the English Catholic Percys has settled down.

Sir Piercie is a clown figure from beginning to end. Why then is Halbert's "altered" self so chafed by this puffball aristocrat that he seeks relief from his rage and help against this inert "enemy" from the frightening White Lady? And why, on the other hand, does the lofty Piercie, confronted by the silver bodkin which the White Lady assured Halbert would place the nobleman and himself "on equal terms," explode in deadly wrath against the nameless rustic like a "gun when touched by the linstock" (p. 174)?

The silver pin, enlarged in the young man's wrath to swords, has a function in the Waverleyan "Romance" which involves a young man and his wraith in a duel to the death for the available single quantum of being, or name, which each desires or represents. Because of the White Lady's magic, Halbert and Piercie engage in such a battle, each waking afterward under the impression he has killed the other, and Halbert flees the glen of his birth to engage in the fleshing out of that acquired identity.

But the silver pin expresses a real truth as well as a magic one, it is a low mimetic tool as well as a high mimetic one. And at this level too Sir Piercie Shafton and the soon-to-be Sir Halbert Glendinning are equals. For the pin was the sign of Piercie's mother, the daughter of a tailor. His origins were not noble, though his end is. Ridiculous as he is, prickable as his inflated language, padded clothing, inflated self are, Piercie too is one of the men who turned the world upside down.[18] And though in the Waverley novels the world continually seeks that upending, and amorally cherishes the men who accomplish it, a punishment is always reserved for them too, some fault or flaw becomes visible to suggest not only the outlaw origins of the march of progress, or history, but, more poignantly, to suggest that the individual can only remain "in step" with that movement whose agent he is for a few steps. After that he is, with most of the others, out of step.

Thus the laughable and laughing Sir Piercie, upending tailor's grandson into nobleman, falls back again, happily enough on the whole, to marry a miller's daughter at the end of *The Monastery*. Thus the political hero of the new Scotland, James Earl of Murray, is barred from the throne he wants and deserves and is warped in character by the fact of his bastardy. Thus the atheist-anarchic baron of Avenel, Julian, whose "profession" it was to "turn the world upside down" and "live ever the blithest life when the downer side is uppermost" (p. 225), and whose alliance with the godly upside-downer Henry Warden and the political reformer Murray showed most clearly the amoral basis of that great historical movement, dies unheeding as his Avenel heir is born. He dies ironically in defense of the Monastery he scorned, because "his fierce and turbid spirit" could not resist participating, on whatever side, in the "strife in which it had so long delighted" (p. 347) And thus the admirable, newly moderate and "bounded" Halbert, arriving as the strife ceases, to take charge for the Protestant forces of the defeated Monastery and its downed world, rescues, in his virtuous neutrality, his carnal reason, the nameless baby who will supplant him, who is actually Julian's son and Mary Avenel's cousin, the rightful heir of Avenel.

He is ridiculed for this action on the battlefield: "'Shoulder your infant!' cried a harquebusier. 'Port your infant!' said a pikeman" (p. 351). But the joke turns a little grim in the opening pages of *The Abbot* as the lady he wedded in the closing pages of *The Monastery* produces no infant to replace—to justify—the gun on his shoulder. The "melancholy depression" that deepens his voice, the "constant pressure of the steel cap" that rubs bald his temples (p. 22), result partly from his decade of strenuous activity in a politically divided and violent country after the takeover of Saint Mary's, but they result more from the inner fragility of a self-made man. "Look at those barren hills, Mary," he muses, on his return from still another successful mission abroad for his Protestant power-brokers, and then, in subliminal association, "let the emergency be passed when they need my head and hand, and they only know me as son of the obscure portioner of Glendearg" (pp. 24, 25). Sir Halbert he is now, and even "Knight of Avenel," but his activities in war, in council, in espionage, do not somehow anchor his self-constructed spirit in its barren hills; these actions seem legitimate and nourishing to him only if he can count them "capacities which are necessary to the foundation of a family" (p. 26), and he had been denied that sanction. For lack of "an heir, in whom our affections, *as well as our pretensions*,might have centered" (p. 25, my italics), Mary Avenel knows that her ego and her husband's, as well as the marriage and the new House itself, is unstable. Her own ego's hollow, and as "fate" would have it, Halbert's, and Avenel's, is filled by the child, Roland, the shouldered infant who was taken from the battlefield on which Saint Mary's Catholic/Pagan world was defeated, by its grandmother, and raised in secret as the Catholic Avenel who would restore the upended world.

Part of the "hardy little boy's" (p. 6) attraction to Sir Halbert's lady, as he arrives by epic accident on her doorstep at the age of ten after an accident in the Avenel lake, is his resemblance to her husband. An anonymous peasant child, she thinks, "May he not be designed, as others have been, to rise out of a humble situation into honour and eminence?" (p. 28) And this unnerving resemblance is part of the reason too why Sir Halbert avoids his lady's new page for the next seven years, his brow "slightly overcast," his neglect, as Roland notes, "not unmingled with fixed aversion" (p. 48). Roland himself, invited by one lady thus to "rise" and secretly pushed by another, Magdalen Graeme, to act up to his high, though hidden, birth, has none of Halbert's problem validating his sense of inner worth, though he has comic trouble making his fellow peasants and servants validate it. What he balks at is accepting his inner worth, his "high" value and destiny, from the hands of women.

Interestingly, in *The Monastery*, when Halbert was a young man he gladly underwent his mystical "change" under the tutelage of the White Lady and gladly accepted his new title at the end from his new wife. In the second novel, however, with its masculine title replacing that of St. Mary's Monastery and its new rational world made by new men out of their outlaw deeds, out of their "unhallowed passion for that clashing of cold iron" (p. 159), the threat that the old feminine "legitimate" powers, Saint Mary at their head, may re-turn the upended world upside down is so strong that even the older, wiser Sir Halbert suffers bouts of resentment about his wife's blood legitimacy vis-á-vis his own "made" legitimacy. And Roland, when he reaches manhood and begins dimly to understand his Catholic grandmother's counterrevolutionary purposes, finds "specially disagreeable" his situation as hooded hawk on a lady's wrist, "slave of a woman's whistle" (p. 88). His heart is set against his competing mothers, mistresses, "tutoresses" (p. 87) from the beginning of his quest for a secure personal identity: "No, by Saint Andrew! the hand that can hold the lance is above the control of the distaff . . . I will know . . . how it is that men, by valour and wisdom, work their way from the hodden-gray coat to the cloak of scarlet and gold. I will be a man amongst living men, or a dead corpse amongst the dead" (pp. 88, 155).

But young women are less easily evaded than old, as are lovers than mothers. And though he escapes the hoods of his "mothers," a Waverley man must, willy-nilly, seek his wife, that queen of the domestic domain which legitimizes his deeds. Roland's ordeal is only half over when he leaves the Lady of Avenel and the Catholic grandmother for the service of the knight and the earl, after the debate between Reason and Unreason. For the Earl seconds him to the service of history's own White Lady, romance's own Queen of hearts, Romanism's own Saint Mary, Mary Stuart. "If they mine," orders the royal bastard brother about the imprisoned Queen and her conspiring ladies, "do thou countermine." Countermine, and more: "Thou art young and handsome," he tells his male spy significantly, ordering him into the bower of ladies (p. 204). On the other hand, "do you become acquainted with each other" (p. 89), had said Magdalen Graeme to Roland earlier, raising the veil of the lovely Catherine Seyton, setting her mine. The old Catholic women expect the young one, chastely to seduce Roland further into their "mine"; the men expect their handsome young page to seduce Queen Mary's maids—Catherine becomes one of them—into countermining the conspiracy.

Roland is again, though at the behest of "the lance," under the sway of "the distaff" when he enters the service of Queen Mary. He once envied the Knight of Avenel the supernatural "help" he received in the glen of the witch; now at Lochleven, suffering that typical longing of the Waverley hero for an awakening into (or is it out of?) the "real history of his life," he bursts out in anguish:

> A land of enchantment have I been led into, and spells have been cast around me—everyone has met me in disguise— everyone has spoken to me in parables—I have been like one who walks in a weary and bewildering dream; and now you blame me that I have not the sense and judgment, and steadiness, of a waking, and a disenchanted, and a reasonable man, who knows what he is doing, and wherefore he does it![19] (Pp. 296–97)

Disenchantment is a painful process, and involves for Roland two choices connected with gender, with resettling the new world sexually with its dominant figure, man, on top. The young heir to power who turned from the Knight of Avenel to the Lady vowing "I will kiss no hand save yours, lady" (p. 28) must go in his turn the way taken by Halbert, who vowed in *The Monastery*, "Tush, man, I will serve the Queen or no one" (pp. 153–54); he must decide in the end "whether I will be kingsman or Queensman" (p. 209). And the young lover must solve for himself "that riddle of womankind, Catherine Seyton, who appeared before the eye of his mind—now in her female form—now in her male attire—now in both at once—like some strange dream, which presents to us the same individual under two different characters at the same instant" (p. 209). The riddle of womankind, Catherine Seyton, is easily solved—too easily, apparently, though I shall have more to say about this in the next chapter. For the lovely and witty but modest and devoted young woman, who had been bred like another Roland in secret to help restore Catholicism and its Queen to the "up" side of the world, has unaccountably a masculine, self-assertive, even weapon-wielding and buffet-giving (p. 287) free-speaking mocking personna. She also has a twin brother, who symbolizes this self. Henry Seyton, sometimes in male dress, sometimes in female, slips around the periphery of the story, fighting like his sister for the Catholic cause, and bristling with hostility at his sister's lover. The anti-marriage "twin" of Catherine, surely allied emblematically to the "mad" side of Diana Vernon, works in uneasy alliance with Roland, because she/he must, to free Queen Mary, but she/he will never consent to give his/her twin in marriage to the nameless page, or perhaps to any man. But given the domestic necessities of the Waverley protagonist we know what the fate of Cath-

erine's masculine "twin" must be. In the last great battle, when the
freed queen and her supporters encounter, too hastily, the forces that
will finally defeat and exile her, Henry and Roland vie for the most
dangerous place on the field, and Mary allows Henry to go, keeping
Roland to protect her. Rescued later out of the thickest press of his
enemies, the dying Henry takes his leave with a startling image, sug-
gesting that fatal cleaving of genders which is to become typical of the
new modern society: "commend me to Catherine—she will never more
be mistaken for me nor I for her—the last sword stroke has made an
eternal distinction" (p. 45).

It is this sword-stroke distinction too which the new world must
impose on Queen Mary Stuart, who is too much the mixture of man-
womanhood to be allowed to keep kingly authority. Imprisoned in the
castle of her illegitimate but ruling brother's mother, Mary plots to free
herself from the imposed "distaff," to take "the lance" for that last try at
righting the upended world. She avoids a poison attempt and handles
with considerable skill the taunts and tricks of ambassadors from "her"
court, who seek to confine her to the role of royal sister to the Earl of
Murray, royal mother to the infant King James, who would just as soon,
in fact, see her dead. Handed the renunciatory deed which, in custody,
she must sign, she goads the brutish Lord Lindesay into manhandling
her and then, baring her bruised arm, asks the company to witness "that
I subscribe these instruments in obedience to the sign manual of my
Lord of Lindesay." Her scorn and wit, as well as the testimony of the
bruise, move the politician momentarily beyond politics—unfortunately for Mary: while he pays tribute to "thy manliness of spirit" he
kneels, carefully making the "eternal distinction," "to Mary Stuart, not
to the Queen" (pp. 240–41). In this way the legitimate Queenship of
Mary, stolen by the outlaw men around her, is guiltily, cunningly,
transposed to her romantic womanhood, a transposition to which she
half consents, half understanding her loss. Freed by Henry and Roland,
later mediating their quarrel over Catherine, she notes, bitterly
prophetic, "with children and boys, at least, I may be a queen" (p. 398).[20]
With her genuine political authority gone, she must use the mythic
authority embodied in her gender, a dangerous and double-edged tool:
"methinks I am like a princess of romance, who may shortly set at
defiance the dungeons and weapons of all wicked sorcerers" (p. 372).[21]

It almost works. Roland and Henry she draws to her side, and even
the scion of the enemy's family, George Douglas; Lindesay she abashed,
and even Murray at long distance. But the sword stroke that has made
her "all woman," princess of romance, that separated her from her
brother, and her newly rationalized masculinized nation, also enclosed

her in a gender-destiny of powerlessness, though it conferred, in another sense, "eternal distinction." In this dire distinction, Roland participates, because he has to. In the new world, if one is to be a man, one must be a kingsman: the new language of carnal reason, forsaking chivalric "tushery," has no word to express the old double-sexed magic of authority and gentility once available to the choice in "queensman."

4   "This Confused Waste": Gender and Imposture in *The Heart of Midlothian, The Pirate, Redgauntlet*

My designs do not admit of female criticism.[1]

In our days, it would have been questioned whether she was an imposter, or whether her imagination was so deeply impressed with the mysteries of her supposed art, that she might be in some degree a believer in her own pretensions.[2]

It is possible that generations of readers and critics took *The Heart of Midlothian* to their bosoms because of the absence from its center of the disturbing Waverley Hero; it is certain that readers, and, I would argue, especially teachers, invested this novel above all with canonical status because of the consoling presence at its center of a quartet of women. It fits so well into "the great tradition" of fiction from *Pamela* and *Emma* to *Portrait of a Lady* and *Middlemarch* that it has been lifted oddly away from Scott. Its place in the Scott tradition is a little more subtle. If for some critics Scott "re-masculinized" a genre in danger of becoming female, for others, for most, perhaps, until the present generation, the one novel where the "prince errant" is a woman has been enshrined as "an Everest of achievement."[3]

    The novel appears to construct a world of efficacious action for women over against the stubborn, blocking inertia of the world of men and their laws.[4] It proceeds from act to act of rescue of women by women, explores and elevates sisterhood and motherhood, celebrates the power of women, they who wield "real power" and not just "the appearance of power," as the narrator approvingly comments of Queen Caroline. But of course this is a lie, whether about the real or the fictional world of *The Heart of Midlothian* or of its writer or readers across the generations, a fiction both within and about the fiction. It has been a lie at least since the evil transformation of Queenship which I have suggested Scott touched on in his treatment of Mary Stuart. Indeed some feminists are disposed to call this entitlement to "real power," that is, private influence, which galvanizes or even replaces "the appearance of power," that is, public sanctioned power, the Great Lie.[5] And with the calculated naiveté which is one of the profoundest tools of this philosophy, feminists are disposed to ask, of a novel acclaimed for its portrait of a woman who declines to tell a lie to save a sister from death for a crime she knows she didn't commit—what bizarre consolations do authors and readers receive from this? What really keeps Jeanie Deans "tugging at the heartstrings" of the author and reader of *The Heart of Midlothian?*[6]

The author of the Waverley novels has been unfixing the boundaries of male identity ever since Edward Waverley rode out from home to be kidnapped, "educated," seduced, and otherwise feminized. The co-opted revolutions and Glorious Compromises which ended political chivalry unfixed the sex roles of chivalry also; now it appears that each gender must journey through the experience of the other, the outlawed, gender, before either one can choose and re-fix the male or female identity appropriate to the new age. "It is never clear why Darsie Latimer should be subjected to female dress in the last portion of *Redgauntlet,*" objects Alexander Welsh (*The Hero of the Waverley Novels*, p. 161). Nor why George Staunton-Robertson should require to disguise himself as Madge Wildfire in the first portion of *The Heart of Midlothian*. In fact, each of these acts functions to initiate this journey. Darsie, the fair hero of *Redgauntlet*, undergoes the experience of the blond woman passivized, literally nailed in place in woman's dress on a woman's saddle board. George, the dark man, kindles his love for his male companion in outlawry and his hatred for that companion's hangman on the mad passions of the dark lady whose clothes he wears to direct the mob which hangs the hangman.

Yet the fair man's experience of female passivity is fleeting and ultimately false; so is the dark man's assumption of dark power. That goes double, of course, for the fair woman's secret accession to "real power" in the sudden revelation of male powerlessness, and triple for the dark woman's usurpation of male power. Jeanie Deans, it is true, bravely takes the journey south to the seat of power that Reuben Butler and George Staunton are too sick to take, and obtains the pardon of her condemned sister from Queen Caroline. But she goes nowhere without the money of the Laird of Dumbiedykes, carries crucial passports to the favor of male aristocrats and outlaws from other males in whose debt they are, and it is King George who grants the pardon. The dark Norna has power over lives, marriages, even apparently over the winds in the superstitious world of *The Pirate*, power, moreover, which she understands to have come to her as a reward for murdering her father. But this usurpation, this "imposture," as the narrator calls it, turns her wits, and is finally ended by the scornful denial—"I deny your powers"—of her own son. Denial of the dark power of woman is the making of manhood and the mark of grace in the world of the Waverley novels, that, and the surrender, which is no real surrender at all, to the powerless power, the "fairness," of the fair woman. When "the Pretender," Charles Edward Stuart, refuses in the political climax of *Redgauntlet* to deny his mistress, he forfeits forever the chance to convert his "pretense," his imposture, into power. Reuben Butler lives in happy ignorance of the little fortune his wife is accumulating in gifts from her exiled sister; he has surrendered his domestic mind to her guardianship of truth. But who could doubt the eventual end of that potential power, given the common sense, or sense of the common, that the fair heroine possesses? When the opportunity to buy land arises, Jeanie turns over her wealth to Reuben; the money buys property in his name and that of his sons, and she has to specify to him, as something a little out of the common, her hope that their daughter should have a good share of it when they die.

If, as Lawrence suggests, we trust the tale first, and then the teller, we will find in the Waverley novels an arresting and true account of the politics of gender, and thus the gender of politics, in these our own Western ages—Chivalry and Modernity. The canonical centrality of *The Heart of Midlothian* makes it the natural candidate for this chapter, and *The Pirate*, set deliberately at the "edge," Ultima Thule, of Scott's worlds, and designed, half-consciously, I think, as a kind of parody of his dark-light schema for manhood and womanhood, offers itself as Chivalric companion. *Redgauntlet*, I want to suggest, is a helpful median and foil, not only because it offers us quasi-brothers to match our sister sets in the first two novels, and our brothers in *The Pirate*, not only because it completes the feminization, and hence the erasure, of the Stuart political line, but also because it brings us as close as we are ever going to get in the Waverley novels to the true nightmare of the new manhood, the new politics. It gives us the mad*man* in the attic, that lover-victim not of passion but of reason, of the law—Peter Peebles.

As for the madwoman in the attic, that Satanic Eve, that woman-who-would-be-king, whose re-animation was to be the hidden desire, whose self-destruction the "cover story" of nineteenth-century woman writers, according to the influential analysis of Sandra Gilbert and Susan Gubar,[7] Scott knows her too. Before Mary Shelley's restored but destroyed female monster there was *Guy Mannering*'s Meg Merrilles, promising the destroying patriarch Ellengowan that each of his blows would fall on his own house. Before Charlotte Bronte's Bertha Mason Rochester there was *The Heart of Midlothian*'s Madge Wildfire, bent on the destruction of her lover's second love.[8] Foremother of George Eliot's great lyric anti-Angel, *Daniel Deronda*'s Alcharisi, is *The Pirate*'s Norna of the Fitful Head, whose attempt to elude the new reality of law and man and restore the powers of "our mother Eve" and of the prophetess-rulers of ancient Norse tradition, acquires in the narrative a curious status somewhere between "Imposture" and the temporary, though fitfully compelling "reality" of a part acted-out with complete self-abandonment.

All acts of power by women partake of this curious status; all Queenship, say the novels of the author of Waverley, truthfully telling the Great Lie, is Imposture, practiced more or less usefully by the female rogue, the madwoman, or her sister within the law, the "sincere actress."[9] These are our protagonists in this chapter, beings trying on roles of gender, roles of power, in the "confused waste" as Madge Wildfire calls it, of post-Chivalric Western society—the Impostor, the Pretender, the falsely named or falsely unnamed person, The Great Unknown—Who *was* that masked man? Who is that unmasked woman? To clarify this issue a bit before looking separately at each novel in the second half of the chapter, I should like to study the three significant acts of power by the three key "imposters" in these novels—Norna's attempt to marry her son to her alter-ego, the pardoning of Effie Deans by Queen Caroline, the last invasion of Britain by Prince Charles Edward Stuart.

Early in the tale the narrator of *The Pirate* delivers this little lesson on the powers of witches:

> superstitions of this nature pass through two stages ere they become entirely obsolete. Those supposed to be possessed of supernatural powers are venerated in the earlier stages of society. As religion and knowledge increase, they are first held in hatred and horror, and are finally regarded as imposters. . . . In our days, it would have been questioned whether she was an imposter, or whether her imagination was so deeply impressed with the mysteries of her supposed art, that she might be in some degree a believer in her own pretensions . . . (Pp. 52–53)

Norna ("the name, which signifies one of those fatal sisters who weave the web of human fate, had been conferred [by the community] in honor of her supernatural powers," p. 53) can heal diseases, because she knows natural biology, can appear and disappear at will, because she has found out all the short and secret ways into and out of places in her town. She can command the tides and winds because she has studied them carefully, can influence and prophesy about the behavior of individuals and families because she has studied them and their history carefully, can save or doom lives because she has a clear personal and political design to accomplish. The Northern Islands in the late 1600s are not so much opposed as politically inert, a fief of the Scottish Earls of Morton, subject to absent-minded economic plundering and occasional levying of troops, suffered to drift and degenerate into dreams of the Norse-Imperial past. But Norna plans a restoration, national and gender-oriented—"If the men of Thule have ceased to be champions . . . the women have not forgotten the arts that lifted them of yore into queens and prophetesses" (p. 51)—as well as personal—"I will be what I ought . . . the queen and protectress of these wild and neglected isles" (p. 104).[10] The forces of Queenship, nostalgically sublimated in the "Marian" tale of *The Monastery/The Abbot* (1820) and subtly mocked in the masculinized Elizabeth of *Kenilworth* (1821), surface as sorrowfully exposed imposture in *The Pirate* (1822).

In her program of female counterrevolution, Norna looks to two young persons, for the old have given in to the corruptions of peace and life. One of these is Mordaunt Mertoun, whom she believes is her son by an old and tragic liaison; the other is Minna Troil, the dark-haired daughter of her cousin, the hereditary "Yarl" of Zetland, whom she was to have married had it not been for the tragic liaison. Minna is her cousin's daughter, might have been, and spiritually is, her own daughter; Mordaunt she thinks is her son. Not for the first time in Scott obsession expresses itself in incest, or apparent near-incest. In this, as in other aspects, Minna is a sister to *Waverley's* Flora MacIvor, whose political and personal energies bound her to live through and with her brother, Fergus, in a more than sisterly union. Minna's romantic imagination too seeks a personal active role in the dangerous and supernatural or mysterious, as it would have to be, enterprise which is to bring political revolution and true Norse identity to her corrupted and sluggard nation. She, like Rob Roy, wants to make use of these "upside-down" times: "why should we not under so many changes as late times have introduced, have seized the opportunity to shake off an alliance which is not justly due from us" (p. 188) argues the "inexperienced" maiden who was "most completely self-possessed and in her own element" while leading the war dance as Queen of the Swords at her father's feast (p. 158). Mordaunt, on the other hand, since he is in fact no kin to Norna, speaks from first to last the Waverleyan language of carnal reason, "resolving within himself to take time for farther inquiry and mature consideration, ere he either rejected or admitted" Norna's claims upon and plans for him, seeking always the shifty middle ground of response, that he might "gratify Norna without otherwise standing committed" (p. 353). These two temperaments will never make the match that, backed by Norna's outlaw powers and Magnus Troil's wealth and standing, could effect the counterrevolution. But Minna is at that time secretly soliciting, with more success, on behalf of the national racial dream, the man who does in fact carry Norna's rebellious blood, who is therefore her spiritual and almost her physical brother, the "pirate," Clement Cleveland.

Both the young woman and the old one have seen in Cleveland a reflection of their own dark ardor and independent spirit; both, therefore, assume that he too seeks to live an unconventional life of imagination and high purposes. But though all imaginists are outlaws, not all outlaws are wedded to imagination and great endeavors. Only to Norna does Cleveland reveal the corrosive Byronic skepticism which underlies his life: "I have been long inaccessible both to fear and to superstition" (p. 408). In this climactic scene she has just rescued him from the law, in order to command him to leave the area and resign Minna Troil to the mate of her own blood that she has designed for her daughter-Enthusiast, leave or die within twenty-four hours. Cleveland refuses to be moved by her "role" as witch and Queen prophetess, but credits her with that "wonderful skill in combinations," that capacity to put two and two together quickly, to anticipate external reality and manipulate internal reality, which *seems* like necromancy and mastery. "For what then do you hold me, if you deny the power that I have bought so dearly?" Norna challenges, in a "hollow" voice, only to hear the denial that utterly deflates her. "You have wisdom, mother," reasons the man who is, unknown to either, her son, "at least, you have art, and art is power. I hold you for one who knows how to steer upon the current of events, but I deny your power to change its course" (pp. 408–9).

As both know in this scene, the current of events, steered on but not controlled by Norna, bears toward the proscribed pirate ship the British warship which will sink it in twenty-four hours. Cleveland can evade this fate by leaving, which is, coincidentally, the will of Norna. But in calling her "power" simply the natural art of "combination," he does more than resist her, he defeats her power. For the power resides fundamentally in her own conviction. What makes her so poignant for a feminist reading of Scott is that along with that "consciousness of power" which was "given me in exchange for innocence and peace of mind" after she had "murdered" her father, she was given a "demon which . . . whispers to me, 'Norna, this is but delusion—your power rests but on the idle belief of the ignorant, supported by a thousand petty artifices of your own'"(p. 355). And that demon takes flesh in the person of Cleveland, as she desperately challenges him to cease meddling in her Design. She calls Cleveland a tool of the specifically male dark Influences which substitute for Principle "a wild sense of indomitable pride which such men call honour," and swears to wrest control of that tool from these male Influences, even though "the demon who presides over it should arise even now in his terrors." "Call your demon," laughs Cleveland, and it is in response to this that Norna plays her last card, calls the male skeptic demon—"for what, then, do you hold me . . . ?" and receives from her human adversary, her demon in flesh, her secret son, her quittance, "I deny your power."

Norna has seen this male power-denying demon before.[11] He was the dwarf who sat on the dwarfie-stone to whom the young Norna, or Ulla Troil, called aloud for full possession of those mysterious powers which her mentor-teacher-father had hinted at, "indicated, rather than explained" (p. 203). The dwarf told her she might have the power, but only if she robbed "the life-giver / Of the gift which he gave" (p. 206). Old Erland's "gift" to his daughter was her life, and her taste for forbidden powers. Terrified at the naked exchange the dwarf exposes—kill the patriarch, receive his power—the young Ulla had attempted to forget her desire until she fell in love with "a fatal stranger." Leaving the house to plan an elopement against the old man's command, she closed the door to her father's room to hide from him, and, and returning, found him mysteriously suffocated in the shut room—"dead through my act—dead through my disobedience—dead through my infamy" (p. 209).

Dead through her desire. The image is stark. When the woman opens her door she shuts the man's; when the daughter leaves the house the father suffocates; when Ulla acts on her freedom she murders her father. On parricide is woman's power built. Yet the demon is a trickster too, for in sealing her to her bargain he seals her to himself, the voice that repeats through all her years of power—it isn't yours, it isn't real. In self-destructive irony Norna chooses for her familiar the dwarf Nick Strumpfer, who takes the message to the English warship that eventually results in the sinking of the pirate's ship, and the imprisonment, almost the death, of Cleveland. As the revelations pile up in the final pages, how little Norna had actually controlled, how the one secret she did not know—Cleveland, not Mordaunt Mertoun, was her son—negated all her secret designs, the prophecy of the demon, against which Norna had striven in vain, is fulfilled: "the parricide shall . . . also be denounced as the imposter" (p. 355).

The heavy hand of Conversion falls on Norna in the last chapter.

Dwarf dismissed, name and dress changed, the sagas and chemicals burned and the "sacred book" always in hand, property willed away from Cleveland and Minna to Mordaunt and Brenda Troil, the fair-haired woman, the Queen turns back her power to its proper patriarchal possessor: "to the poor ignorant people who came as formerly to invoke her power over the elements, she only replied—'The winds are in the hollow of His hand'" (p. 446). But there is something a tiny bit odd in the prose of the author of Waverley, concluding this satisfying male fable. Listen to the (half-conscious?) disclaimers: "From that time Norna appeared to assume a different character. . . . Her conversion . . . seemed to be sincere, and was certainly useful. She appeared deeply to repent of her former presumptuous attempts . . . [but] it was not easy to know how much or little she remembered of the complicated events in which she had been connected" (pp. 446–47). Which, one wonders, does Scott want us to think was the Imposture—the Queen Witch, or the churchgoing granny?

Queen Caroline, or Queen Carline (witch) as those call her who are angry at her kingly behavior,[12] performs two acts of power in *The Heart of Midlothian*. She grants a stay of execution to the soldier, mob-disciplinarian, and murderer John Porteous, and a pardon to the infant-murderess Effie Deans, distributing mercy equally, one would say, to convicted killers of both genders. Neither is exactly guilty (or not guilty), and both have to be convicted, of which more later. The stay of execution is a political act; Porteous, captain of the City Guard in the Edinburgh of the 1730s, executor of British law during the period only a generation after the jerry-built union between England and Scotland, had killed in quelling mob disturbance. To intervene on his behalf is to sanction discipline, enforce, in a way, judicial, as against personal, murder. The pardon of Effie seems a personal act to a woman from a queen who has been "converted" to a woman by a woman's eloquence. Yet a careful study of this climactic scene of pardon reveals an astonishingly complex and truthful picture of patriarchy visibly and invisibly at work subtly corrupting, rather than celebrating, sisterhood and Queenship.[13]

The scene between Jeanie Deans, pleading for her convicted sister, and Queen Caroline, standing in for her royal husband, is in the first place a quartet, not a duet, between three sophisticated politicians and an innocent. And it turns on the responses of the three politicians to three innocent statements from Jeanie, and one statement not so innocent. The Duke of Argyle expects to direct Jeanie in the scene—"Look at me from time to time—if I put my hand to my cravat so (showing her the motion), you will stop; but I shall only do this when you say anything, that is not likely to please" (p. 377). And the absent figure of George II directs Queen Caroline; the king "entrusted to her the delicate office of determining the various degrees of favour necessary to attach the wavering " statesmen of the time, or to "regain those whose good-will had been lost" (p. 380). The Queen has "preserved the power" of retaining and steadying the Argyle allegiance by a friendly alliance with Lady Suffolk, who lies under political obligation to Argyle—and who is her husband's mistress: "By this dexterous management the Queen secured her power against the danger which might most have threatened it—the thwarting influence of an ambitious rival" (p. 382). The Queen compensates for her mortification and resentment at this necessary "dexterity" by allowing herself the "liberty now and then, to bestow a few civil insults" upon Lady Suffolk. The mistress has procured for the statesman a private interview with the Queen, whose general program is to consolidate the royal alliance with the man who held the Highlands in check during the last Jacobite threat, whose specific program is to enforce peace and law in the rebellious capital which rose in revolt the month before at the news of Porteous' respite and murdered the man she had pardoned.

Into this inauspicious tangle of personal grievances and political patchwork steps Jeanie Deans with her request that the Queen obtain pardon for Effie Deans of Edinburgh, convicted of child murder. What a barbarous people yours are, so given to murders that your laws must require conviction without *habeus corpus* in order to control this particular kind of murder, remarks the Queen, "in a kind tone," to which the naif replies, "there are mony places besides Scotland where mothers are unkind to their ain flesh and blood" (pp. 387–88). The Queen kindles at this; disputes between the royal parents and the Prince of Wales are notorious. The king's mistress tries to cover with some light chitchat about causes of the crime of child murder, which draws from Jeanie the observation that some women kill their bastards because they fear the exposure, scorn, ruin, injury, or even death that come in a puritan country to women guilty of "light life and conversation, and for breaking the seventh commandment" (p. 384). Having ignorantly indicted both highborn Englishwomen for the crimes for which her sister begs their mercy ("she has hit with both barrels right and left!" groans Argyle to himself), Jeanie goes on to make her plea, moving and utterly personal:

> When the hour of death comes, that comes to high and low— lang and late may it be yours—Oh, my Leddy, then it isna what we hae dune for oursells, but what we hae dune for others, that we think on maist pleasantly . . . and the thoughts that ye hae

> intervened to spare the puir thing's life will be sweeter in that
> hour, come when it may, than if a word of your mouth could
> hang the haill Porteous mob at the tail of ae tow. (P. 391)

And the Queen, though warning "I cannot grant a pardon," promises
her critical intercession and concludes the scene by giving Jeanie money
and a sewing case.

Two moments are decisive in the Queen's conversion, one when
Jeanie delivers, all unknowing, the insult to the king's mistress, one
when, all too knowing, she tells the Queen a lie. Or rather, not exactly a
lie. A Jesuit might call it mental reservation when the Queen, still
antagonistic to all things Scottish, suddenly challenges—"had you any
friends engaged in the Porteous mob?"—and Jeanie, no friend to the
man who had seduced her sister and led the Porteous mob, but knowing
his name and location, replies, "no, Madam," deeply thankful that "the
question was so framed that she could, with a good conscience, answer
in the negative" (p. 390).

The mental reservation has to do not so much with lying as with that
familiar quietism which is the corruption, that is, the virtue, of all the
Prince Errants of the Waverley novels, the energy which is morally
blocked from attacking, initiating, offensive action, and must therefore
maneuver, procrastinate, and reserve until it can find the defensive,
consolidating, preserving position from which it can act. Any such
hero/heroine, with George Staunton's secret in her ken and even with
his permission to use it if necessary, might have followed up this
reservation with the explanation, "I would hae gaen to the end of the
earth to save the life of John Porteous, or any other unhappy man in his
condition; but I might lawfully doubt how far I am called upon to be the
avenger of his blood, though it may become the civil magistrate to do so"
(p. 390). But only a woman could defer to the law quite so lawfully as
this, make that deference, so comely and natural, the cornerstone of her
plea—by the law, and the Law, are we all criminals, all condemned to
death, and the mercy we receive will be only that which we have given.
As skillfully as Portia does Jeanie marshal the "law" against the law-
givers. But Portia's mercy-loving womanhood is a secret to all but the
audience of Shakespeare's play, where Jeanie's is a visible ironic counterpoint to, even a weapon for, the baiting and rivalry by which the
Queen and the shadow-Queen, the king's mistress, maintain their
shadow power on the periphery of George II's law. Jeanie has Reason
for refusing to endanger a male life to save a female one. But as the
author of Waverley designs the scene, what is emphasized is the
Queen's instinctive and corrupt alliance with the Scotswoman who

innocently condemned the king's mistress and allowed the Queen another one of the "civil insults" to her good friend by which she releases her rage while securing her "power." On that foundation of anti-sisterhood is built Jeanie's power to move the Queen, on that foundation the Queen's power to save Jeanie's sister. The fulcrum is the king's mistress; the weight belongs to the men, John Campbell Duke of Argyle, who is to be conciliated, and George of Hanover, who must be allowed a mistress but who cannot be condemned for light conversation and breaking the seventh commandment.[14]

Jeanie Deans's refusal to play her truth-card in the meeting, her evasion of the invitation to turn in the leader of the Porteous mob because the framing of the question allowed her to answer that she had no "friend" engaged in the assault, is more than a tribute to her capacity for mercy, more even than a sign of her newly learned capacity to juggle the values of truth in the service of the value of mercy. The object of Jeanie's mercy here is a man: the bottom line in this society, the crucial topos of this novel, I believe, is that woman must save, may not kill, man. Man is the tabooed object, woman the eternal forgiver. Queen Caroline commutes Porteous's sentence; Jeanie, Effie, and Madge protect George Staunton; Jeanie saves the life of "the Whistler," George's son. The ghost of murdered Ailie Mushat, who lived with her husband through half a dozen atempts on her life until he finally cut her throat at Mushat's cairn, is adjured by mad Madge to forgive him still, "bygane's suld be byganes." Defending Effie Deans from the charge of neglecting or murdering her lover's child, Effie's lawyer, as we will see, offers the court a new "natural" law—Effie loved George's child and relied on his promise to help her through the childbirth because any true woman, however atrociously offended by him, will cleave to her lover. The court will not accept this in lieu of what the community pretends to believe is *the* "natural" law, that any true woman in trouble will cleave to her female relatives and friends. Finding Effie an unnatural woman because she stayed with and believed in her man, and hid from her sister, the court condemns her. Yet the novel in every significant event asserts, enforces, desires, the earlier truth, the new "natural" law: woman is the protector and forgiver of male lovers, children, parents, not their killer. If she deviates from this behavior toward parricide, male infanticide, homicide of any sort, she is, is made to go, mad, like Madge Wildfire or Norna of the Fitful Head.[15]

Another king's mistress is the fulcrum of another power play at the climax of *Redgauntlet*, where another Campbell walks off with the honors and asserts the king's power. Here the power of influence fictively assigned to the lady becomes the "condition" by which the last

Scottish king loses his last bid for power. Charles Edward Stuart has come from France disguised as "Father Buonaventure" to meet with, inspire, and eventually lead into battle the last remnants of Jacobite supporters. The advocate Alan Fairford, driven into this plot through his attempt to rescue his friend Darsie Latimer from its toils, meets the "Father," the Pretender, and his "penitent," a lady "rather inclined to embonpoint" (p. 326) like Queen Caroline, and Effie Deans, who shadows the Prince's movements and foreshadows his immersion in "domesticity." The Jacobites, roused to their last pitiful gathering in a smugglers' inn, have pretty clearly fictionalized the power of the mistress— "She puts his secrets into her workbag and out they fly whenever she opens it. If I must hang, I would wish it to be in somewhat a better rope than the string of a lady's hussey" (p. 401)—in order to have a reason for rejecting a king so feminized. She for her part, sensing betrayal in the male loyalty he counts on, defines the purely masculine drama—"And thus you will still go forward, like a stag upon the hunters' snares . . . ?" But she is explicitly excluded from it—"be silent, or quit my apartment," the Prince orders, "my designs do not admit of female criticism" (p. 327). On the other hand, the hope of the one genuinely enthusiastic Jacobite to march south, toward the seat of power they covet, is countermanded a few pages later by a dispatch from the House of "Fairladies" where the Prince is staying, and the Enthusiast leaps to the archetypal conclusion about moves of caution—"A female influence predominates" (p. 335).

The author of Waverley designs a double irony into his plot here. The Pretender had privately rejected and ignored the power of his woman, but her caution has penetrated him; at the same time he finds that he must publicly espouse her in order to assert his own power to lead and not be led by his supporters. The power of woman, now pure "condition"—"the note, Number D, of which this is a copy, referred to the painful subject" (p. 407)—becomes the point on which sovereignty and manhood hinge. "I tell you, sir," thunders the last Stuart:

> that I could part with that person tomorrow, without an instant's regret—that I have had thoughts of dismissing her from my court, for reasons known to myself, but that I will never betray my rights as a sovereign and a man, by taking this step to secure the favour of any one, or to purchase that allegiance, which, if you owe it to me at all, is due to me as my birthright. (P.408)

It is not his mistress's wealth or counsel or affection or even her embonpoint which requires Charles Edward to cleave to her here, a cleaving which, his supporters complain with secret relief, "disarms ten thousand men" and "annihilates even the semblance of a royal party in Great Britain" (p. 409). Neither chivalry nor policy requires it, so that the grand designer of the last phase of the Jacobite counterrevolution, Hugh Redgauntlet, cries out in despair and rage aginst both the Prince and the stubborn Jacobite, unable to believe that "so slight an impediment . . . could have really interrupted an undertaking of this magnitude" (p. 408). Redgauntlet half recognizes, in scorn, the Jacobites' motive here. Secretly they needed an impediment, and so they constructed one, note Number D, among their conditions. What he doesn't realize is that the Pretender too needs an impediment, a reason not to become the new Hanoverian Parliamentarian kind of king, the king under condition, the king under law. "My God!" exclaims his last supporter, as the Stuart clings to his degraded and degrading impediment, "of what great and inexpiable crime can your Majesty's ancestors have been guilty, that they have been punished by the infliction of judicial blindness on their whole generation!" (pp. 409–10). In the new world of kingship, judicial, juridical, artificial, Charles Edward Stuart is a Pretender, his actual birthright rendered actual imposture, his sovereignty and his manhood diluted by his female. He is feminized, and then abandoned, by the new generation, for whom the law is safer than the prophets, the witches, the magics of birth and birthright.

As for the inexpiable crime which deserved this punishment—this is unclear. Was it James II's crime, who converted to the ancient religion run by men in skirts, an identity which Charles Edward adopts as a disguise on his return? Was it Mary Stuart's crime, when she refused to hand over her crown to her bastard brother, or Murray's who usurped it, or the crime of James the VI and the I, who received that crown and allowed his Queen-mother to die in her English prison? Or was it, still further back in history, the act of outlawry upon which the whole divine legitimacy of Scottish Stuart kingship was founded, the original sin, the first redgauntleted act to which the author of Waverley returns again and again in these novels. Darsie Latimer, ignorant of his complicit ancestry as a Redgauntlet, mocks that act of origin, "the whole history of Bruce poniarding the Red Comyn in the church of the Dominicans, and becoming a king and a patriot because he had been a church-breaker and a murderer" (p. 21). But Hugh Redgauntlet, his uncle and would-be mentor, explicitly compares the act of rebellion he would have Darsie lead to the moment when "the immortal Bruce stabbed the Red Comyn and grasped, with his yet bloody hand, the independent crown of Scotland" (p. 363). It is the descendant of the Redgauntlet who bloodied his hand and killed his own son in the effort to restore that crown to Bruce who commands Darsie, with his dead father's drawn sword, to restore the crown to that line of Scottish kings, who tells him that his dead father's martyred ghost commands him to be a Redgauntlet, dip his hand in blood, to "be a man" (p. 363). If this is a lie—Sir Harry Redgauntlet, though "out" in "the '45," was essentially a domestic and peaceloving man like Henry Morton's soldier-father—it is only ancillary to the Great Lie. The crime being expiated in the feminizing of the last Scottish king is not the degrading of power by association with women but the outlaw grasping of power by the red hand of man. To this madness law, and the ascendancy of the new men, and kings, of law, have put a stop, creating along the way the fiction that woman, allied with the forces of passion and unreason against the law, the forces of blood against brain, must be put down. But we shall see Scott notice, in somewhat nervous play in *Redgauntlet*, that while repression by law breeds back one kind of madness in women and other outlaws, admission to law breeds back another kind of madness in rational men.

Jeanie Deans, Prince Errant

"The Heart of Midlothian" is, of course, a jail, "a world within itself, and has its own business, griefs, and joys peculiar to its order" (p. 9). Citizens are born into this world through a complex reading of their private crimes by public law, and whether the crime makes the law, or the law the crime, is a point much debated by professionals and amateur lawyers alike. Indeed we learn the story proper from the mouth of a man jailed for "the crime of poverty" (p. 13). Mr. Dunover was released from "The Heart of Midlothian" after he surrendered all his money and goods to his creditors, and he walks the streets now an even poorer man, though, as law would have it, now no criminal. The novel turns on three crimes and their fate-at-law, and it would be well to look at the first two, male, crimes as backdrop to the third, most intimately female crime, which shapes sisterhood for Effie and Jeanie Deans—and the madwoman, Madge Wildfire.

The first crime is committed by one Wilson, an honest smuggler on the Fife coast, whose people have never quite accepted the union with England and the revenue officers who enforce her laws. Ruined by repeated seizures of his contraband goods, Wilson "considered himself as robbed and plundered" (p. 19), stole back the confiscated property, was finally captured and condemned with his young accomplice, one Robertson. Now, I have been arguing that this underworld, or alternate world, "greenwood world" of half-sanctioned outlawry has been on Scott's mind, at Scott's heart, from the very first Waverley novel. On Scottish sea and soil particularly this world of pirates and smugglers is a

kind of mythic national homeland, given that in "Britain" the nationhood of Scotland is a crime. When Wilson was hanged, the narrator
reports, the expression on the faces of many in the crowd resembled
"that with which the ancient Cameronians might be supposed to witness
the execution of their brethren who glorified the Covenant" (p. 29).
When a smuggler dies for resisting that "host of idle English gaugers and
excisers as hae come down to vex and torment us" (p. 37), he "testifies"
in the mind of the crowd to the same Covenant of nationhood that the
religious martyrs did. Morally slippery though this elision is, it is a fact of
life for eighteenth-century British authority, and authority feels it must
respond to this mythic supercharging of private crimes with public
charism by supercharged and public enforcement, making examples.
Thus the encounter at Wilson's execution between the Edinburgh
crowd and the City Guard, captained by John Porteous, is marked by
the demonism of two contending myths, outlaw nation and lawful
Empire. Both sides are "fey," as the narrator says (p. 28), so that when
the last spark of life departs from the hanged outlaw "patriot" it seems
to penetrate the crowd—"at once, as if occasioned by some newly-
received impulse, there arose a tumult" (p. 29). Stones pelt the troops,
the troops respond with bullets, and Captain Porteous "set them the
example" by killing the first man in the crowd.[16]

Scott's depiction of this second crime as taking place in a sense during
the last impulse of Wilson's life, transferred to the crowd, is interesting
in light of the argument later made by the amateur lawyer Bartoline
Saddletree that, had Porteous fired on the crowd before the life was
totally gone from Wilson, he would have been acting still in his official
capacity, to carry out the sentence of the law, and therefore could not be
prosecuted for murder, "being engaged in a lawful act" (p. 38). Five
minutes makes the distinction, if there is one, between a public execu-
tioner and a private murderer. Porteous, on trial, argues of course that
his Captaincy makes all his crowd-control acts "official," just as the
smugglers argued that their national foundation made their acts more
legal than the confiscations of those Pretenders and Imposters, the
English customs officials. Between the imperatives of these two mythic
extralegal realms, the Scottish underground and the Imperial ideal, lies
the agreed-upon *terra firma* of the law, on which ground Wilson's
"trade," in the situation, was thievery, and Porteous's shooting, in the
situation, was murder. As an act less of mercy than of Imperial policy,
the Empire delays and appears to remit the execution of the murderer:
as an act less of justice than of Underground policy the Midlothian
crowd extracts from its "heart" the murderer and carries out, extrale-
gally, by carefully organized mob violence, the sentence of the law.

Two persons refuse to leave the jail when it is "liberated" by the

Porteous mob. One, a notorious thief and con man called "Daddie Rat," or "James Radcliffe," or twenty other names "to pick and choose upon" (p. 138) as he explains disarmingly, has been in jail under sentence of death four times and has made his choice—he will stay in jail, since it likes him so well, and turn policeman, jailkeeper, informer. Daddie Rat is perhaps the most engaging and important example of the shape-shifting, if not coat-turning, figure of Robin Hood in the Waverley novels; he applies for that crucial place within the law reserved for those who break the law in the law's behalf. He knows he will get the job since the law must have its thieves to hunt thieves, its rascals to bring in rascals, for "your decent sort of men, that are put into the like o' sic trust, can do nae gude ava. They are feared for this, and they are scrupulous about that, and they are na free to tell a lie, though it may be for the benefit of the city" (p. 162). Free to tell a lie, free to sell out his old comrades, or his new ones, Daddie Rat is treated with some deference by both sides. His writ runs among thieves as well as lawyers; he will, for his own convenience, try his best to preserve each from the other, since it is the manipulation of each world, rather than the destruction of either, that wins him his warm nook on the interface.

A second prisoner, an eighteen-year-old girl, also refuses to come out of the jail, though urgently solicited by "a person in female attire" who "answered to the appellative" of Madge Wildfire (p. 63). This person, as Daddie Rat proves in interrogation, was not in fact the dangerous and poignant madwoman but George Staunton-Robertson, the man who seduced Madge two years before, which makes Madge sister in fortune to the prisoner who refused to come out to "Madge's" solicitation. For the young woman is Effie Deans, "the lily of St. Leonards," awaiting trial for the third and greatest private/public crime in the novel, the murder of her infant son by George Staunton-Robertson.

It is curious to consider what anxious vibrations this crime sends, is still sending, through Western societies. Though it is clear in Scott's narrative why a woman might be driven to abort, abandon, or even destroy an illegitimate infant—Effie refuses to come out of jail to her lover because as an unwed mother her life is already over, whether or not she hangs as a murderess—it is less clear, because so many unstated assumptions obtain here, why the law might feel driven to put to death the mother suspected of the crime. Indeed the law which condemned Effie did not require proof of guilt, did not even require a child's body as evidence of murder. The law requires Effie to prove the negative: having been pregnant, being unable to produce the healthy child in evidence, she is required to prove that she did not kill it, required to prove further that she made provision to welcome and love and care for it. And what the law will accept as proof of this point is the fundamental "natural" act of sisterhood that did not happen in the novel, that the pregnant woman "communicate her situation" (p. 48) to the other women, her sister, her neighbors, who share, as all women are held to share, naturally and solely share, the responsibility for bringing children into the world. Whether the infant died accidentally or, as Effie maintains (and truly), the child was stolen while she lay fevered after childbirth, if the woman concealed her pregnancy she is presumed to have had murderous intent toward the infant, the infant who is, on the other hand, the incontrovertible evidence of her first, and as women are taught to believe, worst, crime.

The legal mind is uncomfortable with this statute, which substitutes a chain not even of circumstantial but of "presumptive" evidence, in place of that proof positive by which the law usually takes human life (p. 241). The amateur Bartoline Saddletree notes sagely that the chain being so very fragile, presumptive, fictive, "the crime is rather a favourite of the law, this species of murthur being one of its ain creations"—to which Mrs. Saddletree responds still more sagaciously, "Then, if the law makes murders, the law should be hanged for them" (pp. 48–49). Effie's lawyer, doing his best with an impossible situation, contests two of the presumptions in the chain. Far from its being natural that an illegitimately pregnant woman should communicate her situation, is it not more natural that she should conceal it until the father of the child could marry her and restore to her that "good fame" which is life for a woman (p. 227)? Far from its being natural that Effie should go to her sister or neighbor women for help with her delivery, is it not natural that she would rely on the help her lover offered her (in a note produced at trial)? More natural, given, first, that an illegitimately pregnant woman has already broken good faith with the maidens and matrons in the "natural" community of women, and second, that no woman, however "atrociously offended" by him, can refuse to forgive or cease to depend on a man she has once loved (p. 229).

In the trial of Effie Deans we see presumption contest presumption, layer under layer exposed of the "given" about women's nature. The law exempts and even sanctions many categories of life-taking, winks at, hedges or pardons others. But this most heinous, most "unnatural" category it violates its own nature to trace and publicly punish, for this the law and the fathers fear most of all, that a woman may recognize the man's seed in her body as her enemy and reject it. If she does, she forecloses his future, his property (ultimately her own, too, of course). The stakes for partriarchy are so high that a nearly fail-safe psychic system has evolved whereby women do indeed communicate their situation as mothers, pseudomothers, alternate mothers, to each other, where motherhood and female identity merge, where even in the most brutalized masculinized woman, created by the author of Waverley as we shall see to make exactly this point, "motherhood" is the last fragment of female identity to go.

It is in this connection that the madwoman in the attic, Madge Wildfire, becomes the sister of Effie and Jeanie Deans, offering to Effie, via the male imposter George Staunton-Robertson, who wears her clothes and has her name, the "immoral" act of rescue which she will refuse but Jeanie will later accept. This "sister" received from Effie in Jeanie's place the infant in whose imagined murder Effie felt a complicity which only a self-accusation of madness or demonic possession can exorcise:

> Interrogated, whether she had herself, at any time, had any purpose of putting away the child by violence? Declares, never; so might God be merciful to her—and then again declares, never when she was in her perfect senses; but what bad thoughts the Enemy might put into her brain when she was out of herself, she cannot answer. (P. 234)

Madge bore a child the previous year to her father's master, young George Staunton, but Madge's baby was killed and buried according to the way of the world by her mother, old Meg Murdockson, so that she could match her weak-witted daughter with a neighboring merchant. Madge's complicity in this act is hinted at but unclear; she herself believes the act ended her control over her life and her wits. More important, she believes about half the time that the infant she received from her mother—rescued from her mother?—a year later is her own, where, of course it was that of George's next mistress, Effie Deans. Made sisters as well as mothers by that "fatal man," Madge and Effie each rise half-crazed from childbed. Each is confused as to whether the child lived or died, not only because the child in each case disappeared but also because of the "bad thoughts" that "the Enemy" put in her head, to kill the child the lover had put in her body. Effie's child survives because her dark "sister," given another chance with the brother of her own child, elected to save it. She gave it away to a gypsy to save it from the fate of the child who lies buried under the trees near the Staunton house.

The taboo which leads a woman to forgive her seducing lover, no matter how "atrociously offended," operates just as powerfully in the case of the lover's son. No woman can kill her son and remain sane, the author of Waverley would have us know. Even old Meg Murdockson, ripe in "masculine" villainy and enraged at George Staunton's desertion of Madge, tries hard to kill him but cannot enact it, because he was her foster son, nursed by her milk. Thus barred from direct revenge on their tormentors, women turn to the artificially natural, inevitable, objects of destruction, themselves, and each other. Madness results in the sensitive; in the insensitive, murder. Old Meg deliberately manipulates Effie into the situation which brings her to trial and condemnation as an act of revenge on George, "revenge, the sweetest morsel to the mouth that ever was cooked in hell. . . . I have wrought hard for it—I have suffered for it, and I have sinned for it—and I will have it." "But mother," remarks a male thief, "if revenge is your wish, you should take it on the young fellow himself." "No, I cannot," Meg groans, with an appearance of rage against herself, "I have thought of it—I have tried it—but I canna gang through wi 't!" (p. 308). The tabooed object, the eternally woman-forgiven man, meets his death eventually at no woman's hands: his son, abandoned, savagely virile, a Highland chief, shoots the unknown English gentleman for his money in the last pages of the novel. This avenger is certainly Effie's child. And yet I rather like to think of him as Madge's child, the ghost of the boy buried under the hillock, the grandson of old Meg Murdockson, finally going through with it.

Between her two dark sisters, with and against them, stands the fair one, the heroine—and the hero—of this Waverley novel, Jeanie Deans. As heroine her job is to incarnate the still center of the turning world, the blond domesticity that goads and rewards the hero for his journey of self-discovery and self-limitation. As hero, her job is to take that Waverley journey from "romance" to the "real history of her life." She inhabits two dimensions in the novel: uneasily inscribed, palimpsest, under the texts of her dark-light femininity, are the texts of the dispossessed Waverley male, the Prince Errant. If Jeanie is an energized Rose Bradwardine at one level, on another she seems Edward Waverley in drag.

In gentle parody of Jeanie as classic Waverley heroine Scott achieves one of the triumphs of the novel, the relationship between Jeanie and the Laird of Dumbiedykes. This slow-thinking money-holding master is attracted to his tenant like iron to magnet, her "air of inexpressible serenity" is just what he likes, stout, round, short, rough-skinned packaging to the contrary notwithstanding. Neither romance nor marriage nor even speech, really, does the Laird wish, only, "with his old laced hat and empty tobacco pipe, [he] came and enjoyed the beatific vision of Jeanie Deans day after day, week after week, year after year" (pp. 84–85), while they, and the man Jeanie placidly loves, the scholar Reuben Butler, grow past youth toward middle age. When the vision moves to St. Leonards outside Edinburgh, two revolutions occur in this domestic buffoon: dislocated, "he spins round and round his little orbit," his own property, looking into each cottage for The Face, and then, missing it, painfully putting two and two together, it "occurred to him that he was not pinned down to circulate on a pivot, like the hands of the watch, but possessed the power of shifting his central point, and extending his circle, if he thought proper" (pp. 91–92). Shifting, extending, but still pinned to his pivot, the laird buys a "powny" and makes Jeanie's new residence the prime point on his weekly dial, quite to the exasperation of the beatified but plain woman whom the author of Waverley affirms, rather more often than is strictly necessary, is no pretty heroine of old Romance. There is new Romance connected with her, however. The laird is present at the Deans house when the law comes for Effie Deans, accused infanticide. Comprehending nothing but the dismay on the Beatific Face, Dumbiedykes wakes "out of his wonted apathy" and in a touching and ridiculous gesture right out of the Romance of Property pushes his purse full of guineas toward the beloved, ejaculating, "Jeanie, woman! dinna greet . . . winna siller do 't?" (pp. 104–5).

Silver won't do it, of course. And yet, when only one thing is left to save Effie, Jeanie's journey to beg pardon for her from the Queen, we find Jeanie at Dumbiedykes in quest of money for the journey, "opening doors, like the second Calendar . . . in the castle of the hundred obliging damsels, until, like the said prince errant," she gains entrance (p. 263), and the siller to do 't. Dumbiedykes, a slow but pertinent thinker, feels he probably ought to be married to a woman if he is going to give money to her, but Jeanie is finally forced to tell him plainly that for all his money and his kindness she likes Reuben Butler better, and will marry him, if anyone. Forced past astonishment to sagacity, the laird plays his winning, his domestic, card: "Another man better than me? It's no possible, woman—ye hae kenn'd me sae lang." And Jeanie, with Waverleyan, with "persevering simplicity," trumps that card, "Aye, but Laird, I hae kenn'd him langer" (p. 268).

The lady will not marry the laird, so ends Jeanie's heroism; she will travel alone to London, so begins the Waverley hero's saga—Jeanie Deans, prince errant. Jeanie must go to London because she refused to tell a lie, commit perjury, "be mansworn" in court to save her sister. Though she was convinced both by Effie's word and by a midnight interview with George Staunton that both father and mother intended to protect and keep the illegitimate child, she refused to swear that Effie had spoken that intention or "communicated her situation" to her blood sister, the most natural communicant. Though all admire Jeanie, and

Effie forgives her, for putting her own conscience and the letter of man's and God's law first, the journey is not simply an errand of mercy, it has something of a penitential feeling about it as well. For Jeanie recognizes she has, partly because of the difference in their ages, partly because of temperamental differences, never been a true sister to Effie. At most she has been a "mother" to her, no surprise in a partriarchal world in which motherhood is the role women have most practice in, sisterhood the role least understood.

In addition there is even something of a political epic in Jeanie's journey south, as well as a personal one of self-and-sister exculpation and discovery. For there is strong feeling in Edinburgh, after London has refused pardon to Wilson or Effie and reprieved Porteous, that the English don't really "care a boodle whether we dinna kill ane anither, skin and bane, horse and foot, man, woman, and bairns, all and sundry, *omnes et singulas*" (p. 250), so long as they can deal out punishments that enforce their alien authority. Once, a townswoman comments, when authority resided in Edinburgh, the people could "correct" it when it overreached itself—"peeble them wi stanes when they werena gude bairns" (interesting child-murder metaphor there!)—but now that authority has removed itself to London, "naebady's nails can reach the length o' Lonnon" (p. 37). So Edinburgh, like the Laird of Dumbiedykes, must extend its circle, include London on the circumference its hands can reach. And although for Jeanie as for the laird the Beatific Vision waits at that new circumference—"I will see the King's face, that gies grace," says Jeanie, starting south (p. 256)—the pilgrimage, or worship, or penance, includes as well an element of political challenge, to see those stones, those sharp fingernails, reach their target along with the prayers.

Jeanie's Waverley journey can be said to begin even before the trial when, "like Christiana in the Pilgrim's Progress," she dares "the terrors of the Valley of the Shadow of Death" to meet her sister's lover at his chosen place, the home ground of the fatal man, Muschat's Cairn (p. 153). Here, a generation before, Nicol Muschat, after trying and failing several times to ruin, divorce, or kill his wife, finally cut her throat, and suffered the penalty of law for it. Here George Staunton-Robertson threatens the same to Jeanie if she does not agree to save Effie by telling the lie when she is asked in court. Here, secretly following Jeanie and bringing as sister-guide Madge Wildfire, the newly in-lawed Daddie Rat almost captures Staunton. Here Madge comes often of a moonlit night to talk with the dead wife and remind her of the great taboo—no woman, no matter how atrociously offended, can fail to forgive the man she once loved, rather "a's forgotten now . . . bygane's suld be byganes," Here Madge dreams of "a grand boukingwashing . . . in the beams of the bonny Lady Moon" (p. 178) that will one day allow the women, one murdered, one crazed by complicity in murder, to clean their clothes from the blood of the victimization that was, both mistily feel, somehow their crime.

Retreating in terror, Jeanie bolted the door of her house against the female insights and events of Muschat's Cairn and clothed her spirit in the solace of her father's prayers and her God's power. And "it was in that moment that a vague idea first darted across her mind, that something might yet be achieved for her sister's safety" (p. 185), something that would compensate for the lie that she cannot bring herself to tell.

It is necessary once more to be explicit about this lie. George would have her say to the world that the sisters confided in each other, assured each other that bygones might be bygones, washed each other's bloody garments clean. But the painful truth Jeanie tells in court is that Effie said "Nothing . . . she never breathed word to me about it" (p. 240).[17] This crucial withholding took place not only because Effie forgave and relied on her atrociously offending lover but also, because at the moment when she might have told Jeanie she found she couldn't forgive her sister for being morally "better" nor, most terribly of all, believe her sister wouldn't use her moral ascendancy to dominate her for the rest of their lives (p. 99). Behind Jeanie is the inert sisterhood of noncommunication and moral rivalry, sisters falling all too easily into the safer roles of mother and child; before her the poignant mad sisterhood of Ailie Muschat and Madge Wildfire, which she and Effie would join and duplicate if she tells the lie, victim-criminals waiting for the washing day. From this experience comes the desperate enlightenment, the Presbyterian Conviction, which is tantamount to a Fall.

It is not just that Jeanie is deeply attracted, once they let her into the "heart of Midlothian" to see Effie, to tell the lie and establish corrupt sisterhood—"say what ye wad hae me do, and I could find in my heart amaist to say that I would do 't" (p. 214). It is that Jeanie recognizes that she *was* guilty, she scarcely knows how, of the innocence that separated her from her sister. In this condition of dark enlightenment, paralysis, powerlessness, like Bunyan's Christian or Christiana, Jeanie decides to undertake her romance, Pilgrim's Progress. Given that Waverley's pilgrims subconsciously seek the earthly rather than the heavenly city, however, we can expect that Jeanie's journey will rather cause her to discard the ideal and grapple with the real. And since her specific romance, and her fall, come from her love of telling truth, we can expect to see this grappling with the real take the form of an education in the uses of fictions, of mental reservation and canny speechlessness, of lies.[18]

So it proves, right from the start. Jeanie needs her father's blessing for the solitary trip south, but David Deans, whose pride in the propriety of his fair daughter is matched only by his high moral condemnation and outlawing of his "harlot" daughter, would never give it. So she doesn't tell him, extracts a general blessing from the broken old man, and continues her preparations, arguing to herself, "He has blessed mine errand . . . and it is borne in upon my mind that I shall prosper" (p. 254). Then, rather than apply for help to any who would lay conditions upon her journey, who might involve her in "such a series of explanations and debates as . . . might deprive her totally of the power of taking the step" (p. 259), she resolves to "think and act as firmly as I can, and speak as little" (p. 257). She accepts the Rogue's Latin note from Daddie Rat to negotiate accommodation with outlaws on the road, and solicits the monetary help of the impotent Dumbiedykes and a letter of intervention from the bedridden Reuben Butler, whose ancestor made the last Duke of Argyle his debtor. It is easy enough to speak truth to these two powerless lovers, but the meddlesome Bartoline Saddletree is another matter; she lies to him about the reason she wants to see Reuben, and even though, "instantly feeling ashamed of the fiction to which she had resorted . . . she corrected herself" (p. 278), the correction was not the truth but another evasion.

Halfway through the long journey south Jeanie encounters her own particular Apollyon again, and undergoes at her/his hands a complex version of the typical Waverley hero's self-discovery—kidnapping, outlawing, escape back to the law with the power to destroy the outlaws, which, out of hidden sympathies, she does not use. Apollyon, falsehood, tempts her on the public road north of Grantham, in Robin Hood's old domain of Sherwood Forest: "Hark ye, my lass," says the thief who has been paid by the vengeful Meg Murdockson, "Mother Blood," to strip, rob, and turn Jeanie back north. "If you'll look up to heaven, and say, this is the last penny you have about ye, why, hang it, we'll let you pass" (p. 297). Practiced now in evasion—"I am not free . . . to say what I have about me"—Jeanie counters Mother Blood's orders with Daddie Rat's passport, and is forced by the thieves "in a direction more and more from the public road" (p. 298) until they come to the thieves' hideout. This evasion/admission, "I am not free," links Jeanie in the following scenes with her jailed sister, and Madge Wildfire's welcome in the thieves' hideout completes and makes explicit the trio of jailed sisters: "Jeanie Deans—in a gypsy's barn, and the night setting in; this is a sight for sair een!—Eh, sirs, the falling off o' the godly!—and the t'other sister's in the Tolbooth at Edinburgh!" (p. 300). "Were ye ever in Bedlam?" inquires Madge later, with an eye to further familiar sibling exchanges, "Never in Bedlam! . . . But ye'll hae been in the cells at Edinburgh?" (pp. 301–2). Jeanie's "never," an interesting echo of her admission of nonsisterhood with Effie in court, merely convinced Madge that she herself has somehow been made to bear the deserved punishments of the "godly"—"I think thae daft carles the magistrates send naebody to Bedlam but me." But now that Jeanie has come at last where she belongs, into captivity, Madge takes charge, as elder sister and "playfellow" of Jeanie. Feigning sleep in her "cell," Jeanie hears part of the story of old Meg's wish for revenge on Effie; playing along with Madge's mad fictions and games, guiltily but effectively "abusing the simplicity of this demented creature" (p. 316), Jeanie extracts all but the final detail of Madge's history of her dead child and her treatment of Effie's child. Playing further, Jeanie joins Madge in a game of escape from "our" mother, during which Madge names the game: "Did ye never read the *Pilgrim's Progress*? And ye shall be the woman Christiana, and I will be the maiden Mercy" (p. 314).

Jeanie reaches the nadir of sisterhood with Madge as "Christiana" and "Mercy" reach the next major station on the Progress. The madwoman, taking a village church for "the Interpreter's house," disorders Jeanie's dress and tears her hair to make her appearance as Bedlamite as her own, and then leads her "in captivity up the whole length of the church" (pp. 321–23), forcing her with painful kicks and punches to perform the whole ritual of Anglican Sunday service with the madwoman and the irate and scornful congregation. In this remarkable humiliation scene, pitched somewhere between farce and melodrama, the sensible unromantic Jeanie is fully "womanized" at last, reduced to "dishevelled hair, downcast eyes, and a face glowing with shame" (p. 324). Madge, her sisterly office done, having communicated her situation to Jeanie, falls asleep, leaving Jeanie in the hands of the Interpreter, the clergyman, who turns out to be George Staunton's father.

Jeanie's escape from this situation of degraded womanhood requires the shaking off of Madge, lest the village continue to think Jeanie "a bird of the same feather" (p. 325). With the help of the clergyman she distinguishes herself from the madwoman after the church service, and watches her alter-ego exit, pursued by "all the mischievous imps of the village . . . some pulling the skirts of her dress, and all exercising some new device or other to exasperate her into frenzy." Jeanie watches her departure "with infinite delight," for though Bunyan's Christiana refused to be parted from Mercy at the Interpreter's house, insisting that their salvation must be mutual even though Mercy was without an "invitation," this Christiana, pitying Madge, nevertheless has another sister to save, another task to do. And the plight of Madge—"God help me, I forget my very name, in this confused waste" (p. 328)—might be more than our Waverley heroine can face, though it is, we recall, the necessary condition for the Waverley hero's apotheosis. Shaking off regrets about Madge, resolutely narrowing her attention to her task— "Do not tell me any of your secrets" (p. 341), she warns the bedridden George Staunton—Jeanie completes the journey to London. There she invokes the ambiguously sisterly mercy of the Queen, mentally reserving, as I have described, the secret which George Staunton forced on her, the secret that would have traded his life, as leader of the Porteous mob, for Effie's pardon.

But Madge is not so easily shaken off. Returning north, successful, carriaged and attended by the fairy godfathership of the Duke of Argyle, Jeanie sees the nightmare sight she has rescued Effie from, "the outline of the gallows tree," with its human furniture, and "one of the objects, launched into the air, gave unequivocal signs of mortal agony, though appearing in the distance not larger than a spider dependent at the extremity of his invisible thread" (p. 413). Shortly afterward, she feels at the door of her carriage the mad grip of her erstwhile sister-cellmate and playfellow: "Eh, d'ye ken, Jeanie Deans, they hae hangit our mother?" (p. 415). "Some degree of violence" is needed this time to dislodge Madge, but she is shaken off, though it is clear that the circle of tormentors in which she "dances" intend more than impish insults this time, they intend her death. Jeanie and her friends send her help, when it is too late, and witness a death song uneasily veering, split like the womanhood she personifies, between angelic hymns and outlaw love-ballads. But by the time our fair Waverley heroine/hero emerges on home territory, after the usual circuitous route through outlaw identification with the dark sibling, Madge is dead and even Effie has removed herself, cleaving to her atrociously offending lover, leaving Jeanie, as her father biblically phrases it, "the ae and only leaf on the auld tree" (p. 430). As such it is her fate, without an action on her part in her own behalf, to claim the hero's reward—mate, property, peace.

It is astonishing to consider how radically the author of Waverley departs from his source-story to arrange this characteristic ending for Jeanie, his hero. Helen Walker, the original pilgrim, returned from London on foot, without further patronage from the Duke, lived and died a rough life, unmarried and poor. The author, in his introduction and postscript, emphasizes these very facts, reporting that his source on Helen guessed at once from her "cheerful disengaged countenance" that she had never been married, and concluding piously that "a character so distinguished for her undaunted love of virtue, lived and died in poverty, if not want, serves only to show us how insignificant, in the sight of Heaven are our principal objects of ambition on earth" (p. xiv). Alexander Welsh has shown how even the Waverley hero forfeits virtue if he shows ambition; the Waverley heroine's virtue is utterly dependent on self-lessness. "You are a singular young woman, you seem to me to think of everyone before yourself" (p. 370), marvels the Duke of Argyle. But Scott has him respond to this archetypal singularity not as the world does, but as a romance does, effecting the interview with the Queen, and the pardon, sending Jeanie home in a carriage, like Cinderella, even providing her wedding dress. "The rod of the same benevolent enchanter" (p. 435) transports to the property prepared for Jeanie—since she cannot own it herself—her mate and her father. Accepting these rewards of Jeanie's ambition (for everybody but herself)—the farm at Roseneath for David Deans, an arranged "call" from the Duke's parish of Knocktarlitie for dominie Reuben Butler—is morally tricky for the men, scorners of the world and its pelf. But they had now, says Scott with equanimity, "to go to work to reconcile [their] speculative principles with existing circumstances" (p. 439). And they did.

So does Jeanie, when the time comes for her to accept the specifically female inheritance which her sister's corruption has bought. For Effie, once merely "a banished outlawed creature" (p. 469), has married George Staunton and taken the place appropriate to her beauty, her newly educated wit, her acquired rank, and her still archetypal womanhood. That is, to society she is "the ruling belle—the blazing star" (p. 486), the woman of power. But the woman is inevitably, especially to herself, "a miserable imposter" (p. 481), in constant danger of self-incrimination, indebted for her power to the husband to whom she is bound in terror and outlawry and deceit as well as in that love that never ends, however atrociously offended.[19] Effie has "lost" her first child, has miscarried twice and become barren, while Jeanie has borne three children; the woman's legacy of fertility has clearly passed to the elder sister. With Effie's secret letters to her sister come a steady stream of fifty-pound notes, which Jeanie knows is partly "hush money" (p. 483). But Jeanie has learned to reconcile principles with existing circumstances; hidden in "the darkest nook" of this exemplary housewife's pantry—leaved between the pages of David Deans's old Bible (p. 492) like the new interpretation of that ancient text—the money becomes one of the several secrets that her elasticized conscience requires her to keep from her husband and her father.

That secret sisters' wealth is crucial in the last reward of Jeanie's virtue, the purchase, at last, of an estate of their own, the full domestication, more, the bourgeoisification, of Jeanie Deans Butler. "Surely," says Reuben, still in the dark, counting over the money "as if to assure himself that the notes were real," surely "there was never man in the world had a wife like mine." To this Jeanie replies, twinkling, "Never, since the enchanted princess in the bairns' fairy tale, that karned gold nobles out o' the tae side of her haffit locks, and Dutch dollars out o' the t'other" (pp. 493–94). One sister coins money for her husband and children out of her silence, keeping secrets with her sister, and the other coins money for her sister out of her notoriety, keeping secrets with her lover. But both sisters live in the same world now, manipulating an imposter's power to assuage a natural powerlessness. It is the dark sister who says of the fair at the end, "you have been truth itself from your cradle upwards, but you must remember that I am a liar of fifteen year's standing" (p. 505). But the fair one might surely, from another perspective, say the same to the dark.

Brothers and Sisters

Mad Madge Wildfire's lament, "God help me, I forget my very name in this confused waste!" is a fundamental subtext in the Waverley world, as we have seen. But one might also hear in Madge's cry, as she stands in her man's cape and lady's scarf, carrying her boy's willow switch and her high-heeled satin slippers (p. 321), testimony to an equally serious amnesia. In this confused waste she has forgotten her gender. Many are the identities established in these novels, or consolidated, only after a wearying journey through a maze of no names, mis-names, false names, type names, to the right name. But the shifting and shaking down into one's proper gender is an equally traumatic operation in the unstable world of post-chivalric sexuality. Once a man was the human who led the advance; now he hesitates at the bridge, like Henry Morton, wondering about the safety of his flank, or makes short erratic dashes, leading and being led captive, like Frank Osbaldistone and Edward Waverley, or he edges round the action, like Ivanhoe or Reuben Butler, tracking "circuitous routes" between the jailhouse and the criminal's den, the sickbed and the marriage bed. Once a woman was the human who stood at the man's back, unchanging, guarding his retreats, and securing, in childbed, his future. Now she is a wanderer like the man, Die Vernon, Edith Bellenden, Jeanie Deans, making dashes across the new landscape of action, carrying on a ceaseless interior monologue, reconciling her actions with her womanhood as he integrates his inactions into his manhood.

Since the remaking of gender, with the class, religious, and racial components which arise from gender archetypes or figure into them, is the woman's job as well as the man's, the two genders appear to redefine

themselves with and against each other in intimate and fascinating ways
in the novels. The author of Waverley, giving up as lost or as myth the
chivalric or Edenic natural man and woman, now sends his male and
female protagonists adventuring through each other's territory, often in
each other's clothes. I should like to isolate for brief treatment here two
such groups of adventurers, one a classic quadrangle of dark/light men/
women, the other a tense triangle of two fair men and a woman, to see
how the remaking, the tactful poetic patching together of a lost sexual
stability, is accomplished.

The Pirate, the novel that "George Eliot's" Maggie Tulliver stopped
reading when she realized that once again the author of Waverley would
undermine the dark woman and establish the fair one, contains the
Waverley gender archetypes[20] in so ostensibly pure a state as to raise the
possibility, as I suggested, that some self-parody is at work. The patriarchal pirate himself, Basil Mertoun, is a near psychotic misogynist who
turned outlaw—no Robin Hood he—after the illegitimate birth of one
son to the young Norna, or Ulla Troil, and the legitimate but clouded
birth of a second son to an adulterous wife. The elder son distinguished
himself in his father's line of work until, his control over his pirate crew
slipping a notch when the Captain performed some minor good deed, he
was abandoned by them and presumed dead until the arrival, drowning,
on the "Zetland" coast some ten years later, of a dark piratical stranger
named Clement Cleveland. On the spot to rescue him, all unknowing, is
the younger son, Mordaunt Mertoun, a climber of cliffs, a half-believer,
like Edward Waverley, in the Romance tales of this land of extremities.
The fair men of the Waverley novels often are tested or manipulated by
apparently being cast off by their fathers or father-surrogates: unique
among them, Mordaunt Mertoun is actually hated by his father as the
living reminder of the blight and fraud that he thinks woman is to man.
In a curious sense Mordaunt is half a daughter to his father—the elder
man is content to educate his son strictly in the sciences and arts of a
gentleman, but occasionally, "in the perusal of history . . . or the study
of classical authors there occurred facts or sentiments" (p. 13)—facts
about Cleopatra's or Catherine de Medici's power, the intenser moments of the *Orestia* or of Juvenal, perhaps—which would bring on the
"dark hour" in which Mertoun loathes the sight of his changeling child
and throws him out of the house.

Such treatment has bred no outlaw resentment in Mordaunt—the
emotion is of course taboo to daughters, though not to sons. Instead, a
wanderer-guest among the hospitable islanders, he comes inevitably to
settle down as "an attached brother," almost a sister, to the daughters of
the great landholder Magnus Troil. Minna and Brenda Troil have been
poeticized by the islands as "Night" and "Day" (p. 21), and Scott makes

it clear that it was the fancy of the beholders which transformed a trifling and pleasing difference of character, the one sister graver, more elevated and self-contained, the other gayer, more humorous and accessible, into these potent archetypes. Mordaunt, their "playfellow" for years, is the talk of the island during his adolescence for amiable behavior which gives no hint of which woman-archetype, the dark or the fair, he will "choose." Yet there is more to this "hesitation" or "vacillation," as the onlookers, in some dudgeon, term it (p. 23), than the usual young man's wish to remain free, or even than the usual Waverley hero's instinctive balancing act. Mordaunt does indeed affirm, in the language of carnal reason, that "he could see no excellent quality in the one that was not balanced by something equally captivating in the other" sister (p. 67). But he does so in subliminally wary response to an unprecedented inquisition by his father on the state of his affection—"you have been gravely brought up, and this Minna, I suppose, pleases you most? . . . [the gay active Brenda is then] best qualified to amuse the young man who has a dull home and a moody father?" (pp. 66–67)—which is designed to pin down and define the youth's character and render him, thus pinned down by and to a woman, comfortably contemptible, fully feminized, in his father's eyes. In Mordaunt's own eyes the choice of a certain kind of woman would make him a certain kind of man, would make him, at last, fully man, change him from undifferentiated and undifferentiating sibling to male lover. Maintaining the tense openness of the triangle safeguards his freedom but insults the women's, postpones his surrender to gender archetypes but reinforces theirs.

The event that first stretches, then collapses the triangle, which forces/allows the three playfellow siblings to choose gender and subgender types, is the arrival of a fourth figure, the catalyzing outlaw, Clement Cleveland. Rescuing his half-brother and wraith alter-ego, Mordaunt feels the same immoral and visceral disquiet that Frank Osbaldistone experienced with Rashleigh, as if, while consciously striving to preserve both lives the men feel subliminally in competition for a single quantum of life. Purchasing a silver box from a peddler who had stolen it from Cleveland, Mordaunt returns the box to the stranger, hoping to get rid of his debt and his disquiet, and accepts the male-emblematic gun Cleveland insists on giving to his rescuer.

The sparks of magnetic opposition struck between the two men, the gun tossed to Mordaunt, the box handed to Cleveland, shape and disclose male identity, hardening the first, softening the second. For the owner of the box is by it identifiable as the pirate son of Ulla Troil, Norna of the Fitful Head, and by disarming himself and arming his half-brother Cleveland passes his captain's authority and his male power into Mordaunt's hands. As "the Pirate," Cleveland solidifies his interest in Minna Troil's eyes; in acting out what he half-consciously recognizes as a "role," he turns his outlaw energies first to Minna's half-outlaw dream of Zetland nationhood, and finally, when both recognize that as a dream, to the fully legitimized piracy of Britain's war against Spain in which, satisfyingly, he is killed, leaving Mordaunt alone to claim all the legitimate inheritance of the Waverley hero.

As his half-brother veers away from the daylight toward death, Mordaunt makes his choice between the women who signify "night" and "day," moving toward the erotic domestic commitment which signals both his retreat from a kind of sisterhood with the Troil sisters and his arrival at Waverleyan manhood. It is Brenda's anger at his rumored belief that he could have either of the Troil sisters to wife, interestingly, that reveals her erotic attachment, first to her, and then to him. From the moment of that revelation Brenda is Mordaunt's choice, not because she is "fair," or "Day," not even (entirely) because "her cheerfulness . . . mixed itself with the everyday business of life" and, instead of merely accepting and being carried forward by the stream of dailiness, took action "to aid its progress by efforts of her own" (p. 20). These indeed are the qualities of the Waverley woman which consistently attract and anchor the sexual confusions and diffusions of the Waverley man. But the true attraction, one might even say the primary erotic charge here, is that of possibility. The Waverley man defines himself against the suddenly seen possible, and by this act he narrows himself, but he contributes to and enlarges for the world, the domain of the possible, as his dark alter-ego defines for the world, by thrusting himself upon it and perishing, the domain of the impossible, the suddenly seen newly impossible. Once, his play-actor henchman reminds Cleveland, it was possible for a man to work both sides of the borders of law, to be Sir Francis Drake at home and a pirate abroad, or the pirate Harry Morgan in early manhood and a landed gentleman at maturity. But now, says Jack Bunch, striking a tragicomic attitude from his old acting days as "Altamont," even though Cleveland can show "that you were as gentle a thief as Robin Hood himself . . . that is all ended now—once a pirate, and an outcast for ever" (p. 334).

As for the female side of this duel between new possibility and new impossibility, the author of Waverley has the same lesson to teach, though the dark sister must suffer loss of love, not life, barrenness, not death, as the price of her discovery. Clinging to the last archetype, the ultimate philosopher's stone for transmuting outlaw into Robin Hood, Cleveland argues to Bunch that one woman will love and legitimize him, but bows to Bunch's unarguable "then she does not know what a pirate is" (p. 335). In a sisterhood scene cleverly contrived by the author of Waverley to take place while the two women dress, and Brenda tightens Minna's laces, they argue about the nature and dimension of their knowledge of their men. Brenda insists she knows Mordaunt for a modest, reasonable, if confused, man, despite the rumors of his arrogant delay of choice until he sees how much land Magnus will settle on each daughter, despite the mystic aura lent him by Norna's patronage, and she knows rightly. Minna insists that to believe only what one can rationally understand or engage only with what one can emotionally control is to blaspheme God's creation, and insists further that she knows what a pirate is—a viking lord, "or what else modern times may give that draws near to that lofty character" (p. 217). In this estimate of Cleveland she is wrong, or near enough to wrong to have to forfeit her lover. Seeing his pirate crew, sensing that the attempt to master them must inevitably, even for a good actor, result in his becoming like them, she withdraws from Cleveland, urging him to change his mask from outlaw to in-law not in order to gain her but for his own sake. In his final moment onstage Cleveland makes the switch of masks clearly—manfully shooting the pirate who would have taken him and Minna forcibly back to the pirate ship and its life, but casting his pistol into the lake, disarming himself, as Mordaunt, uncertain which mask is the real Cleveland, rushes, armed, upon him. The next iron mask Cleveland takes up is the gun he fires as a legitimate member of the British navy, and the final mask Minna takes is that of Rebecca, and Flora, and Effie Deans, a life lived as if in, if not actually in, a convent, devoted abstractly to good works and/or penitence, "detached from the world" (p. 449) as surely as her dark lover-brother is.

Where in *The Pirate* the Waverley hero learns manhood by relinquishing the genial neutrality of a brother for the tense possibility associated with the role of lover, the hero of *Redgauntlet* reacquires and consolidates his identity only by relinquishing the pretentions of a romantic lover for those of a brother. Or rather, as the *eclaircissement* strikes, Darsie Latimer becomes the *sister* of Lilias Redgauntlet, for he is dressed at that moment, like her, in women's clothes, and virtually tied on horseback, like her subject to the direction of the patriarchs who run their world. It is the usual Waverley world, however, in which, as a merchant in *The Pirate* expresses it, "the tae half of the Mainland . . . is lost, and the other is running to and fro seeking it—awfu' times!" (p. 344), in which like the landscape itself the definitions of manhood are shifting, leaving some men suddenly beached, some whales suddenly trapped, some suddenly drowned, suddenly lost in quicksand. In the first pages of *Redgauntlet* the two youths raised as brothers, and more than brothers, "all in all" to each other, chafe each other about the proper definition of courage, Alan Fairford arguing that Darsie's rash bravado only serves to get him into scrapes, while his, the true courage of "self-possession," allows him to extract them both from, or avoid, situations of danger (p. 15). In the first major scene Darsie's direction-less curiosity strands him between quicksand and the sudden advance of the Solway tide, and he is rescued by the very embodiment of powerful manhood, the tall, harsh, and mysterious Laird of Solway, who instinc-tively finds his footing among the dangers and sweeps the hero to safety. He challenges his adversary, the Quaker net-fisherman, on the superior virility of spearfishing—"you and your partners are using unlawful craft to destroy the fish in the Solway by stake-nets and wears; and we, who fish fairly, and like men, as our fathers did, have daily and yearly less sport and less profit" (p. 50). The Laird has speared his fish in Darsie, yet appearances here deceive; no one familiar with the gender politics of the Waverley novels can fail to recognize in the Laird's certainty the doom of his kind of manhood, in Darsie's need of rescue the beginning of his journey toward certainty and the new manhood.

As the Laird's rescue becomes coercion, and finally kidnapping, as Darsie's wandering leads him first to play the role of a peasant fiddler's assistant and then, forcibly, a gentlewoman, as the young lawyer Alan Fairford seeks his truant classmate/brother and is pursued by his mad client Peter Peebles, the old association of manhood with instinctive outlaw strength falls away, and unlawful craft, jimmied hastily into lawful craft, becomes the measure of man. Darsie's adventures begin when he literally runs away from his studies in law toward the borders of England which were forbidden him by the unknown patron who pays his bills. Alan's begin when he receives, under the stern eye of his father, his barrister's robe and his first two clients. Darsie resists for two hundred pages the kind of masculinity that comes with his true identity as a Redgauntlet. He is, as he dreamed, the son of an English aristocrat, but also nephew to the Laird of Solway, Hugh Redgauntlet, who is plotting to bring back the Stuart king even while he labors consciously under the doom of his house—to expend energy always on the losing side of the age's cause. Alan embraces, somewhat restively, the rational masculinity of his lawyer father, which expresses itself in rigid devotion to business, and tolerance, under that First Principle, of all the personal and political vagaries of those who are, or may become (and whom does that exclude?) clients. But a letter recording the dangers and possible disasters which have overtaken Darsie in the land of the Laird appears magically among the papers Alan is commenting on, pleading his first case in court. And he dashes off to the rescue, breaking his father's heart, jeopardizing his career, and giving his client Peter Peebles warrant to pursue and arrest Alan Fairford, outlaw to his proper business.

The two surrogate brothers find one another in front of Father Crackenthorp's Inn, where the Pretender awaits the supporters who were to have been gathered by Hugh Redgauntlet and led—if the uncle has to kill the nephew to make him lead—by Sir Arthur Darsie Latimer Redgauntlet. Forced by Redgauntlet to dress in women's clothes to hide the fact that the semi-mythical "Arthur" has come to support the counter revolution, Darsie tangles himself in his dress dismounting and falls with feminine helplessness and more than feminine excitement into Alan's arms (p. 369). In assisting the masked lady, "a little surprised at the solid weight of the distressed fair one," Alan joins battle briefly with the elder Redgauntlet, who behaves like a jealous and irritable father over the young lady of whose "charge" he "releases" Alan. As a young lady, Darsie cannot, with propriety, run to the young man whom he knows is seeking to rescue him from the personal and national "history" which has kidnapped him. The only self-assertion open to him/her is to say no. No, Darsie will not lead the armies of the Jacobites, of whom he knows little but suspects much; no, he will not, from his feminized, neutralized, position, Redgauntlet or not, join the losing side of the cause. As Alan waits, fuming, in another parlor of the commodious Inn, as the Jacobites seize like canny businessmen the male-rational initiative from their feminized would-be king, opting for the escape clause (p. 407) planted in "note Number D" (for defeat?), as the blind fiddler plays "The Campbells are coming" to warn of the approach of the government's troops, the Jacobite cause, the Redgauntlet masculinity, vanishes. And in one of the most telling phrases in all the novels the dark uncle recognizes the neat trick, the tainted, patched, but legal-logical plot by which fate, and the author of Waverley, have accomplished the transformation of his house, ending its curse through the masterly inaction of its last son—"you pass under the service of the reigning monarch without the necessity of changing your allegiance" (p. 430).

The careful plotting by which the last Redgauntlet, without striking blow or turning coat, nevertheless passes under the aegis of the winning, the artificial legal, side of the cause, is matched only by the artful dodge which insures success for his "brother" the lawyer, who deserted the court and his father, carried messages for Jacobite traitors, made friends with smugglers, and eluded the lawful pursuit of his client Peter Peebles, while in fact carrying out his legal business. For his *first* client, the nameless muffled woman he called Greenmantle, hired him to warn and rescue Darsie, and it was by playing truant to that business that he fell into the clutches of his second, mad, pursuing client, Poor Peter Peebles. Alan hesitated on the Greenmantle case because it jibed too closely with his personal wishes; as a rational man and a lawyer he feels uncomfortable making business out of the rescue of the quasi-brother whom he loves and the service of the lady he fell for at first half-sight. He hesitated the more when the "pretty chaplain" who lives under the thumb of the saturnine Laird of Solway with the rescued kidnapped Darsie turns out to be that very Greenmantle. The cheer with which he assigns her to his friend, and shelters himself in the identity of "a smoke-dried young sophister, who cares not one of the hairs which it is his occupation to split for all the daughters of Eve" (p. 133), masks his alarm at the possibility of finding himself rivals with his brother for the lady.

The stratagem by which Scott saves him involves one of the oddest enlightenment scenes in all the novels. For Darsie, seeing Greenmantle so busy in his affairs, so anxious for his welfare, makes the judgment that Frank Osbaldistone had made of Diana Vernon, that she is in love with him and, unwomanly, showing her love before it is asked for. Frank's self-satisfied, half-contemptuous fantasies on this score receive no worse deflation than a sharp speech from Diana, but Darsie's fantasy actually seems to constitute a pre-Freudian "family romance." For Greenmantle is his sister, Lilias Redgauntlet. When they begin their ride toward the Inn and the Jacobite conspirators, the womanized Darsie dreams of loving his pretty female companion. When she, thinking he knows her identity as she knows his, frankly kisses him, the taboo shatters his romance: "If a hermit had proposed to him to club for a pot of beer, the illusion of his revered sanctity could not have been dispelled more effectually than the divine qualities of Green-Mantle faded upon the ill-imagined frank-heartedness of poor Lilias" (p. 333). He cannot perceive why the "sudden flame should have died away so rapidly," from his mind and tries to "coax back" the passion (p. 336). When she tells him she is his sister the shadow of the worst evil Romance can inflict upon a man passes over him—he "started in his saddle, as if he had received a pistol-shot"—and disappears, leaving relief, and "reality"— "he really felt himself more relieved . . . than disappointed by the vanishing of so many day-dreams. . . . He had been already flung from his romantic Pegasus, and was too happy at length to find himself with bones unbroken, though with his back on the ground" (p. 339).[21]

This scene, paralleling the entry into "common day" of Mordaunt Mertoun when he sees and chooses possibility in Brenda, also parallels Edward Waverley's entry into the "real history" of his life after he has been wounded in the battle of Prestonpans and finds himself relieved of his infatuation with Flora and Fergus MacIvor. To discover in place of a lady-love a practical sister, who has her whole life been temporizing with and cleverly evading in womanly fashion the tyranny of their uncle and the various schemes of blackguards, is for Darsie to discover not a fantasy but a model. Shedding his woman's clothing, he takes Lilias's advice and temporizes, delays, finally outwaits the man of action, and receives his legitimacy without—this is, as Welsh pointed out, the secret fear of Waverley heroes—having to strike a violent or traitorous or even egoistic blow for it. His discarded skirt becomes the screen behind which Lilias and Alan Fairford begin their romance, when client and lawyer meet in the Inn to see completed the contract she initiated and he fulfilled, to go to the rescue of her (and his) brother.

A second contract, however, is still to be fulfilled, the one to which Fairford is outlaw. This is the mortally tangled legal case which is the great tragicomic "harlequinade" of Edinburgh, the case of Poor Peter Peebles versus Paul Plainstanes. The case, of more than fifteen years' standing, originally involved Peebles suing Plainstanes for his fair share of a dissolved partnership, but has since, like the Jarndyce case in *Bleak House* which it startlingly prefigures, accreted countersuits and parallel suits in the very ecstasy of law, forming "lawsuit within lawsuit, like a nest of chip-boxes" (p. 140). It is old Fairford's shrewd judgment that the case is now beyond solving or curing, like a dead body passed from the doctors to a medical apprentice, "to cut and carve on a departed subject, to show your skill" (p. 135). But Alan untangles the case in his first speech, presenting his client as a man owed the money he claims, though a subtle adversary, his own obstinacy, and, most of all, the hunger of law and lawyers for business, have wrought from this simple matter the present monolith and circus of a Case. This clear-headed exposition threatens to bring the circus to a conclusion, until Alan finds the letter about Darsie's danger among the Peebles correspondence. He runs off; his father runs after him. The attorney for Plainstanes in rebuttal "quietly and imperceptibly replaced all the rubbish which [Alan] had cleared away, and succeeded in restoring the veil of obscurity and unintelligibility" (p. 164); and the judges agree that the case is archetypally calculated to drive to madness everyone—judge, client, advocate, observer—who touches it (p. 156).

The specific madness of total immersion in the law is perfectly expressed in Peter Peebles himself, "the man of rags and litigation" (p. 149), that "wrecked ship" and "scarecrow" of a man who haunts the precincts of the court and ought to serve men as a warning (p. 138). Instead it seems to serve as an invitation—to small boys to torment him in the streets like they tormented Madge Wildfire, to young lawyers practicing the skills his case gives scope for, to all who attend on the law and depend on it. The madness has a name—megalomania. Like "shadow to substance" (p. 149), Peter Peebles follows Alan Fairford to court, and from court through the fields of Ayrshire to the Inn at which Fairford finds Darsie, like a shadow attached to the man upon whom he can serve warrants in the gigantic Personna of the Law, like a shadow taking ever larger and more fantastic shapes, like a shadow showing, however, where the light is.

Peebles versus Plainstanes is for him the Great Cause: it makes him great, equalizes him with other giants in the service of Great Causes, with Hugh Redgauntlet himself, for instance, who lodged in Peebles's house during "the 45," the time when the Jacobite's Great Cause was simply an annoying interference in the Greater Cause of Peebles versus Plainstanes. Redgauntlet firmly denies this brotherhood—"you have confused me with some of the other furniture of your crazy pate" (p. 208). But the brotherhood was unmistakably there. It is enforced by the image of brandy, drunk by the plotters of "the 45," smuggled across the water like the monarch himself, symbol of Peebles's intoxication with the inflated self created by Peebles versus Planestanes. The addiction is at once a waster and an inflater of its victim, but oh, the rapture of the inflation. It is in a tone of "sustained rapture" that Peter praises his case at the end:

> it is grandeur upon earth to hear ane's name thunnered out along the long arched roof of the Outer House . . . a' the best lawyers in the house fleeing like eagles to the prey—to see the reporters mending their pens to take down the debate—the Lords themselves pooin' in their chairs, like folk sitting down to a gude dinner. . . . To see a' this, and to ken that naething will be said or dune amang a' the grand folk, for maybe the feck of three hours, saving what concerns you and your business—O, man, nae wonder that ye judge this to be earthly glory! (P. 418)

Here Scott has hold of a truth about law deeper even than those Dickens will pursue in *Bleak House*. The rapture of law consists not only in its apparent promise to magnify the power of private greed or revenge; the paralysis attendant on the rapture consists not only in the law's impersonal mysterious tendency to magnify and reproduce itself rather than its promised products of equity and justice. It is true that these qualities are part of Peebles versus Plainstanes as they are of Jarndyce and Jarndyce. It turns out that Peter is not just an innocent entrapped by lawyers and an unscrupulous partner, for he entered the arena voluntarily, and originally as pursuer, not pursued, suing and bankrupting an old widow twenty years before, not just for the money but the pleasure, even grimly, the justice, under law, of it all. "What business have folk to do to live," he asserts, unblushing, when this episode is uncovered, "that canna live as law will?" (p. 382).

No, the true rapture of law consists in the power it gives the ordinary man, Poor Peter and Plain Paul, to come into the midst of, to sit down to dinner with, to grip and "arrest," the grand folk, the lords themselves. Even if, fundamentally, the ordinary man is the dinner, not the diner. Peter halfway understands this—"to see all a' ane's worldly substance capering in the air in a pair of weigh-bauks, now up, now down, as the breath of judge or counsel inclines it . . . there are times I rue having ever begun the plea-wark." But his madness, as well as his peculiar truthfulness, and his mental survival, requires the conversion of that rue to joy, of that underlying despair to celebration, of what is really a mid-air state, to solid ground. On this ground, knowing it can toss "substance" up and down in the air, live lawyers, and the new law-endowed men, even the best of them harried by qualms: "my profession had need to do a great deal of good," Alan Fairford notes, "if, as is much to be feared, it brings many individuals" to the condition of Peter Peebles (p. 138).[22] This fear remains, even if, in exchange, the study of the law offers solid manhood to its practitioners, shaking off from the young Alan "that native air of awkward bashfulness of which I am told the law will soon free me" (p. 77). In the prime of his manhood, as a male and a citizen feeling himself especially invited to it, Burgess Peter Peebles stepped onto that airy ground and was lost. He died at last, a "Dr. Dryasdust" elucidated for the author of Waverley in the last chapter, of a "Perplexity fit" when his adversary offered to give in and end the Great Cause (p. 433).

Thus *Redgauntlet* offers us, in a fictional conjunction of the two Great Causes, the male madnesses of violent irrational revolution and rational law. Suffering the madness of Jacobitism, the last Stuart capitulates to King George because of "judicial blindness," that is, a refusal to become judicial, in the 1760s. And Peter Peebles flares and goes out, with his cause, the insistence on becoming judicial, in the 1770s, as Walter Scott is born. Thus far, and no farther, the author of Waverley follows the madman in the attic. On the madness of King George himself, which struck first but not last in 1788, just as young Walter Scott, like Alan Fairford, put his head in the yoke of the law, the author of Waverley holds his peace.

5   The Salted Mine of History: *The Antiquary, Woodstock, The Talisman*

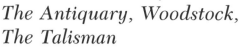

One can study only what one has first dreamed about.[1]

For nothing else is history
But pickle of antiquity,
Where things are kept in memory
         from stincking,

Which otherwaies would have lain dead,
As in oblivion buried,
Which now you may call into head
         with thinking.[2]

History, says Joyce's Stephen Dedalus, pretending, like all the others of his century, not to have read Scott, is the nightmare from which he is trying to awaken—so that he can fall, like Edward Waverley, into a more comfortable dream. "Araby," says the young hero of that *Dubliners* story, pretending to have liked Vidcoq's *Memoirs* better than *The Abbot*, is the enchanted home of his soul.[3] The adolescent, whether Stephen or Edward, undergoes an awakening which establishes the history, the romance, as a dream, as play. But in Scott no less than in Joyce, the state of awakening is more intolerable than the nightmare, more damaging than the quest-romance. If the Holy Sepulchre is empty and dark like the vault of the boy's bazaar, another crusade must be fabricated; if the chalice is spilt and the exposure of one's "vanity" burns out the old priesthood in anguish, anger, and shame, another priesthood must be composed.

     The old artificer stands us all in good stead in such deadly epiphanies. For turning history, romance, adolescence, into object, surface, packag-

153

ing it as picture, as Waverley (and *Waverley*) does Fergus MacIvor in the
final pages, as *Woodstock's* Cromwell has done with Charles I, solves
little. The subject is no less packaged, no less "abandoned," than the
object, once the split has been accomplished. That is why Stephen
"sleeps" again at the ends of his chapters, composing another tableau for
the portrait of the artist; that is why, as I have argued, Scott contrives
that Edward Waverley is somehow "the stranger" again at the end, even
at home in the domestic paradise of Tully-Veolan, even with his past
history-romance ostensibly packaged in Highland dress in the portrait
on the wall. Here Scott's modern perspective on history meets the
contemporary perspective on fiction: like Milton's hell history, as nightmare, is here, nor are we out of it.

Students of Scott's historicism may distinguish two methods, the
antiquarian and the theoretical, as well as two "matters," the Stuart
Jacobite and the "chivalric," in his works.[4] The antiquary digs up or
uncovers parts of the past, the theorist "re" constructs the artifact
herself. Yes, herself. Like Carlyle's Sphinx, history seems a mixed
being, the future a beast, the past a goddess, the present, the Meaning
of *this* day, is the active/passive forwarding of the transformation of the
one into the other. Being in time changes; the idea of history requires at
least three points on the line of process, requires a shapely past, a
wilderness present, and a void or dimly sketched future. From that
perspective *The Heart of Midlothian* is a characteristic history; the novel
dimly sketches a future for Jeanie and Effie Deans, then returns after
ten years to realize it in the death of George Staunton and the purchase
of land by Reuben Butler. By this measure his most perfectly characteristic history is *Old Mortality*, which seems to end in the wilderness for a
separated but loving Morton and Edith, returns after ten years to realize
that loving future, ends with the lovers joined by the deaths of Lord
Evandale and Burley, but gazing into the suddenly void future in the
rigidity of awakening which only the ostentatiously fictitious dream-
weaving of the last chapter can relax, for them or us.

This progressivist, meliorist, enigmatically elegiac as well as optimis-
tic theory of history, whereby the past becomes more beautiful as it is
found lost, more clear and shapely as it is (because it is) relinquished, fits
the Stuart-Jacobite "matter" like a glove, not least because the Sphinx
figure behind it, to be "re" constructed/repudiated, as I argued earlier,
is Mary Stuart. And its artifacts and arguments lie close to Scott's hand,
secularized and valorized in the eighteenth century by the new science
of party politics and the Scottish intelletual renaissance which were the
stuff of Scott's own early personal history.[5] But the "matter" of chivalry
was less tractable. He was not only both more ignorant and innocent

here than on the ground of the Scottish immersion in English history but also more knowing and guilty. For chivalry, the ground of *Ivanhoe* and the medieval and Renaissance novels, is the territory not only of the British national myth but of the Christian international one, of "Christendom." The survival of the nation being transformed from Stuart Monarchy to multi-party Empire seemed in the early nineteenth century brilliant enough to afford secure ground to the contemplation of the past which was the lady and the future which is the beast, humanly productive and morally just enough to afford safe territory for the exposure and analysis of the corruptions, compromises, and losses which made up the survival. But, the "present" of Christendom offered shaky ground. Where was Christendom tending? Where did it preserve its domain? Where was the hidden outlawed heart of its light, its Robin Hood, its guerilla jesus? Its antitheses, paganism/freethinking, held stronger ground than ever; its thesis, the Scarlet Woman of Catholic Rome, fanaticism of all Christian descriptions, held strong ground too; its synthesis, tolerant Belief, seemed indistinguishable from the secular landscape.

This anxiety about Christian Belief seems one of the most important points to bear in mind when considering the impression so many readers have had of the diminished vitality, the tableau-quality, of the realized historical worlds in Scott's chivalric novels, the so-called emphasis on costume and staged convention, the impression, in James Simmons's words, that in the medieval novels the stories are "always played out *against* a historical setting, never *in* one."[6] If to some extent the author of Waverley held himself more aloof from the passionate fanatics and bewildered compromisers of Christendom than of Stuartdom it was not only that he knew less than we do, enriched as we are by the explosion of Victorian medieval scholarship which was partly triggered as a response to the Waverley novels.[7] Access "inside" the medieval setting was for Scott partly blocked, I think, by a subversive quailing before the supreme Being in whose presence he clearly always felt himself, about the history of disestablishment, self-destruction, and loss he was presenting of His Kingdom. Crossing the divide of *Ivanhoe* into Britain, into Christendom, the author of Waverley found himself already describing the disintegration of that kingdom and the "uselessness" of its ideal figure, Richard Coeur de Leon. He would have to travel further, in time and space, to find its origin and its "use" and simultaneously the root contradiction, the contrastor-figures who would undermine the kingdom. He would find them, of course—deeply historical, deeply ironical—in "Araby." Riddle within riddle, his narratives of the Crusades, like the Crusaders, would never reach home, would halt in the moral paralysis explicit in the contrastor figures of *The Talisman* first sketched in *Ivanhoe*—the Christian chivalric ideal embodies itself, arrow within secret desert leaves, in the Arab, Saladin, and its enemy is the atheist warrior-priest, the Templar.

"The only Thought which Philosophy brings with it to the contemplation of History, is the simple conception of Reason; that Reason is the Sovereign of the World; that the history of the world, therefore, presents us with a rational process. . . . Passion is that which sets men in activity, that which effects practical realization. . . . The Idea is the inner spring of action; the State is the actually existing realized moral life." Thus Hegel, introducing his lectures on universal history in 1822–23, refining them through the decade, through the term 1830–31, arguing that history is the progress of the consciousness of freedom.[8] In the fall of 1831 the author of Waverley, collecting his notes for his Magnum Opus, dug up in the British Museum the evidence for, indeed the argument for, his kind of history, a poem on the episode which is the triggering device for his novel of Puritans and Cavaliers, *Woodstock*. "For nothing else is history," says the anonymous author of the poem, "But pickle of antiquity, / Where things are kept in memory, / From stincking. / Which otherwais would have lain dead, / As in oblivion buried, / Which now you may call into head / With thinking."

What I like about this Waverleyan description of history is its anonymity, its operative images of history as buried treasure and buried bodies to be dug up, ghosts to be called up and Resurrected, and above all the duplicity hinted at in the picture of the historian as "pickler." The historian's pickle, as applied to his object, both preserves and disguises—both operations are necessary for the act of thinking. Does the savory disguise the stink of actuality and lie about its gaps? Or does it preserve the actual from the disintegration that stinks, and imaginatively restore its lost parts? The historian's pickle, as applied to himself and his intentions, is just his consciousness of the duality inherent in the game of hermeneutics, historical interpretation.[9] The inspired understanding he brings to the identification of his "finds" changes them: does the "salt" of his enlightened imagination stabilize and reveal the truth, or does it contribute a fixity, coherence, and beauty that are actually a falsehood? The historian-interpreter cannot touch the treasure without salting it—but perhaps he, or his predecessor-interpreters, have already salted the mine?

In this context it seems to me quite wonderful that Scott chose for the triggering plot artifice of his novel *The Antiquary* a salted mine, for that of *Woodstock* a false apparition, for that of *The Talisman* a parody resurrection.[10] All three of these incidents—the faking of an antique

treasure trove by the greedy Dousterswivel in *The Antiquary*, the
faking of an apparition of the Devil and of dead men by the anti-Puritan
villagers of Woodstock, the apparently miraculous Resurrecting operation of the talisman in that novel—have been seen as side issues, mere
artificial backgrounds or plot excuses for the character studies. But I
should like to make readings of these three novels the focus for an
examination of Scott's understanding of the matter of the Stuart-
Jacobite adventure, of the Christian-Chivalric adventure, and of anti-
quarian-historiography itself. As an introduction I want to isolate these
three triggering artifices, and to suggest that Scott's recourse to them
was not simply his habitual mask of the entertainer-folktale spinner. Nor
is it simply his continuing return to the leitmotif of the hidden reality,
the treasure under the secret leaves. It partakes of both these reflexes
but signifies in addition his commentary, as a shrewd and learned man
embedded like all his characters in the superstitions of his age, on the
infant science, the ancient superstition, of universal history. Scientist or
dreamer, the historian may well penetrate the leaves only to find that
this treasure, history, like the arrows that protect it and the arrows that
beguilingly point to it, is, after all, an artifact.

The Antiquary is about the Romance of Property when the property
is history. The true-love gleam in the eye of Jonathan Oldbuck as he
surveys his dearly bought ditch at Kinprunes, scene, as he argues, of the
final conflict between the Romans and the Caledonians, the erotic
tremble of his hand as he carries off from the unsuspecting book dealer a
blackened volume or fondles an ancient shard of medallion, is kindled
by the instinct of acquisition and possession of objects, yes. But the mark
of the ditch is "indistinct,"[11] and the inscription in the texts, on wood or
metal, are most often illegible. And that is what makes them peculiarly
his. Only the antiquary can possess the secret treasure under the
"barren" (p. 29) surface, only he can "own," through his educated
imagination, the time extending three dimensionally from the object in
space he grasps. "I was unwilling to say a word about it till I had secured
the ground," whispers Jonathan to the stranger, Edward Lovel, but now
he can display his new possession in its wholeness: "From this place,
now scarce to be distinguished, but by its slight elevation and its greener
turf, from the rest of the fortifications, we may suppose Agricola to have
looked forth on the immense army of Caledonians" (pp. 29, 30). The
"ecstasy" in this scene is cut short by a challenger, though; appearing
suddenly, like magic, "unseen and unheard," the old beggar Edie
Ochiltree, gossip, trickster, popular historian, affirms, "I mind the
bigging [building] o't." Further he insists, "I . . . built this bit thing
here . . . for a bield [shelter] at auld Aiken Drum's wedding." And

further, digging out the mentally withheld treasure of the appalled young stranger, Lovel, "I'll tell him whaur he was yestreen at the gloaming" (pp. 31–32).

There is explicit comic deflation of the aristocratic romanticizing of history-property here, of course; many critics see only this.[12] There is, more subtly, the suggestion that the populist history revolving around the celebrations and artifacts of ordinary folk is as usefully historical as the aristocratic idea implicit in the antiquary's ecstacy over world-historical clashes. This would make the substitution of Edie's translation "Aiken Drum's Lang Ladle" for Oldbuck's translation "Agricola Dicavit Libens Lubens" for the indistinct "A.D.L.L." traced on the stone at Kinprunes less a deflation than an addition to the stone's historicity. For if the most insisted on trait of Scott's characters is that they are none of them free of the superstitions of their particular age, the most insisted on trait of his landscapes is that they are all palimpsests, ruin within ruin, structure upon structure, inscription under inscription.

More subtly still, since the author of Waverley chooses here as elsewhere a rhetoric of mystery and prophecy for the intrusion of Edie onto the scene, he becomes an archetype as well as a vivid personality, an oracle as well as an ironist. Like Jung's Little Old Man, or Malory's Hermit, he might almost as easily have been present at Agricola's defense as at Aiken Drum's bachelor party. On the other hand, Edie might surely have invented his translation and the whole story of Aiken Drum's wedding just to tease and frustrate the antiquary, as someone of his prankster temperament delights to do.[13]

Or—he may be making it up, yet hitting on the truth.

Or Oldbuck may be. When the antiquary proposes the event to Lovel later on as the matter for a poetic epic entitled "The Caledonian: Or Invasion Repelled" ("but the invasion of Agricola was not repelled," protests Lovel on the authority of Tacitus) set at the disputed ditch of Kinprunes (but the ditch is only twenty years old, protests Edie Ochiltree on the authority of his experience), Oldbuck is only partly swayed. His version has been twice disconfirmed, but on what authority, after all? Every text, Father Eustace in The Abbot says, has its paraphrase, One intelligently imagined text may confront, or even replace another, if Lovel writes as he directs, and "I dare say, ye may unwittingly speak most correct truth in both instances, in despite of the toga of the historian and the blue gown of the mendicant" (pp. 121–22).

Though Scott is gently mocking the antiquary here, he has created in Jonathan Oldbuck an imaginative historian neither frenziedly credulous nor grimly skeptical. He simply has a sharp side, where other people's fantasies are concerned, and a "blunt side," about which he is ruefully aware, for his own. As a digger up of history's treasures and diviner of time's indistinct inscriptions he is often fallible, but his crochety humility comes not only from his personal consciousness of the historian's "fall"—his eternal capacity to deceive himself—but also from his sense of the real paradoxes and imponderables of history itself, his sense that whatever the undoubted benefits of painstaking proof-collecting and rational skepticism, there may be occasions where the evidence lies and the inspired or legendary guess is the truth.[14]

Edie Ochiltree, the ragged independent beggar who affects to tell common or gross truth and yet in his semi-mythic way plays imaginatively inspired pranks, is one of the digger-diviners who can "find out the blunt side" (p. 145) of the antiquary. The other is Herman Dousterswivel, salter of the mine of history, swindler and fake "exorcist," who affects to dig up or resurrect buried truths and treasures with the help of the Rosicrucian spirit-masters. Once burned in a Dousterswivel mining scheme in the eloquently named "Glen Widdershins," Oldbuck watched his antiquarian enthusiast friend Sir Arthur Wardour sink deeper and deeper into the German's toils, taking the old coins and plate found by the diviner as evidence he can deliver on his promise of finding and unbinding untold riches hidden by spell-binding monks. But of course, as Edie comments, watching the scam from a secret observation post built by a suspicious Prior in what are now the ruins of St. Ruth's Priory, "they that hide ken best where to find" (p. 199), and Dousterswivel has already supplied the half-obliterated sixteenth-century grave with the coins that he expects will breed more coins from the credulous Sir Arthur. The baronet has had reason, in this early scene, to doubt the word of the German magician, for Edie, "who began to enter into the humour of the scene" (p. 197), had sneezed and howled and imitated one of the master spirits, to the surprise and terror of the imposter.

Insisting on the evidence of "mine own eyes" (p. 198), Sir Arthur is gulled entirely when Dousterswivel allows him to turn over the gravestone and handle the supposed antiquarian treasure himself. For though, as Oldbuck has earlier commented loftily, "too many of our historians" have "followed each other's blind guidance" instead of taking pains to "satisfy their own eyes" (p. 8), the evidence of the eyes is no simple way out of the historian's dilemma. In choosing at random a mine for his salt, a grave for his fake resurrection, Dousterswivel has chosen better than he knew, has chosen a truth that will erase his falsehood, has chosen in his mechanical greed the very place where actual history resides, waiting to develop its consciousness. The stone casually removed bears the recumbent figure of a knight and the coat of arms of one

Malcolm the Misbegot, or Malcolm Misticot to the commonality, a half-mythical figure of the twelfth century. And he himself, Edie takes Dousterswivel aside to say, is the only man in the county besides Sir Arthur who can tell the real story of the man. Edie and Oldbuck accompany Sir Arthur back to the ruins to prove that any treasure present can be discovered without the aid of spirits or magic, and to the German's astonishment a large cache of coins is discovered beneath the grave where Dousterswivel had hidden his own small cache. The false "divining" was a true one, it seems.

The trickster then tells the swindler the story of the illegitimate Malcolm, begotten between two first cousins, who usurped the Knock-winnock-Wardour land from Sir Richard "Red-Hand" (another one!) Wardour for a generation until his legitimate brother took them back again by force and confined the usurper as a monk in that very monas-tery of St. Ruth's. Here, Edie ends impressively, "he died soon after, of pure despite and vexation" (p. 229), leaving a mysteriously depleted treasury and an enigmatic prophecy—"If Malcolm the Misticot's grave were fun', the lands of Knockwinnock are lost and won" (p. 220).

The true history of Malcolm Misticot engages the swindling but credulous Dousterswivel to take part in the plan Edie proposes, of returning a third time without Sir Arthur to search the grave for the fullness of the treasure which, surely, must be buried beneath the found/lost treasure which was beneath the false/lost treasure which the German had secreted there. At that third visit the swindler is first terrified by the apparent ghastly visitation of ancient Knockwinnock-Wardours, and then hit over the head. The comic punishment applied, we learn at the end of the novel that there was no third treasure, that the second casket, like the first, was false, not historical, "salted" this time not by a villain for a greedy purpose but by young Lovel, as a way of helping Sir Arthur pay his debts.

Fooled again by fake history. But not exactly. For the ghostly funeral at St. Ruth's which terrified Dousterswivel had in fact interred the old Countess of Glenallen, and her death triggers a series of revelations which makes clear that Lovel is the very image of Malcolm the Misbe-got, resurrected and cleansed, just in the nick of time, of the bar sinister. And his treasure, symbolically buried and dug up as a trick, does lose and win back for the legitimate family this property whose true history stands revealed in the popularly recorded prophecy. Like the individual Waverley drama of father and son, the larger drama of univer-sal history travels on the near miraculous coincidence of duty with desire, of the unconscious burden of the past with the rogue personal will. History is the progress of the consciousness of our freedom to dig up and act upon the massively accumulated, already assembled, meaning of the day.

But who buried the meanings? One's fathers?—misbegotten, everyone of them, all their inheritance branded "red-handed" with crime? Or the poets and tricksters of the present—inspired liars, with their laughter and their secret signals? Or the antiquarians and historians, on the interface, trying to speak of their fathers and listen to the inspiration and laughter in the air, and divorce the object from the subject? Playing with the salted mine image in *The Antiquary*, Scott seems almost to hint at a catastrophist God of history, who plants false clues to a long evolutionary sequence purely to give us matter for this new obsession of conscious freedom.

The plot of *The Antiquary* veers strongly toward the safe areas of recent common history and the legitimate white-handed inheritance, of course. We feel that Agricola's presence on the land and Malcolm the Misbegot's treasure are in fact too deeply buried for recovery, and we welcome the newer inscriptions of "Aiken Drum's Lang Ladle" and Edward Lovel's neat little cache in the box from the brig *Search No. I*. In *Woodstock*, placed one hundred and fifty years further back into history, we recognize something of this same motif; here the comedy of historical interpretation we saw in *The Antiquary* becomes farce. Again, mysterious supernatural apparitions seem to guard a deeply buried historical treasure. The treasure is the monarch, the young Charles II, escaping from the royalist military disaster at Worcester, and the territory where he has gone to ground, the abandoned but still "live" mine, is the ancient feudal house of Woodstock, where Henry II poisoned the "Fair Rosamond" and the folio of the works of William Shakespeare, "the king and high priest of these vices and follies" (p. 41), rests beside the Bible in the Master's study. [15]

As the novel opens the Cromwellians who have taken over the house, dispossessing the Royalist Ranger, Sir Henry Lee, have already been visited with every kind of terrible light, noise, push, trick: the supposedly empty house seems to put forth its "guardians" from the past which lives so strongly there. The worthy Puritan pastor sees the ghost of the loyalist scholar-friend he could not save from the army, and even the genteel hero Everard hears and sees accusing supernatural visitors whom he cannot fully rationalize as tricksters.

They are tricksters, of course, royalist servants and friends engaging in Shakespearean farce and fooling, who have salted the looted royalist stronghood with false inhabitants to keep usurpers from taking or destroying Woodstock. The alarms at Woodstock are fake, yet they are true too, for as one of the ghosts accuses Everard, "Those only hear the alarm whose consciences feel the call" (p. 176). Both Puritans and Royalists, red-handed from ancient and recent despoilments, both fanaticists and moderates, heads turned by arguments they sense are hollow, feel that alarm.

As in *The Antiquary*, the first half of *Woodstock* is given over to the tricks which suggest that a historico-mythic treasure can be dug out of a materially empty hiding place. At midpoint in the former novel, however, the tombs at St. Ruth's receive a real corpse and a genuine secret begins working its way to the surface. At midpoint in the latter novel a "masculine" or "denaturalized" (p. 217) woman appears at the ruined solitary spring where the Fair Rosamond once received her Plantagenet, the same face looks in like a goblin at a second-story window, and then enters as the much scratched and patched visage of a Scotch page, and the empty mine of Woodstock has its history back in it. Charles II, female gypsy, "Louis Kerneguy," "the Young Man," "the King of Scots," a hunted fox, has come to ground where both his friends and his great enemy have expected him; the king is in the King's Oak again. Cromwell arrives at the end of the novel to lay hands on his treasure, and destroy it; his soldiers pursue the figure of the king from secret chamber to hidden passage, from parlor to tower, whispering fearfully of the "devils of Woodstock, who might be all the while decoying them" (p. 124) with fake images of their treasure. They finally blow up Rosamond's tower and the figure of the king, the historic monarchy, with it. But the dead man in the ruins turns out to be "our own sentinel," the fleeing figure of the king was really the disguised royalist Albert Lee, and the devil (or angel) of Woodstock, the true meaning of this day, has disappeared again.

It is one thing to play ambiguous tricks about secular history—Is there anything behind the arras but rats? Anything behind the long adventure of Divine Right Monarchy but red-handed Robert Bruce cutting his rival's throat i' the church? Anything in the ruins of St. Ruth or the tower of Rosamond but contemporary rivals and new men on the make manipulating old stories? Moving toward sacred history, where the same questions must be felt, the author of Waverley tightens his spacious narratives into Romances, giving rise to the kinds of subliminal tensions that issue in satire. What is this "insanity, which brings you hither to obtain possession of an empty sepulchre," marvels Saladin of the Western Christians.[16] Who is this "dog of a Prophet" whom the Moslems blasphemously think still lives and guides mankind, rages Richard Coeur de Lion; "It makes me sick to think the valiant and worthy Soldan should believe in a dead dog" (p. 85). "It is justly spoken," says Saladin, "with serene gravity," playing the part of an ignorant desert sheik listening to a Scottish knight tell him about the frozen lakes of the north, "list to a Frank and hear a fable" (p. 10). "Hark, thee," Richard of England warns the Saracen physician who has just cured him with "the talisman" and is arguing that Richard is in the power of that mystic object; "I have no objection that leeches should wrap their words in mist, and pretend to derive knowledge from the stars, but when you bid Richard Plantagenet fear that a danger will fall upon *him* from some idle omen, . . . you speak to no ignorant Saxon or doting old woman, who foregoes her purpose because a hare crosses the path, a raven croaks, or a cat sneezes" (p. 182).

Yet the Frankish fable of the empty sepulcher, which must be repossessed precisely because its emptiness signifies its holiness, is the origin of the cosmopolis of Christendom and must be, or be rendered, true. The slain hero-sacrifice must arise. As Scott's narratives of the crusades climax in *The Talisman*, a tenderly ironic parody of the Resurrection occurs in the tent of Richard Plantagenet, its agent that worshipper of dead dogs, that "pretender" to the talismanic powers of the grail, the Sultan of Araby, whose kingdom the Crusaders have come to despoil.

The talisman, in the keeping of the infidel, is a hidden substance in a small red silk purse, which "changes" water into a healing elixir, though the change, like the substance itself, is mostly conjectural—"it seemed to the spectators as if some effervescence took place during the operation, but if so, it instantly subsided" (p. 91). The scene in which Richard "drained the cup to the bottom . . . and sunk back, as if exhausted" (p. 105) is his Gethsemane; it is followed by a scene where Richard's and Christendom's major true enemy, the Templar, urges a greedy fellow crusader to join him in killing the too-popular king—"Richard arise from his bed, sayst thou?—Conrade, he must never arise!" (p. 112)—and concluded by his Resurrection. When "the critical hour" arrives, at which the dead-looking body in the royal tent might be awakened, Richard not only wakes safely (demanding to know how much money he has in his coffers, a nice Waverleyan touch), but, hearing that the standard of England has been abused while he was in his "grave" he shouts his anger "in a tone which might have waked the dead" (p. 123), and goes to his harrowing of hell. He strides to the mound that contained the standard and hurls an offending warrior bodily down the hill in an "almost supernatural display of strength" (p. 127).

This parody resurrection of a figure whom the author of *Ivanhoe* described as "useless" and the narrator of *The Talisman* suspects may be a species of madman shows the theme of history-as-trickery still operating in the Waverley novels even as they seek back through time for the sacred origins of the trick. For the antiquary of secular or sacred history, national, or universal history, the digging seems always to bring them back to the illegible inscription, the rifled casket, the empty sepulcher. Only after this blankness has been possessed, often bloodily or corruptly, does the work of the historian begin in earnest.

Kunst Macht Gunst: The Stuart Matter

The Waverley hero of *The Antiquary*, nicknamed "the phoenix Lovel" by his avuncular companion Jonathan Oldbuck, spends a phantasmagoric night in the Green Room at Oldbuck's manor Monkbarns. The room is haunted by two forefathers, the monk John of the Girnel, who received rents there in the sixteenth century as the last bailiff of the Abbey of Trotcosey, founded in the fourteenth century, and Aldobrand Oldbuck, the printer-ancestor of the present owner, who drew the first sheets of the Augsburgh Confession and, driven out of Germany for it, came in the early seventeenth century to purchase the lands of the dissolved monastery. Edward Lovel himself is haunted by the blank on his ancestral escutcheon: he doesn't know who he is in his insomniac visions—"He was a bird—he was a fish—or he flew like the one, and swam like the other . . . and whatever attracted his attention underwent, as he attempted to investigate it, some wild and wonderful metamorphosis while his mind continued all the while in some degree conscious of the delusions from which it in vain struggled to free itself by awaking" (p. 87). The empty background upon which he irresistibly projects and loses his dozens of identities, in which the phoenix agonizingly dies and lives, finally stabilizes, in a dream, a fiction, a goal—he imagines one of the room's haunting fathers, the Protestant printer, pointing to an inscription in an unknown language, an inscription which reads, as Jonathan Oldbuck proudly repeats and translates the motto of his house, of the Reformation, of the modern world, of the Waverley novels—Kunst Macht Gunst (p. 95).

This inscription the tales in this novel and all the novels themselves translate roughly thus: birth counts, of course, and money talks, and land is lovely—but it is skill that wins favor, craft that brings success, patient application that makes power, accomplished deeds that make history. Art that creates value. In the postchivalric world in which the Stuarts contend for kingship and the Scots seek to avoid extinction, experts are the new aristocrats. This is the context in which so many of the Waverley heroes are called on, soon after their appearance, for demonstrations of expertise, displays of exotic or unexpected skills which are not necessarily central to their characters or used more than once in the novel. Henry Morton wins the marksmanship contest and never shoots again; Ivanhoe witches the world with horsemanship; Edward Lovel, a virtual stranger to the Fife coast and, as we learn, an inland-bred man, climbs like a native cragsman down a sheer precipice to rescue Sir Arthur and Isabella Wardour from the incoming tide. The author of Waverley constructs this scene partly to suggest that a "daring adventurer" (p. 64) lives repressed within the reticent gentleman, partly to complicate the love between the two young people by a service which he is too proud to take advantage of and she too fearful of her repressed passion to show proper gratitude for, partly to render the exhausted Lovel prey to the ministrations of Oldbuck, who "drags" him back to his home after his dizzy swing over the precipice, "Like an agitated pendulum . . . like an idle and unsubstantial feather" (p. 71), to spend the night haunted by his unsubstantiality in the Green Room at Monkbarns. And partly so that the first term of the Waverley Topos, skill-patience-craft, will have been established in Lovel before the inscription itself is read, translated, and, in the course of the narrative, accomplished. When Lovel, restored to his substantial identity, marries Isabella at the end of the novel with a ring of antique massy gold inscribed Kunst Macht Gunst, he unites the two ancient houses the young people represent under the sign of the third and premier house in the novel's world, that of the bourgeois Protestant printer whose father-hood Lovel accepts in his dream.[17]

Thus Jonathan Oldbuck is not a side issue, a comical character on the periphery of his titular novel; he has as much at stake in the resolution as the Wardours and the Glenallens at whose rescue he seems simply a scholarly observer. The young man whose identity knits the Wardour and Glenallen fortunes binds the Oldbuck future to theirs; for as much as Lovel is, interestingly, his own phoenix, burning, dying, and return-ing, he is also, as the childless antiquary somehow knows from the start, *his* phoenix too.

As antiquaries, the current Oldbuck and the current Wardour are friendly rivals for imaginative control of a royal past which this genera-tion of the 1790s has emphatically put to sleep, pickled, sculpted, and completed, so they think. The Roman-Celtic past, where the borders of the kingdoms were established, is still a matter for dispute between Jonathan Oldbuck and his nephew Hector M'Intyre, whose mystic Highland royalty and Ossianic pride the uncle begs leave to doubt. The debate about the faking of MacPherson's poetic "history" which the antiquary hotly participates in, focuses both Oldbuck's skepticism about the legendary M'Intyre family history and his running cynicism about the glorious Celtic antiquity of the English kings with whom Sir Arthur

Wardour, descendent actually of "red-handed" rievers, identifies himself. If Sir Arthur's aristocracy (rather newer-minted than he would like to admit) makes him defend the "good fame" (p. 41) of Queen Mary Stuart, it is clearly Oldbuck's antiquarian monkhood that fuels his skepticism about her and all such "womankind." If Sir Arthur's imprisonment as a boy in "the 45" cemented his proud loyalty for the losing side, it is clearly Oldbuck's pride in the quick action of his own merchant Provost father in arresting the Wardour of the last generation which keeps the antiquary so staunch a Hanoverian. The "historic" passions which once embattled knights and merchants, which created as values, as identities, finally as Parties, the Protestant and Catholic, Puritan and Cavalier, Whig and Tory, are now, in the "far-descended knight . . . and the representative of the typographer" (p. 42), recognizable mainly in their "mode of disputing" about that completed object, the past. The "petifogging intimacy with dates, names, and trifling matters of fact" which allows Oldbuck to get the better of Sir Arthur in arguments the knight traces to his "mechanical descent" (p. 43). Attacking in his turn, Oldbuck ascribes the propensity of the knight to credit any stories which display the power of pride-of-descent or the chivalric power of love and "trumpery womankind" (p. 53) to the egoism and secret anxiety which the aristocracy has inherited from their actually unchivalric and low-descended feudal forbears, "brawling, bullet-headed, iron-fisted old Gothic barons . . .—not one of whom, I suppose, could write his own name" (p. 54).

The dispute about history carried on in *The Antiquary* turns not so much on the continuing collision of the two great forces, old and new, Stuart and Hanoverian, aristocrat and mechanic, passion and reason. That, the novel tells us, has been resolved on the island, though it is being renewed, artifically, in the nightmare of present invasion from across the water that underlies all the peaceful wrangling of historians about the island past. What really concerns Scott and his character-historians is the destruction, the disappearances, the racial and personal losses which make up the fabric of history, the wiped-out voids which the persistence of ruins, or even the sudden discovery of hidden fragments, only emphasizes. No wonder the phoenix is the icon of this dispute; "the phoenix Lovel" speaks exactly for this sensibility. Oblivion has been Lovel's own background, for he had been raised in Yorkshire to believe himself the illegitimate son of Geraldin Neville, and has received hints that a "deeper stain than that of ordinary illegitimacy" obscures his birth. This stain, incest, is in fact a fiction composed by the domineering old Countess of Glenallen, who like several women in the ancient histories governing the present crises of Waverley novels had been driven to cruel and criminal actions in order to maintain some control over their lives and lands, so captive to the laws of male inheritance.

Distinguishing himself as a soldier against this worse than blank escutcheon, Lovel rises a self-made man from the ruins and fragments of his criminal identity, and receives by the end of the novel the reward of his distinguished and legitimate birth, new interpretations reordering the false clues to his illegitimacy dug up at St. Ruth's Priory. As legitimate heir of the ancient Celtic Catholic Glenallens, Lovel marries Isabella, the heiress of the newer Gothic chivalric Wardours and Knockwinnocks. But he is also in a manner the heir of the newest blood on the island, for the northern English Eveline Neville was also the boyhood love of Oldbuck the typographer's descendent, and it is his family ring, which might have married him to Eveline, which instead marries her child, his phoenix-son, to Isabella Wardour. Lovel has thus already undergone the ritual Waverleyan outlawing and disinheritance before the novel opens, and been in a manner forced to the profession in which the illegitimate man-of-old, Malcolm the Misbegotten, made his new name.

The history of his birth and the lie that tainted it was buried in the ruins of St. Ruth's the same night that Edie Ochiltree and Steenie Mucklebackit tricked Herman Dousterswivel into returning for more of the faked treasure salted in Malcolm the Misbegotten's grave. It rises the next day in the breasts of the popular historians, beggars, and old women, as Steenie's grandmother Elspeth, hearing that her old mistress the Countess of Glenallen is dead, rises from her decrepitude "like a mummy animated by some wandering spirit into a temporary resurrection" to "unlade my mind" to the wrecked Earl (p. 252). Dousterswivel was comically punished by a clout on the head for faking acquaintance with historical secrets. The day after they witness the interment of the real secret Edie is arrested for the attack on Dousterswivel and young Steenie is drowned. The boy's father, who earlier pulled Lovel and Isabella out of the approaching tide, but could not save his own son, shoulders his grief at the wake the following day in the scene which Virginia Woolf's Mr. Ramsay so identifies with. Meanwhile the dead boy's grandmother, who was once paid for robbing another man of his son and his peace, prepares to give up her guilty secret, now that her own grandson has paid for it, to the Earl of Glenallen, whose knock on the door Woolf thought an unwarranted imposition of "plot" upon "life."

But "plot" makes "life" in the Waverley novels—kunst macht gunst. In a world of competing plotters the young Waverley hero has no life in his own eyes until, falling from sinless drift into outlaw craft, he allies himself with, or remakes for himself, one of life's ongoing plots, Stuart or Hanoverian, Gothic or rational. Allying himself with Edie and Steenie to salt Malcolm's grave and retrieve its treasure, the phoenix Lovel resurrects the Wardour fortunes, the Glenallen name, and the triumphant Oldbuck bourgeois ethic. Under his borrowed motto, kunst macht gunst, he settles down at novel's end to manage the lands of three houses while his co-conspirators disappear, the young one, connected with the unchanging orders of fisher-folk life, into the sea in Lovel's place, the old one, pursuing his "vocations" of wandering wit, beggar, and oral historian as best he can, into the land.

Though he has his legitimacy and his aristocracy restored on the last page of the novel, Lovel is still fundamentally the stranger expert, the man on the make, the man-made man. This is emphasized in the final scene of *The Antiquary*, where, Dousterswivel's fake digging apparatus having been burned and mistaken for a beacon signaling the awaited invasion of Hanoverian England by Republican France, the countryside marshals its forces to await the London military authority, the man on horseback, who will lead them to battle. To "the surprise of all present, but most especially that of the Antiquary," the warrior turns out to be "the pacific Lovel" (p. 408), restored to the officership he had laid down to come north for the sake of Isabella Wardour.

This final phoenix disclosure of the military pacifist is of course crucial to the novel's historical point, to that of the first trio of the Waverley novels, to Scott's general picture of universal history. The author of the first two Waverley novels had, as he says, "embraced the age of our fathers . . . and that of our own youth" (p. v); the author of *The Antiquary* embraces his own manhood, the age in which he feels himself to be living. In this age the intelligent muse and write about the passionate, divided, vulnerable past; the foolish quarrel about it; the crafty play tricks with it; and the guilty heap stones over it. And the young hero, of the past but not in it, hedges and observes and picks up protective coloration from his surroundings until his benefactor the antiquary takes him for a traveling actor, one of those who hold the mirror up to our nature, not their own; who function, in their ambiguous chameleon versatility, as the abstract and brief chronicles of the time. "The time" is one in which a general "polish" has "assimilate[d] to each other the manners of different nations" (p. v), in which Norman, Saxon, Roman, and Celt have become British, in which the wars that accomplished that assimilation have been finished, polished now into history. It is a "pacific" time, and man-made man is a civilized man, but the natural man is still a warrior. The central point of the last episode as the novel constructs it is not the emptiness of the French invasion alarm but rather the preparedness of even the least likely persons to go to war. The pacific Lovel finds a town "unanimously devoted to defense," finds the wandering beggar, in a famous passage, shouldering his pikestaff as he had in "the forty-five," as ready "to fight for his dish as the laird for his land" (p. 401), finds the antiquary himself with a sword stuck through his breeches pocket.

This last readiness is the key. Lovel has been a soldier, so has Edie; the town knows that in defending the present government it is defending the system of tariffs and treaties that has brought it prosperity. But Jonathan Oldbuck has been strenuously, oddly, anti-war all through his life and through the novel. His rhetoric has emphasized that war ruins records, war opposes knowledge. His laments over the ruin of libraries counterpoint his running sarcasm over his military nephew's rash chivalric pursuit of—and comic repulse by—a seal. "I hate a gun like a hurt wild duck—I detest a drum like a quaker," he affirms early on, damning the "military frenzy" which has driven the population of Edinburgh "mad" and caused its lawyers, clerks, merchants, and doctors to break out in a feverish rash of warrior-disguises and gestures (pp. 49–50). He, as civilized man and historian, is finished with war—all but one war. For when the alarm sounds, and his "womankind" offer him the weapons which lie at ease, as collectibles, round his study, neither the Roman falchion nor the Crusader's two-handed sword nor the riever's Andrew Ferrara sword tempts him. "Give me the sword which my father wore in the year forty-five," he cries (p. 405). Though the author of Waverley will not tackle directly, anymore than the author of *Pride and Prejudice*, the great international conflict of their time, the French Revolution, the sense that the sword of "the forty-five" is somehow appropriate for it, tragically and foolishly but also naturally-historically, is strong here. For in the 1790s no less than in the years of the writing of *The Antiquary*, between Waterloo and Peterloo, it was apparent that just beneath the easy platitudes of anti-French patriotism lay the old ground of civil discord, new men against old, class against class, money against land, Protestant Kunstler against the "far-descended." The classes Scott was attempting to preserve in their vitality and antagonism before they disappeared into the victorious assimilation had only gone undercover and would reemerge under the Great National Myth, under the free-suffrage Greenwood Tree. Robin Hood against the Game Preservers. As the author of Waverley lived his time forward from the alarms of French Republican invasion to Reform Bill agitation, writing his way backward from Jacobinism to Jacobitism, he was neither escaping nor prophesying, simply studying, as even the most self-conscious historian must, the undertow of the tide he himself moved on. The vision he had as a historian was the nightmare or the satire Jonathan Oldbuck experienced in Edinburgh, where the clerk must put on the soldier, in both senses of the phrase. The novels he wrote followed the single undertow to its farthest reach, as he understood it, from the sword of the forty-five to the New Model Army, to the Crusader's axe, till it merged in the surf of the first great assimilationist tide, the civilization that the eighteenth century historians claimed as their own ancestor—the Roman falchion.

Kunst Macht Gunst—the creator of the New Model Army fashioned from the discontented classes of his time the instrument that broke the old mold of feudal monarchy. But what interests the historian of the Waverley novels in *Woodstock* is the existential discomfort of the Great Man, and of the middling one who supports him, who rides the tide rather than watches the undertow.

In Oliver Cromwell Scott shows a man maddened by the kingship he murdered, well ahead of its appointed time, on January 30, 1642, haunted not only by the picture of the dead Charles I but, more terribly, by the desire which he must not desire—for kingship. It is that contravened desire which makes a shambles of Cromwell's language. Though Cromwell can speak to the point when he wants to, and though he can deliberately evade the point when he wants to, his discourse seems often seized by the very gremlin of carnal reason: it surrounds his meaning with "so many exclusions and exceptions . . . fortifying it with such a labyrinth of parentheses," that hearers account him, as Scott accounts all the original matter of history, including Great Men, "unintelligible" (p. 85). In the two scenes Scott gives him in *Woodstock*, one early in the narrative when his purpose is to free the Lodge from his Commissioners so that the escaping Charles II may come there to hide and be trapped, one at the end when he arrives to spring the trap, Cromwell's language turns parenthetical, self-reflexive, at the crucial moments when his purpose is to commit the final regicide.

When Roger Wildrake, a disguised Cavalier being protected by his Protestant friend Markham Everard, approaches the General with Everard's petition to put the king's supporters back in possession of Woodstock, Cromwell clearly decides immediately how to trap the young king of Scots. Yet he requires a long "ambiguous" and "periphrastic" oration, which usurps that of the messenger—"answer me not: I know what thou wouldst say. . . . Do not answer—I know what thou wouldst say . . ." and comments often upon itself—"Now, when communing thus together, our discourse taketh, in respect to what I have said, a three-fold argument, or division" (pp. 88–89), an oration punctuated by "dead pauses," before he can speak directly his regicidal purpose. Being spoken, the purpose provokes a "blush . . . agitation . . . distemperature," finally a "spontaneous unburdening"—"it was a stern necessity,—it was an awful deed!"—then a recognition of his desire to supplant the king—"The weak rider is thrown by his unruly horse, and trampled to death—the strongest man, the best cavalier, springs to the empty saddle,"—and finally a "shamed" giving way to the "constitutional taint of melancholy" which undermines his air of command (pp. 99–100). When the General and his lieutenant stand before the tower in which Charles II, as they think, is trapped, Cromwell astonishes his man by a delaying digression on the quality of *his* language. Pearson, normally a blunt man but a time-server, has made a foray into Puritan-ese, what I have called "Scripture," to please his chief—"All is as silent as the valley of the shadow of death—Even as the vale of Jehosaphat"—which in fact annoys the shrewd Cromwell— "Pshaw! tell me not of Jehosaphat . . . these words are good for others, but not for thee." The lieutenant then segues into Cavalierese or "tushery"—"Well, then, nothing has been stirring, yet peradventure"—which truly irritates him—"Peradventure not me, or thou wilt tempt me to knock thy teeth out. I ever distrust a man when he speaks after another fashion from his own" (pp. 409–10). But this digression turns Cromwell's conflict with himself outward upon Pearson, frees it for use against the Cavaliers holding Woodstock, and enables him to carry on the pursuit of the king, and, ambiguously, of the kingship. Leaping up to a dangerous ledge from which he can see the chasm over which the "king" jumped to safety in the tower, Cromwell provokes his officer's admiring fear—"I tremble to see your Highness stand there, balancing yourself as if you meditated a spring into the empty air. . . . I would scarce stand so near the verge as does your Highness. . . . Your Highness may feel such calls" to heroism (p. 426). The language and the situation seem to remind Cromwell of his forbidden desire to leap into the empty saddle, the high space just vacated by the legitimate king. Pearson has named that desire three times, but a fourth naming hangs ambiguously in the air: "thou has thrice, yea, four times, called me Your Highness," muses Cromwell, and backs down from the high place a bit, physically, and metaphorically—"it were fitter for a simple soul like me to return to my plough. . . . Nevertheless, I will not wrestle against the Supreme will, should I be called on . . . " (p. 427)

In Cromwell, as to some extent in *Old Mortality's* Balfour of Burley, Scott attempts to imagine the Great Man whose greatness, unlike that of Richard the Lionheart or even Bonnie Dundee, is founded not on unconscious rights of birth but on conscious right of worth, the self-constructed expertise, the expertly constructed self, whose very consciousness of its origin is a worm of doubt and melancholy. To hold on to that greatness, as Scott depicts it, the man must somehow render himself unconscious of the origin of his right, must displace it upon God, the Cause, or the tide of history or destiny in a reflex which is fascinatingly not hypocrisy, not even pitiful self-deception, but a genuine species of invoked unconsciousness almost, but never quite, approaching innocence.

Thus, Cromwell's final scene is a triumph of "greatness" as well as a punishing comedy. Having given explicit orders for the killing of all at Woodstock presumed to have aided in the hiding and escape of the king, he forgets he has done so, and rises in wrath half a day later when the orders are mentioned—"What execution? What malignants?" (p. 447). Greatness builds on a double and duplicitous right. First there is the right that first made itself known as a species of "might," that same red-handed and sacrilegious murder which confirmed Burley's identity and Cromwell's, and Robert Bruce's, and Mary Stuart's as Scott never tires of reminding us—but then, argues Cromwell, joining that line, "what can they see in the longest kingly line in Europe, save that it runs back to a successful soldier?" (p. 448). And then there is the right to forget that origin. Kunst macht gunst.

World-historical figures may define "right" in this paradoxical way, marking and then erasing their marks. Middle-management, which senses on either practical or ethical grounds that "right" is simply that which preserves life, must cope in different ways. Cromwell's lieutenant, Pearson, has simply not carried out Cromwell's orders to execute the Lees, Wildrake, Dr. Rochecliffe, and Markham Everard, because he has become used to Cromwell's peculiar ways. Wildrake, disguised in the first meeting with Cromwell as a Puritan, agrees to Cromwell's order to tell his commander Everard to spy on the Lees and their mysterious guest, but ignores that because he supports the royalist cause. And Mark Everard, perhaps the most nervously self-doubting of the Waverley heroes as long as he is associated with the winning side, that is, the Presbyterian Cromwellian side, must, by various twists of the plot, remain innocent of the identity of the young stranger in Woodstock up to the very moment when he is about to kill him.

Since Mark does not aspire to greatness, however, but only to that foggy, and from some perspectives ridiculous, definition of "right" which consists in "preservation," he invokes no passion, no madness, no covering innocence when the Scottish page "Louis Kerneguy," who has insulted his manhood and mysteriously captured the total allegiance of his love, Alice Lee, puts himself suddenly at his mercy with, "I am Charles Stuart" (p. 344). Disarmed, but in another sense restored,

Everard "stood for a time utterly confounded," then "awoke at length like a man from a dream" (p. 345). And though as Charles shrewdly and genially realizes, the Puritan Colonel cannot embrace the King or the King's Cause and still "maintain an honorable consistency" (p. 347), the two take hands as private gentlemen who owe each other a signal private service, Charles having revealed and imperiled himself to save Everard from the misery of separation from Alice Lee, Everard now pledging his life, on a purely private ethical basis, for the safety of the man he is indebted to.

I have emphasized "private" here to show that the typical Waverley "suppression" of private dilemmas or paralytic contradictory desires in the action of public life is a reversible equation. The story of Edward Lovel's military career, like Henry Morton's, acts out this type. And the first part of Woodstock depicts this conventional suppression in Everard. "When we were poor and you had power," "he tells Alice's father bitterly, the young lovers were forbidden each other, now his own party's power and his personal success have only deepened the division. Turning from this hopelessness to study papers on politics, he prays that "the thought of public affairs may expel this keen sense of personal sorrow" (p. 68). But for the man with some power, whose choices actually help govern public affairs, this arena is even darker than the personal one. No one ever wrote a more eloquent expression of the dread of the common Liberal than the author of Waverley gave to Everard, the Commonwealth's man: "it appears that every step we have made towards liberty, has but brought us in view of new and more terrific perils, as he who travels in a mountainous region is, by every step which elevates him highest, placed in a situation of more imminent hazard" (p. 68). The undertow of history is the progress of the consciousness of the terrors of freedom. Observing the classic split among the parliamentarian libertarians, between civilian moderates and military and religious radicals, Everard agonizes over the fundamental responsibility of the winning party, "Someone must be trusted with power," he argues, and among the contending men Cromwell is "perhaps not the most dangerous" (p. 74). On the one hand Everard suffers the personal mockery of his committed royalist friend—"thou art a milksop . . . such a prig as thou art . . . " (pp. 68, 70); on the other hand, touching public power even so far as to trust someone else with it is inevitably a deflating and corrupting thing.

It is this guilt which makes even Everard a prey, momentarily, to superstitious dread in the presence of what he knows must be the human contrivances of the "devils of Woodstock." Afterward, his claim to Alice Lee that "I choose the line of policy best befitting the times" only cheapens him in his own eyes, "and though unshaken in his opinion, that it were better the vessel should be steered by a pilot having no good title to the office, than that she should run upon the breakers, he felt that he was not espousing the most direct, manly, and disinterested side of the question" (pp. 152, 153). In other words, choosing public policy according to the commonsensical needs of the national "times" makes one indistinguishable from those who are simply acting according to pusillanimous private interests—means that inevitably one's private interests will govern one's temporal choices. To act on the basis of pure personal loyalties, clear, though inevitably "impractical" and almost inevitably "outlaw" private principles, may, paradoxically, be the best basis for a "right" public policy.

This anxiety, again only possible to the winning side, to those whose choices matter publically, gives the dream-quality to Everard's life before the king reveals himself—it was in a dream that he struggled with the rationally impossible question, "wherefore not Oliver as well as Charles?" (p. 72). With Charles before him the wherefore is answered emotionally—"sire" is the first word out of the Parliamentarian's mouth, and "oh, were better times to come" are the last (p. 347). Here it is in fact the sublimating thought of *private* affairs that expels the keen sense of *public* sorrow. In this scene the private gentlemanliness of Charles and the personal love-life of Everard function as a cover for the public principle—legitimate monarch with parliament—which is Everard's, and Scott's, fundamental desire. No longer struggling and anxious, Everard lends active countenance to Charles's escape. Achieving the outlaw status which is most congenial to the Waverley hero, Everard is taken into custody and almost executed by Cromwell, collaborating with the Cavaliers in masterly delaying tactics during which he endures "calmly, with unaltered countenance, and brow neither ruffled nor dejected" (p. 403).

Looking forward now, without anxiety, to the "better times" to be produced by "disinterested" personal bonds between subject and king, Everard tells the king, "If your plans are soundly considered and securely laid, think that all which is now passed is but a dream" (p. 345). As it happened, the dream of escape, exile, outlawry, the monarch hidden in the oak tree, the arrow out of secret leaves, was to last some nine years longer for that prototypical Waverley hero, Charles Stuart.[18] But his odyssey, we should remember, is what gives primal historical legitimacy, reality, both to the Jacobite enterprise which became only memory in Scott's young manhood, and to the modern psychodrama embodied in the hero of the Waverley novels. A tainted but legitimate inheritance, a violent disinheritance, an enforced passivity with attendant muffling or masking which shatters the given identity and requires a new self-making, a personal public choice of identity which miraculously coincides with the old imposed one, a "masterly inaction" which reaps all the rewards of violent action without the attendant guilt, a repression whose compensation is ultimately the very desire repressed; this is the history of Charles II. It is in fact the topos of the Stuart monarchy to be outlawed in the female or Catholic form and called again in the male and Protestant form. It had happened with Mary Stuart and James VI and I, with Charles I and Charles II—who could doubt it would happen again with James II and the first nonfeminized nonprelatized Stuart who could cross the water to "enjoy his own again," sanctioning all good owners in their own as well?

Yet no such figure presented itself, as the Waverley novels describe Jacobite history. We have seen how *The Abbot* described the enforced disenfranchisement into romantic femininity of Mary Stuart and *Redgauntlet* the feminized "conditioning" of Charles Edward Stuart. *Woodstock* actually introduces Charles II disguised as a "denaturalized woman" wearing his/her clothes so "indifferently adjusted and put on" that they looked as if they had been stolen (p. 218). In his next apparition, as a loutish Scots page of Albert Lee, Charles shovels food into his mouth as if he were "the very genius of famine himself, come forth from his native regions of the north" (p. 237), enjoying his own again in mythically degraded fashion, which leads the conversation to certain legends of the royalists as cannibals, "babe-bolters" (p. 241). Diminished thus into a woman and a cannibal Scot, Charles embarks on a discreditable but half-hearted seduction of Alice Lee, taunting Everard, the "round-headed Colonel . . . the man of texts and morals," into the duel which "might, at the moment, have changed the destinies of Britain" (p. 295).

Charles at this moment comes close to the same pigheaded refusal to disencumber himself from "womankind" (whom he doesn't really care for except as the sex typically signifies "his own") that was, in the closing moments of *Redgauntlet*, to mark the end of the Stuart adventure. The refusal, it is important to stress, would be fatal to his public authority, not dishonorable to his private affection or dignity; yet again as with Everard himself the avoidance of this public pitfall is camouflaged as an act of private generosity. Man to man, seeing Everard turn away from the supposedly compromised Alice Lee with "a look of unspeakable anguish," "Louis Kerneguy" comes to a "sudden resolution" and reveals his identity (p. 344), ending the charade of private loverly interest in Everard's cousin, escaping the self-set snare of feminization which is in the end to foreclose Stuart public authority. Charles's reward, in the last pages of *Woodstock*, is the splendid tableau-scene of the Restoration. There the Lees, and even the triumphantly domestic Markham Everard, sit like a sculpture group in a wayside bank to welcome the king to his own again. And the most active participants in the scene, emphasizes the author of Waverley, sardonically approving, are "all those craftsmen, who, having hunted the father from Whitehall, had now come to shout the son into possession of his ancestral palace" (p. 459)—Kunst Macht Gunst.

Chivalry: Cutting the Cushion

When Jonathan Oldbuck imagines his adopted ancester, John of the Girnel, steward of Trotcosey Abbey, at work, he imagines him collecting rents, taking in the poor and sick, and, most intimately, drawing "a flagon to entertain a wandering minstrel, or palmer, with the freshest news from Palestine" (p. 77).[19] Three years after *The Antiquary* the author of Waverley created, in Wilfrid of Ivanhoe, that very palmer, who returned Cedric's hospitality with the news of the fall of Acre, the failure to take Jerusalem, and the victory of King Richard and his secular Saxon knights against the Franco-Syrian priest-knights who were more enemy than the Saracens. Six years later, in 1825, came the first of the *Tales of the Crusaders, The Betrothed*, which elaborated a tale referred to in a *Waverley* footnote and was, like *Ivanhoe*, about the multi-racial anarchy released in the lordless homeland deserted by the Third Crusaders rather than about the spiritual homeland they sought to repossess. *The Talisman*, the second Tale, finally left Britain to describe the Crusaders before Acre. *Count Robert of Paris*, dictated-written in 1831, followed the First Crusade as far as Constantinople, and in 1832, while journeying through Malta and Italy, Scott began his last (unfinished) novel, "The Siege of Malta," about the conflict within the Order of priest-knights who represented for him the fundamental and fascinating paradox of chivalry, Christendom and Western civilization. If, tentatively, we put together a chronology of chivalry from these five novels of the Crusades we find *Ivanhoe* and *The Betrothed* and *The Talisman* describing the late-twelfth-century high point of the Norman and Celtic imaginative reach back to the looted, usurped, and empty center of ideal Christian behavior, *Count Robert* the romantic-satiric beginning of that reach, and the "Siege" the final obliteration of that reach, the Crusading impulse having been pushed back to the doorstep of Italy in the sixteenth century, whence the call—Deus Vuelt—had issued more than four hundred and fifty years earlier.

It is certainly fair to say that Scott's attention to the Crusades and the drama of chivalry showed rather less historical scholarship, certainly less original thinking, than his attention to the Scottish-Stuart drama. And yet the myth that emerged from his treatment of the chronicles of chivalry was equally, or even doubly, important, to the generation of readers who first absorbed it. Fundamentally the myth is this: vivid individual nations and races must die, be absorbed or replaced by another less vivid more amorphous race called, in its various manifestations, "the Romans." The first great effort to sublimate this loss, to construct a super race and ultra nation of Christians in chivalry, failed because the mass of men, that is, "history," loved the tragic battle of nations more than the comic reconciliations of Christendom. Even the noble Scots hero of *The Talisman*, fighting with the English King for the Holy Land, shows a "hasty and fierce" flash of national passion under his Christian surface: "If the King of England had not set forth to the Crusade till he was sovereign of Scotland, the Crescent might, for me, and all true-hearted Scots, glimmer for ever on the walls of Zion" (p. 25). This being the history/fact, the proffered reconciliations and universalities of Christendom and its enabling psychosocial construct called chivalry become, in the historian's backward-gazing eye, unstable, not just comic but risible, even mad, a dangerous process for a historian who is a believer, but an inevitable subject for one who is himself, as an Anglican Briton, a "roman."

Scott had glimpsed history as cycle yielding barbarians, romans, roman barbarians, new romans, in Gibbon, of course. It is the ground of the Arthurian iconography, and contributes too to the Robin Hood Myth. The Waverley novels packaged and dispersed this myth-history to common consciousness. The last novel, *Count Robert of Paris*, guided by Gibbon to the manuscript of Anna Comnena, Byzantine historian of the First Crusade, states it directly. The Greek writer, in a "lost fragment" created by the narrator of *Count Robert*, calls herself and all characters within her history and in her lifetime, all civilization, and all politically aware opinions, "roman," while the rest of the world, all "innocent" passionate actions, above all the Saxon warrior Hereward and the Frankish warrior Robert who unevenly divide the protagonist's role in the novel, "barbarians." This despite the narrator's Gibbonite comment that any such designation is pure fiction, since the actual Rome and its principles had disappeared with the Antonines, "that brilliant spark no longer remained for Constantinople to borrow, or for Rome to lend."[20]

The political situation is the same in all the Crusaders novels: in *Ivanhoe* the Norman and Saxon races struggle to recreate that spark of romanism; in *The Betrothed* the Norman advance begins to push back the Welsh and other Celtic races, while the Flemish or "Flammards" bide and grow strong; in *The Talisman*, as we shall see, antipathy between Scot and Norman English, between Frank and German Austrian, makes the European-Saracen conflict more than irrelevant, actually absurd. Above this conflict rides the religious issue, so that medieval Christianity, shaken by history's roman-barbarian conflict, veers unstably in one direction toward the superstitious barbarian "paganism" of the Greek and Oriental models it sought to transform, and in another toward the cynical roman, or freethinking, or atheist alternative which crops up in so many of the medieval novels, from the gypsy cynic Hayraddin in *Quentin Durward* to the cynic Aegisthes in *Count Robert of Paris*. And below this political and religious conflict, as the novels see it, rides an experiment in the deep structure of the individual psyche, an experiment called chivalry.

What is the human construct called chivalry? The author of Waverley wrote a learned essay on it for a supplement to the Encyclopedia Brittannica in which it appears as a form of that most respected of traits, "military valour . . . blended with the strongest passions which actuate the human mind, the feelings of [religious] devotion and those of love."[21] But dramatically, chivalry functions quite simply in the Waverley novels as the myth that sanctions male wrath, releases the joy of violence in the new Christian channel. It contains the Dionysian element in Christianity, purged in the Reformation, purged again in the Anglican restoration, and again in the Hanoverian ascendancy that ended the Stuart adventure and assimilated the Scottish nation. Chivalry spoke of high loyalties and personal mastery, encoded a ritual abasement before Christ and his Mother politically elaborated as the Lord and the Lady. But as Scott sees it, the grafting of humiliation upon desire in fact produces a personal egotism almost unmanageable by public principle, results in a Lord whose explosiveness is either brilliant but useless, like Richard the Lion Heart, or a joke, like Count Robert of Paris, who gravely consults The Code at every corner and every encounter, hoping it will sanction a fight to the death. The Presbyterian hero of *Woodstock*, offered equally hopeful provocation by chivalry's descendent, the Cavalier Henry Lee, passes, "purified" by the carnal reason of language:

> my religious principles . . . are no less sincere than your own, and this far purer—excuse the word—that they are unmingled with the bloodthirsty dictates of a barbarous age, which you and the others have called the code of chivalrous honour. Not my own natural disposition, but the better doctrine which my creed

has taught, enables me to bear your harsh revilings without
answering in a similar tone of wrath. (Pp. 52–53)

Personality, as well as history, in fact has its uses for wrath, as we
know. And the dramatic sublimation of his own forms of wrath is one
of the interesting accomplishments of the many-masked author of
Waverley, as I hope to show in the conclusion. But "romans" have
agreed to call wrath a sin, or at least to surround it with rue, to withdraw
from it that sanctity with which the people endowed Norna of the Fitful
Head, or Habbakkuk Mucklewrath. Here again *Count Robert of Paris*,
that very odd final Waverley novel, offers an instructive incident. For
Anna Comnena's history the author of Waverley invents a newly translated lost fragment called "The Retreat of Laodicea" in which the
"roman" part of the troop was to retreat cannily and to keep to the
middle, protected, part of the moving army, while the "barbarian"
Western Christians in their employ not only jealously seized the epic
part of defending the rear, but when the army was outflanked and
attacked a second time at its head, they joyously pressed through the
ranks to defend that as well. This virtually tactically impossible and mad
maneuver, as the author of Waverley allows the Princess Anna to write,
with smooth sarcasm, was made "doubtless by the wise directions of my
serene father, distinguished for his presence of mind upon such difficult
occasions" (p. 67). Chivalry, the encoded right of personal violence, is in
the private sphere of the Waverley novels what monarchy, the Stuart
monarchy, is in the public sphere, the last holy flare of divine fire before
the presence of mind "romanizes," secularizes, outlaws, and secretly,
behind the leaves, valorizes it.

The appropriate place to pause for a look at this secret valorization is
The Talisman, that late-career flashback to *Ivanhoe*. For I want to
suggest that *The Talisman* reworks more than the one character from
that important watershed novel. The triangle which pivots on King
Richard in both novels links not only the one typical Waverley protagon-
ist-hero with another, Ivanhoe asleep at the Crossroads with Kenneth,
knight of the sleeping Leopard, but also one canny half-mythic outlaw-
king with another, Robin Hood, the arrow out of secret leaves, the
splitter of wands, and Saladin, the face behind the veil, who can cut a
cushion with a sword.[22]

Ivanhoe opens deep in a sumptuous magic forest, *The Talisman* in
the treeless waste of the Dead sea, the "awful wilderness of the forty
days' fast" (p. 26) of Jesus. This does not prevent King Richard from
attempting to enforce in Palestine his personal forest-laws, to keep all
the hunting and its products in his own authority, nor the author of

Waverley from allowing his Scottish hero, Sir Kenneth, to assert his national identity and liberty by keeping a hunting dog to provide him (in the desert!) with venison. "We have heard of late by minstrels and pilgrims," Sir Kenneth challenges, reversing the form of *Ivanhoe*, "that your outlawed yeomen have formed great bands . . . having at their head a most stout archer, called Robin Hood. . . . Methinks it were better that Richard relaxed his forest-code in England, than endeavored to enforce it on the Holy Land" (p. 8).

The proposal that the king relax his codes rather than make outlaws of free men who would be his supporters is linked with the worse outlawry which Kenneth is engaged in, the outlaw love which is actually enjoined on him, in a way, by chivalry, sanctioning lust as it does wrath by the imposition of fragile codes for containing it. For the knight blushes in the presence of the feverish king when accused of "presumption," and relaxes when Richard speaks directly only of the outlawed hound, at which Richard, who knows of the Scot's dangerously personal, as well as chivalric, love for the Lady Edith Plantagenet, "smiled inwardly" (p. 95). In the code of chivalry a knight in good standing may keep a hound or a lady—within bounds. Even the monarch has his limits. And it is these limits, which make of both private and public chivalric life so complex a pavane of rules and excesses, which give objective correlatives to that drama of "suppressions" which Scott understands is the key to human personality and politics in all ages. Richard balks at but fundamentally accepts the limits, the villains of *Ivanhoe* and *The Talisman* cannot abide them. The Grand Master of the Templars, Sir Giles Amaury, and Conrade, Marquis of Montferrat, have developed on the contrary "some attachment to the Eastern form of government," the "simple and primitive structure" of pure despotism unconstrained by the "artificial and sophisticated . . . internal chain of feudal dependence." "A king should tread freely," Conrade argues, "and should not be controlled by here a ditch, and here a fence—here a feudal privilege, and there a mail-clad baron, with his sword in his hand to maintain it" (pp. 108–9).

The external structure of chivalry thus tempted men in both their private and public actions to gestures "wild . . . extravagant . . . fantastic," which nevertheless were "pure from all selfish alloy" and therefore unfortunately were "inconsistent with the frailties and imperfections of man," says the narrator of *The Talisman* (p. 133). But the subtle awareness of all this produced the internal reality of chivalry, an evolving "sophistication" of checks and balances which lead from the Crusades to Magna Carta to the Glorious Revolution in the public sphere, from rape to courtly love to Waverleyan domesticity in the private sphere.

The Templar, half-paganized and wholly orientalized, suggests they kill Richard rather than let this dangerous confederation of Western princes, with its demeaning system of debates, charters, and balances, take root in the "Holy Land" as it has in the West. His confederate, seeking some "substitution for the sacrifice—some ram caught in the thicket" (p. 114), foments between Richard and Leopold of Austria a quarrel about precedence centered on their respective banners, and the Scottish Kenneth is set, with his freeman's hunting dog, to guard the banner of England for his lord and, through that perhaps deadly risk, win a freeman's courtly love from his lady Edith.

The Waverley hero, uprooted, exiled, kidnapped and/or outlawed, always suffers humiliations, but never was a man so humiliated as Kenneth, knight of the Couchant Leopard, never was a fairy-tale atmosphere so deliberately created to allow for bizarre degradations as in *The Talisman*. Though the novel emphasizes the complex public degrees of rank and sophisticated political balances chivalry exacts in the sphere of government, it is Kenneth's boast that man to man chivalry equalizes everyone of the rank of gentleman, rich or poor, monarch or knight errant: "Were Richard of England himself to wound the honour of a knight as poor as I am, he could not, by the law of chivalry, deny him the combat" (p. 23). But the knight experiences no moment of glory which is not directly or indirectly degraded. Even the very fine opening scene, where he faces the lone mysterious Saracen bowman Sheerkohf (really the Robin Hood of this novel, Saladin) in single combat, performing feats of exemplary defensive horsemanship, enduring the other's arrows, felling him with an axe and nearly capturing him with a trick, is edged invisibly in satire by the emphasis on the burdening armor, the enveloping sand, the mercilessly exposing sun—all calculated to remind us, by its parodic distance, of Spencer's high chivalric opening to his epic. Scott's enervating, deadening landscape allows no "pricking on the plain," however gentle the knight. After the opening the degradations only get worse, a series of dishonors and cruel mockeries culminating in the tragico-farcical scene where Kenneth is lured away from his feudal duty of guarding Richard's banner on a whim of the bored Berengaria, Richard's Queen. As punishment (and secret restoration) he is virtually sold by Richard to the Arab physician who cured the monarch with the talisman.

Kenneth will not willingly become an outlaw, even though he, like Richard himself, occasionally looks away from the corrupt intrigues inside the Western camp toward the outlaw in the desert across the political, religious, and social border, whom he imagines is his brother in honor. So the plot, as usual, must kidnap him into outlawry. The physician who takes Kenneth forcibly away to his own land reveals himself as Kenneth's adversary in the opening duel at the Diamond of the Desert, Sheerkohf. The protean physician-Emir, who like Kenneth himself "is not what I seem," rules this Waverley hero's actions in the endgame—"Take then, the guidance of this matter" (p. 245), says the banished and disoriented knight. He entraps him in one final humiliation; as a Nubian slave, "a black chattel there, that is bought and sold in a market like a Martlemas ox" (p. 221), Kenneth returns to Richard with a message to Edith from Saladin and a watching brief for the person of the legitimate king from his brother the outlaw king. In his disguise Kenneth both saves Richard from the Templar's assassin and aids in the discovery, through the use of his guardian hound, of the man who stole the English standard, Conrade of Montferrat. But his worst humiliation and hardest test follows this success. For in delivering Saladin's letter to Edith he must, as he promised Richard, speak no word to his lady: obeying his lord even after Edith has recognized him and asked for his allegiance and understanding, means insulting his lady and risking the loss of her love. Where passing the test—adhering to the lordship side of the chivalric code—earlier involved active fighting and perhaps killing for the standard, and Kenneth failed, here it involves the passive restraint, muteness, of the typical Waverley hero. And here, of course, Kenneth passes the test, to be chosen champion by Richard, to fight and defeat Conrade in his place under the patronage of the true and secret lord of the land, the great public adversary and heretic outlaw king, the man who confronted Kenneth as Sheerkohf and cured Richard as El Hakim, Saladin himself.

We know Saladin, the true monarch of the novel, as we know Robin Hood in *Ivanhoe*, by the many disguises which suggest we never quite have his measure, by his capacity for the secret or overt management of events and persons, and by a single metaphorically illuminating skill he demonstrates—Kunst macht gunst. Most memorable in *Ivanhoe* was Bend-the-Bow's victory in the archery contest, shivering his opponent's arrow where it sat in the eye of the target, then splitting a willow wand no wider than the arrow which struck it. And perhaps the most memorable tableau in *The Talisman* pits Richard against Saladin at the end in a trial of skill. The two kings are together in the outlaw king's domain, the fountain oasis Diamond of the Desert corresponding to the Great Oak of Sherwood Forest. Richard strikes a bar of iron in half with a terrific blow of his great broadsword: Saladin asks him to do the same to a cushion.

"No sword on earth, were it the Excalibur of King Arthur," replies Richard, "can cut that which opposes no steady resistance to the blow." His brother king eyes the target, measures his aim, and balances his footing and his finely tempered scimitar, then splits the cushion with such speed and restraint that it "seemed rather to fall asunder than to be divided by violence" (p. 289).

Excalibar has returned, to intimate the new facts in the once and future world—that the forces that will now make history, irresistible and enveloping, flowing like water or gauze but opposing no steady resistance (or invitation) to the blow of the strong man, will be mastered by guile or tolerance, not strength, indirectly by him who can wait, or who can move so swiftly or obliquely that he looks like he's waiting, until the matter of history falls asunder for him. The Robin Hood who shakes hands with Richard and refuses to come out out of the secret leaves to take his title and its commitment to the direct encounters of politics, knows this. Saladin, who smilingly exchanges pledges of brotherhood with Richard but refuses his offer of direct single combat to decide the future of Palestine and retires into his desert enigmatically promising to "yield to any fair demands . . . as yonder fountain yields its waters" (p. 314), knows this.

David, Earl of Huntington, and Prince Royal of Scotland, senses this dimly, for when the national politics of England and Scotland forbade his joining Richard on Crusade, he took the oblique identity of Kenneth, knight of the Sleeping Leopard, and in that "sleep" drifted around the obstacle to the fight for Christendom and to Scots-English union, attaining both these historically inevitable goals in his saving of Richard's life and in his eventual dynastic (though fictive) marriage to the English heiress. Col. Markham Everard, Presbyterian soldier, senses this, for he meditates, as he aids both Cromwell and Charles II, that whereas Enthusiasm "is a stream . . . that is sure to bear down every barrier which is directly opposed to it" (p. 109), it is the indirect or hidden or guilefully accepting channel which will contain and direct the flow of history.

As for Christendom, that kingdom reared on the holy emptiness of a tomb—as a material historical entity, something to be ferreted out or dug up or politically "re"-constructed, it is doomed. Its heroes in Scott's narratives never approach it; they are always deflected by the national secular aims which are their true desire, and that of "history." As a material historical entity it is in fact humanly and politically devastating, inviting to barren violence and tipping the precious unstable complex amalgam of Belief toward pagan cynicism. In *The Talisman* as in *Ivanhoe* (as in a slightly different way in *Old Mortality*) the priest-soldier who is the archetype of Christendom dies of his own contending passions, tempted by his too earthly possession of the God-home to that self-divinizing which ends in atheism and despair. Though it is the sword of Saladin that strikes off the head of *The Talisman's* villainous grand master, it is Sir Giles Amaury's guilty start at the words "Accipe hoc" that condemns him.

"Accipe hoc"—take this—said the Grand Master when, coming to the wounded but recovering Conrade to give him the sacrament, he instead drove his dagger through his heart (p. 311), and "Accipe hoc" repeats the dwarf who overheard him, as the Templar reaches for a cup of cool sherbet in Saladin's tent later. If the Templar "started, like a steed who sees a lion under a bush" (p. 310), it was not only because he sensed himself discovered, not only because he is reliving the moment when he murdered his ally. For in substituting the dagger for the sacramental cup the priest-knight pronounced the words which, I believe, Scott means to associate both with the liturgical formula marking the distributing of the Eucharist and the chivalric formula conferring knighthood. If consciously the formula was on the traitor priest's lips in derision or parody—"Come, shall we to this toy?" he had earlier contemptuously invited Conrade to confession (p. 299)—its unconscious meaning is surely desire, for the priest-knighthood he has profaned. When the words are spoken and the guilty start recorded, the Templar, "to hide, perhaps, his confusion," takes the cup, "accipe hoc," but dies before he can drink the sacrament.

The prominence of the cup in the death of the priest reminds us of the prominence of the cup in the restoration of Richard early in the novel. "The talisman," a secret infusion, makes a healing Grail out of the various cups of the novel; it is potent to heal or destroy in the hand of the Saracen owner of Jerusalem, the veiled outlaw king of the Diamond of the Desert. When at the end of the novel the talisman travels from its origin to Scotland as a wedding present, it loses much of its power, becoming a mere herb good enough, in a natural way, to relieve minor ailments. The true talisman, the real Grail, it seems clear, was found and lost again, as is its nature. As such it means in Scott's narratives what it has always meant, was to mean still more intensely in the directly Arthurian narratives of the Victorian medieval revival which Scott's novels helped to prepare—that the profoundest experience of the citizens of the kingdom of Belief is the experience of that kingdom's hidden proximity after its tangible loss.

Conclusion, with Prefaces:
"The Author of Waverley"

I have seldom felt more satisfaction than when, returning from a pleasure voyage, I found *Waverley* in the zenith of popularity, and public curiosity in full cry after the name of the Author. The knowledge that I had the public appreciation was like having the property of a hidden treasure . . . from the instant I perceived the extreme curiosity manifested on the subject I felt a secret satisfaction in baffling it, for which, when its unimportance is considered, I do not well know how to account.

(General Preface, *Waverley*, pp. xvii, xviii)

Is this criticism or high comedy?[1]

Scott found it difficult to account for the satisfaction with which he regarded, and baffled approaches to, the hidden treasure of his authorial identity. And so shall we. The difficulty, and the treasure, have a moral as well as an aesthetic dimension which must be kept in mind as we assess, here at the end, the beginnings, the prefaces, the opening chapters and counteropenings which contain the subcharacters and the psychodramas where is constructed, like a labyrinth of mirrors, what Scott came to call the "eidolon" of "the author of Waverley."[2]

Scott's first novel, *Waverley*, offered its authorial persona both in an introduction and in the last chapter, "A Postscript that should have been a Preface." Thereafter he constructed almost all his novels with an opening section, or even two or three, elaborating the origin of the tale and characterizing the tellers through whom it came. This "front matter" has often seemed just an inert barrier to the story, so that in this century it became a commonplace warning, reader to reader, especially teacher to student, to start Scott novels at chapter 2. Yet I find this material fascinating, not only because it (inevitably) repeats, as aesthetic self-characterization, many of the key images—outlaw king, parricide, usurpation—of the novel's plots, but also because it offers material for a new assessment of Scott the artist. The authorial matter that surrounds the Waverley novels is unmatched in size and complexity. Such an abundance of trees will, properly viewed, reveal a consistent forest: so obsessively maintained a cover pulled tight reveals the shape of the author.

What Scott understood of his motives he told the reader directly or dramatically through the alter-egos of his introductions, explanatory chapters, and eventually his "magnum opus" prefaces and notes. He wanted the private peace of anonymity, the personal delight of the elaborate trickery, the freedom to disown his mistakes and lapses, the more mysterious freedom to disown successes. He wanted the extra sales that came with the intrigue, and the special glow that came with being not only the most productive author of his time but the most productive *two* authors. The critical truism that Scott is his own best (or at least first) critic Scott accepted; indeed, he invented it, creating out of himself complaining antiquarians, antagonistic historians, keen-eyed editors and literary philosophers of the realistic and romantic schools, the criminal author of Waverley himself, who gaily admits all charges. These occupied all the critical positions except the two left for us: that the author of Waverley wanted to be a great and serious, as he understood the terms, artist, and that Walter Scott hid (pretended to hide) the treasure of his identity/ambition because he was afraid (pretended to be afraid) to claim that immoral, that outlaw, booty.[3]

The spirit of the outlaw—rage, pride, obsession, competition—surfaces over and over in the introductory materials and the cast of narrating characters with which the author of Waverley guarded his work. The prefaces of the magnum opus edition, so disarmingly revelatory of the history of the stories, so sweetly candid about the history of their composition by Walter Scott, finally allow him to claim his property. But of course he made that claim from the relative moral safety of his near-bankruptcy in the late 1820s, when all of his property, novels written and yet unwritten, was in the hands of other men. Even here, what he owned up to he did not (quite) have to own.

Before looking at the author of Waverley in his incarnations, it is worth reminding ourselves, as Scott reminded himself in a series of reviews and essays written in the teens and twenties, what traumas the "nineteenth-century novelist" inherited from the eighteenth-century novelist as part of his or her identity.[4] His job was to teach and to delight, to invent and to represent; his business was with men, not manners, unless, of course, reversing the terms for the same concepts, with manners, not men. Behind this schizophrenia lay the whole post-Reformation effort to redefine and recover sacredly revealed Truth as humanly knowable "nature." Not only did this knowing require personal delight and individual invention working alchemically upon just representation and general nature, it is only definable, laments an anonymous reviewer of the anonymously authored *Tales of My Landlord* (both anonymities were Walter Scott) as a "sort of freemasonry," by which one mind invents and another recognizes, "nature," that is, truth, in art.[5] Novelists dramatized this schizophrenia by an effort to displace themselves as the origin of their stories. Only Fielding stood forth boldly as the inventor of his true world in *Tom Jones*.

But Fielding did not begin his career thus boldly: his imagined legitimizing source was not history or autobiography recovered by its editor-novelist but rather one novelist, Richardson, recovered (parodied) by another. Scott takes special notice of the animosity this provoked in Richardson in his introductory essay on Fielding in *Lives of the Novelists*,[6] and it is in his mind as late as the introduction to *Count Robert of Paris* (1831). I think it possible that the spectacle in the previous generation of two "masters" competing, as well as the spectacle during his early manhood of critic partisans of the Romantic and the Realistic schools of novelists each denying space and legitimacy to the other, is a deeper element of his satisfaction at the "accidental" anonymity of the fiercely public and popular author of Waverley than the more obvious and admitted relief at abandoning (secretly, of course, continuing) his competition with Byron. Gentlemen and Christians do not compete. Englishmen and Scotsmen do not compete (anymore). Artists, God forbid, do not compete, nor do they allow their disciples to belabor other artists with their eidolon. "Eidolons," however, may do all these these things, and the evolution of the author of Waverley from a straightforward apologist in the first trio of novels to a set of Cervantean tale-tellers and editor-historians in his next group, to an "eidolon" with a "family" of narrators after the watershed novel *Ivanhoe*, forms a fascinating commentary on the dynamic of evasion and enhancement, of self-deprecation and self-enlargement, of criticism and creativity, which enabled the Waverley novels.

Scott had one timely precedent, as many have noticed, for his prefatory self-definitions and elaborations, in the Preface to the second edition of *Lyrical Ballads*, where Wordsworth had argued, as the author of Waverley would, for the natural poetry of the speech of the common man. But a profounder model was surely the continuing Prefatory

Chapters of *Tom Jones*, where Fielding writes the rules of the new genre—flexibility, multiplicity, autonomy—into the text. "These critical introductions, which rather interrupt the source of the story, and the flow of the interest at the first perusal, are found, on a second or third, the most entertaining chapters of the whole work." Thus Scott on Fielding in 1821,[7] with the elaborate prefaces of *Ivanhoe, The Monastery/The Abbot* just behind him (1820), and the more elaborate ones of *The Fortunes of Nigel* and *Peveril of the Peak* (1822) just ahead. Between Fielding's prefatory jokes on the self-generated story he is feeding the hunger of the reader with, and Henry James's prefatory complaint about "story" as "the spoiled child of art" (spoiled by readers and in another sense by critics), lie Scott's prefatory debates about whether story is the occasion for "fine things" in the way of analysis, description, and dramatic gesture, or vice-versa. Fielding's and Wordsworth's prefaces argue the egotistical sublime of their narratives. The preface to *The Ambassadors* reveals at the heart of James's principle of the displaced central narrating consciousness his fear of the "terrible fluidity of self-revelation" in first-person narration.[8] Between these classic descriptions of the relation of artists to story lie the prefaces and introductions to the Waverley novels, where the alter-egos of Walter Scott, the first nineteenth-century novelist, competitive, obsessed, violent and dreamy, ideal and amoral, the virtue/vice figures of his imagination, mechanical, opportunist, practical and loving, the captains of his immense industry, take shape.

In introductions to *Waverley, Guy Mannering,* and *The Antiquary* the author of Waverley stood forth in his own persona to describe the aesthetic strategic dilemmas in which a novelist of the time finds himself. It is the ur-situation of the novelist, of Defoe and even Bunyan and Cervantes behind him: How shall he find, that is, extract, his product, from the degraded environment of "romances and fables" in which it is embedded, distinguish it aesthetically, and justify it morally? Two associated strategies have been tried—the autobiographer's, and the historian's. The author of Waverley will be the latter. "The most romantic parts" of *Waverley* "are precisely those which have a foundation in fact," he assures us in "A Postscript that should have been a Prelude" to that novel (p. 448), and the most "forced and improbable" event in *The Antiquary*, we learn in the 1816 "Advertisement," is based "on a fact of actual occurance" (p. v). At the same time the remarkable "Introductory" chapter to *Waverley* contains the description of the author's efforts to displace all the reader's expectations about the actual "occurrences," contemporary or ancient, which form the basis of all novels, and to claim for himself, through a careful historical placement "sixty years since"

and through the choice of an "uncontaminated," that is, morally ambiguous, title, a blank space, a "maiden shield," on which to invent the
actual. The reader of Waverley was thus from the beginning taken to the
work through the workshop. And as the author offered his gloss on
Fielding's principle that men, not manners, the unchanging heart, not
the changing coat, should be the subject of the historian-inventor's
narrative, an apparently casual example from the "Book of Nature,"
which is said to be the moral origin of the novel, shows us something of
the heart in the coat of the author of Waverley, a heart that knew the
heart of Poor Peter Peebles, the madman in the attic of the law:

> The wrath of our ancestors, for example, was coloured *gules*; it
> broke forth in acts of open and sanguinary violence against the
> objects of its fury. Our malignant feelings, which must seek
> gratification through more indirect channels, and undermine
> the obstacles which they cannot openly bear down, may be
> rather said to be tinctured *sable*. But the deep-ruling impulse is
> the same in both cases; and the proud peer who can now only
> ruin his neighbor according to law, by protracted suits, is the
> genuine descendent of the baron who wrapped the castle of
> his competitor in flames. (P. 4)

Scott made no boast more proudly nor more frequently than that he
prosecuted no literary rivalries and remained the friend and supporter
of all his competitors: the accomplishment was genuine and, in its way,
great and moving. Yet I have already argued that "wrath" is unmistakably one of his main subjects in the Waverley novels, and law its indirect
channel. The laws of the new genre, laid down by Fielding, Richardson,
Radcliffe, and Maria Edgeworth, were rewritten by the author of
Waverley to absorb all these territories, and that of Wordsworth and
Byron as well. The personal sources of Walter Scott's subtle wrath are of
his gender and of his time—a wife not his first love, a family to support, a
lawyer-father to love and subvert, a lost male heroism to harness in
work, a schizoid national-imperial identity to attack and defend. The
sources of "the author's" wrath are what they always are—a kingdom of
fantasy leased, not owned, a "maiden shield" invented in whorish
negotiation with progenitors, competitors, and critics.

Scott created a telling fable about this negotiation in his first "original" work, a tale of Border wrath channeled into song, *The Lay of the
Last Minstrel*. His minstrel tells Scott's ancestral kinswoman the Duch-
ess of Buccleugh how her ancestral Scott kinswoman, Margaret of
Branksome, married her true love and feudal competitor, Henry Cranstoun, after the latter entered her castle and heroically killed her

family's enemy. He was aided by a magical spell illegitimately stolen out of a "Book" owned by their still more ancestral kinsman, "the Wizard" Michael Scott. Cranstoun's enabling genie is a dwarf, a "goblin page" who appeared out of nowhere, and dogged him until taken in service. Spiteful and sly and grasping, he appeared crying enigmatically "lost! lost! lost!"; he stole the spell from the dead wizard's magic book and altered his master. Then, at the betrothal celebration, he plays pranks from group to group of the tenuously knit revelers, Scotts and Carrs, Scotsmen and Englishmen, trying to rouse debate and jealousy, and restart the old feuds. The dwarf, a projection of wrath and competition whose source is Scott's ancestor Michael Scott, has gotten loose, lost, somehow, and the wizard, dealing invisible "buffets," still cannot reclaim him until, at the betrothal, Margaret's mother gets all the minstrels to play one by one their songs of "wrath and vengeance" in an expressive channeling of ancestral feudal passion. After the final song the dwarf, felled, and muttering "found! found! found!" disappears back into the wizard's breast, and all the characters disappear back into the Minstrel's Lay.[9] The power to arouse and channel this spirit of wrath and rivalry is a dangerous one, yet it was the minstrel's job to do it. Warning—legitimizing—this dwarf inside, the author of Waverley knit to himself that fable in the second novel, *Guy Mannering; or The Astrologer*. This novel bears as its headnote, as sufficient introduction to its "unknown" authorship, the lines from *The Lay of the Last Minstrel* which refer to the macroscosmic magic that parallels the microcosmic fatality signified by the continuing presence of the dwarf:

> Tis said that words and signs have power
> O'er sprites in planetary hour:
> But scarce I praise their venturous part,
> Who tamper with such dangerous art.

The next two novels both contain magus-dwarfs in their narration. In the former, Scott tells us disarmingly in the magnum opus preface, an original minstrel-like interest in The Astrologer as harbinger/interpreter/accomplisher of the fatal destiny faded in favor of the novelist's desire to paint manners in *Mannering*, the enactment of wrath shifting from the male astrologer-hero to the first of Scott's witches, the gypsy Meg Merrilies. As Scott characterizes this wrath figure—Meg, Madge Wildfire, Allsie Gourlay in *The Bride of Lammermoor*, later Norna— self-insertion into the ancient role of the Curser is equal, for a time, to the genuine power to curse. The imposture creates the truth, a transaction, as Scott remarks later in his journal, worthy the name "sublime" (*Journal* for 22 July 1827, p. 331). The male magician of *The Antiquary*, on the other hand, is a deflated scarecrow dwarf from the beginning: Dousterswivel's role-playing Rosicrucian wizard is farce.

In the (1816) Advertisement to *The Antiquary* the author tells us we will find wrath safely displaced away from the classes and gender closest to him, "to that class of society who are the first to feel the influence of that general polish" overtaking civilization, who can therefore be relied on to illustrate the operation of "the higher and more violent passions" in "the strongest and most powerful language," as "my friend Wordsworth" has already pointed out. Partly because of this schizophrenic assignment surely, the author of Waverley has to report that he has been unable to fully integrate "those two requirements of a good novel," character and action, passions and plot, "truth of colouring" and "artificial [that is, artful] narrative." Trusting, surely, that an audience even further from the source of its schizophrenia than he is will forgive him this disclosure of their mutual paralysis, and clearly intrigued by the prospect of disappearing after the three claps of thunder, three novels which illustrated three different periods of Scottish manners, the author of Waverley takes "respectful leave, as one who is not likely again to solicit their favor" (pp. v, vi).

But in the antiquary himself, as we have seen, the author of Waverley lodged a kind of madness, a competition for "authority" in the present about the past that partakes of thievery, blasphemy, paranoia, and even murder. The rivalry of writing antiquarians is rationalized and lovingly satirized in the person of Jonathan Oldbuck, but there is material here from Scott's authorial nightmares, a preview of the soul-destroying adventures of George Eliot's Casaubon among his competitors and critics "Pike," "Tench," and "Carp." And, by one of those astonishing non-coincidences of the controversy that would be generated by the next Waverley novel, the volumes called *Tales of My Landlord* contained (who could doubt it) a story called *The Black Dwarf,* and *Old Mortality*.

To midwife and mother these texts, to Carp and Care for them, the vanished but still monitoring author of Waverley creates a new cast of narrator-characters in a setting which once more recalls and absorbs Fielding. The stories originate in an Inn whose Fieldingesque host, shrewd, witty, generous and sarcastic, tolerant yet manipulative, politely deferential yet king in his precinct, remains mysterious and voiceless. He presides at the Wallace Inn at Gandercleugh, "the navel . . . of this our native realm of Scotland" from which are born the human shapes of the quasi-magic legends of "various tribes and peoples" who pass through this navel.[10] Resident midwife is the teacher-antiquarian Jeddediah Cleishbotham, collector and arranger but "NOT the writer, redacter, or compiler" (p. xii), he emphasizes, of *The Black Dwarf, Old Mortality* (first series, 1816), *The Heart of Midlothian* (second series, 1818), *The Bride of Lammermoor* and *A Legend of Montrose* (third series, 1819), and, interestingly, as Scott's health made major inroads on his conscious control at the end of his life, of *Count Robert of Paris* and *Castle Dangerous* (fourth series, 1832).

Jeddediah, a middle-aged martinet, a rule-giver, an arguer upon trifles, litigious, acquistive, a jealous upholder of his rights and dignity (Scott as he hopes he is not), has heard the first three series of tales from Peter Pattieson, a youthful, active, merry schoolmaster, escapee from schoolrooms, part-time preacher, empathic with outlaws, vagabonds, and eccentrics (Scott as he has been, and hopes to remain). This sweet-natured poet-outlaw, who collected and wrote but apparently felt no need (or capacity?) to publish, the tales, is, by curious potent necessity, dead—of what we do not know. And so Jeddediah can trump the critics, an addiction of his: "And now, ye generation of critics, who raise yourself up as if it were brazen serpents . . .bow yourselves down to your native dust." The originator of these tales was one too many for you—he is dead: "waste not your strength by spurning against a castle wall; nor spend your breath contending in swiftness with a fleet steed" (pp. xii, xiii). Notwithstanding an affection for the young collector as strong "as if he had been the offspring of my own loins" (p. xv), Jeddediah reserves to himself the praises for the Tales, "when any is due," and to Pattieson the censure, "if at all due." Pattieson receives the tales from people who pass through the umbilicus of Gandercleugh, *The Black Dwarf* from Bauldie the Shepherd, who feigned skepticism but underneath believed in the tale of the wrathful dwarf-misanthrope, *Old Mortality* from the Covenanter himself, encountered in the graveyard grimly recarving the names of his martyred kindred on their tombstones, *The Heart of Midlothian* from Mr. Dunover the bankrupt formerly resident in that famous Edinbugh prison, *The Bride of Lammermoor* from Dick Tinto, traveling artist, and *A Legend of Montrose* from Sergent More McAlpine, a dispossessed Highlander emigrating to Canada who stopped for good at Gandercleugh.

Unlike Jeddidiah, Pattieson had not pretended to be the passive conduit of the received tales; in each case, he says in documents included by Jeddidiah, he has taken the individual source tale back to the countryside and "as is my habit," balanced it and often combined it with other versions of the same or similar tales, from the desire to elaborate his own structure. But this enterprise will raise "The Demon of Criticism" in two forms to challenge him. The Covenanter bias of *Old Mortality*'s oral narrative has been "corrected," he says in the introduction to that novel, by information from Bishops and Lairds representative of the Royalist side (p. 9). He hopes that current partisans of one side or the other will neither think him unbalanced in his presentation nor resent his balance: "O rake not up the ashes of our fathers! Implacable resentment was their crime/and grievous has the expiation been" (p. 11). But he suspects they will resent him for both reasons. After all, he is raking up the ashes. And he is right; the resenting Covenanter scholar-critic Thomas McCrie protested vehemently in *The Edinburgh Christian Instructor*, provoking both the anonymous reviewer of the novel in *The Quarterly Review* (Scott) and later Jeddediah himself in his next "series" to defend the historical authenticity of the portraits, and to vouch for the objectivity and "veracity" of the defenders.

The Demon of Criticism is not merely political-historical, it is also aesthetico-popular, as Peter Pattieson found when he decided to "waive the task of a concluding chapter" to *Old Mortality* (p. 407), to evade the final tying up of the structure and the drawing of the moral (these are perhaps the same thing). Gandercleugh, the world's navel, contains not only tellers but readers of tales. To the most experienced of these, Miss Martha Buskbody, Pattieson applies for approval of this evasion, and he is roundly criticized. The reader, it seems from this characterization, not only requires "a glimpse of sunshine in the last chapter," in the form of the attested "marriage of the principal personnages," she also requires details of the further lives of secondary and tertiary characters right down to the history of Guse-Gibbie, the clown peasant. Requires, in other words, that the Tales never be concluded, a discovery so appallingly congenial to his own deepest guiltiest wishes that Pattieson/Scott grabs his hat and fairly runs from the room "ere the Demon of Criticism had supplied her with any more queries," any more continuations to be called for (p. 410).

Knuckling under to (or parodying?) this Demon, Jeddediah concludes *Tales of My Landlord's* first series, whose first story had been concluded abruptly by truncation in a single volume, like the misshapen being it created, in order to make room for a second story which expanded until it had to be abandoned, with the promise of more tales for a "devouring" and "demanding" but yet "discerning" public (*A Legend of Montrose*, p. 411). It unmistakably tickled Jeddediah's fancy to begin—and end—the second series with one tale, *The Heart of Midlothian*, which, having "filled more pages than I opined," makes room in Peter Pattieson's voice for the famous moral address to the reader at the end, a well-nigh blinding glimpse of sunshine in the last chapter: "Reader; this tale will not be told in vain, if it shall be found to illustrate the great truth that . . . " (p. 538).

Confident he may sound as he continues. But in fact an argument over what is "illustrated" forms the aesthetic interest of Pattieson's Preface (chapter 1) to the first tale in the third series, *The Bride of Lammermoor*. There Peter Pattieson is taken to task by one Dick Tinto, portraitist and landscape artist descended in his poverty to sign painter, for relying too much on words, dialogue, "patter,"[11] to tell his stories, where a carefully chosen and colored dramatic gesture, posture, or incident should be able more effectively and briefly to convey the point. Demonstrating this proposition, so dear to the heart of Scott's critics, Dick Tinto offers a sketch he made of a story, expecting that Pattieson will receive from it "that instant and vivid flash of conviction" (p. 12) which contains as one gestalt the past and future history of the story whose key moment is pictured. The writer tells the painter he cannot catch the full story from the illustration but shows elsewhere in the chapter that he does. The painter tells the writer that the sketch is all he has, or that the other needs, but in fact he provides with the sketch a parcel of notes on the story containing both writings and drawings, evidence of his, and Scott's, and Scott's reader-critics' schizophrenia. "My attention was divided between the wish to draw . . . and to represent, in a history-piece," he says, a division dramatized on the painter's (and eventually the writer's) "representation" of *The Bride of Lammermoor*, where "outlines of caricatures, sketches of turrets . . . disputed the ground with his written memoranda" (p. 13).[12]

As the third series came to a close, the volumes filled out with the Highland tale called *A Legend of Montrose*, the narrator invokes the conclusion of *The Tempest*; both the story and the storytellers "melted into thin air" at the end, as the end, of the novel. Though the author of Waverley calls Jeddediah his Ariel here, I would argue that he illustrated the dynamic of *The Tempest* better than he knew in *Tales*, raising up in Pattieson a gay productive tricksy Ariel, and in Jeddediah Cleishbotham an earthy pinched Caliban. Like Prospero he renounces his magic and fades, "himself a phantom," into the text, taking leave like the actor of Shakespeare's final speech, with the duplicitous promise that, exhausted, he will never return—unless, of course, he is called in another incarnation. He has "exhausted one individual's powers of observation," says the author of Waverley; still, since "there remains behind not only a large harvest, but laborers capable of gathering it in," the reader need fear no "conclusion" yet (p. 357). Recommending with unfeigned generosity the present and future work of "a brother, or perhaps a sister shadow" who wrote the novel *Marriage* (Susan Ferrier), he disappears deeper into history, into cover, into myth.

Into *Ivanhoe*. The novels beyond that watershed text, *The Monastery/The Abbot, Kenilworth, The Pirate, The Fortunes of Nigel, Peveril of the Peak,* and *Quentin Durward* and the rest, take the author and reader of the Waverley novels into international, medieval Shakespearean times, well beyond the almost verifiable oral histories of the first Scottish novels. To "conduct" these tales out of legendary history and into veracious fiction is the job of another cast of quarreling narrative characters who are by degrees revealed to be part of the "family" of a newly fleshed out and dramatized author of Waverley. In the introductory epistles of these novels Scott offers a picture of the author of Waverley himself, member of the *"irritable genus,"* and lusty pursuer of the "wrathful trade" of book writing ("Introduction" to *The Monastery*, p. lii). The subnarrators are conceived to be imitators, disciples, and hence critics of this powerful figure, but never a match for him. The competitions and debates are often muted, usually comic, but they are there.

Ivanhoe is said to have its source in a manuscript jealously guarded by Sir Arthur Wardour, one of the two quarreling antiquaries in *The Antiquary*; its Dedicatory Epistle contains a defense by an English antiquarian, Laurence Templeton, of his popularizing and condensing techniques, to another "graver" antiquary, Dr. Jonas Dryasdust. Dryasdust, whom Carlyle will resurrect, slightly caricatured, to be overcome by his own popularizing narrator in *Past and Present*, argued against Templeton's attempt to assume for England the task the author of Waverley performed for Scotland, not only because English myth-history is less accessible but also because the English reader will not give to English (or perhaps any) history that willing suspension of disbelief which the magic and magnetic "North" evoked (p. xxi). Undaunted, Templeton put the manuscript in press, whence (to move from a fictional adventure to the adventure of a fiction) Scott hoped to have it issue in genuine anonymity, since a recent "continuation" of *Tales of My Landlord* by a fake "author of Waverley" had clouded the trail of the true one. But his publisher objected to the probable loss of sales thereby, and Scott accepted his complaint, noting later in the magnum opus introduction that "trick upon trick . . . might reasonably be considered as trifling with [the public's] favour" (p. xii).

Ivanhoe came out under the aegis of the author of Waverley, therefore, making it inevitable (returning to the fictional adventures of the author of Waverley and his family) that when a disguised Benedictine monk passed a parcel of memoirs about two sixteenth-century Border families over to the antiquarian "Captain Cuthbert Clutterbuck" in exchange for help in unearthing the heart of his Abbot ancestor from the Ruins of Kennaquhair Abbey, Clutterbuck should pass them on for editing to the author of Waverley, hinting, as had the phantom himself, that "the deepest well may be exhausted" (p. xliv) and need new springs opened for it. By no accident, surely, the tale they create together, *The Monastery*, is governed by the figure of the White Lady's fountain of fire in the magic cave which produces and frees a book, and then, exhausted, disappears.

Responding to this hint, the author of Waverley twits Captain Clutterbuck on the artifice he has caught him out in: amazing, he marvels, how often innocent antiquarians and editors have manuscripts forced upon them by mysterious Benedictines, or they "step into a chandler's shop, to purchase a pound of butter, and behold! the wastepaper on which it is laid is the manuscript of a cabalist" (p. xlix). He himself, he affirms now, was the source of all his stories. Yet of course the author of Waverley not only creates in Clutterbuck another guilty alter-ego to take responsibility for the two-part (and perhaps monkishly biassed) story of *The Monastery/The Abbot*, he tells him that he will not give him credit on the title page, will take him "as a sleeping partner only," lest the partner-puppet gain fame enough to be stolen and manipulated by another anonymous storyteller as "Jeddediah Cleishbotham" was the previous year (p. li).

Such wars among artists for control of their stories and storytellers can be deadly, the author of Waverley observes: the eidolons of art are such portable property that after "Don Quixote" and "Cid Hamete Benengeli" were stolen from Cervantes and put to work by another author, the creater was forced to kill them in the next continuation, lest they fall into bad hands (p. l). And so does the author of Waverley serve Jeddediah Cleishbotham, reporting his death in a footnote to *The Monastery*'s introductory material. "It is a wrathful trade," the author of Waverley admits (p. lii).

The agent and object of this wrath reprehensibly and satisfyingly cherished by the gentle, responsible Walter Scott, this energumen, this "eidolon" as he is called, surfaces as such in the introductory chapter of *The Fortunes of Nigel* and *Peveril of the Peak*.[13] In the former, Captain Clutterbuck finds himself in Ballantyne's publishing house and, driven by curiosity despite a "holy horror" (p. xv) at the primal scene he is about to uncover in "the penetralia of their temple" (p. xxix), interrupts "the person, or perhaps I should rather say the eidolon or representational vision, of the Author of Waverley!" (p. xv).

In this incarnation the author of Waverley is a veritably Gothic figure, hidden in a vaulted room, communicating at first only by gesture, "veiled and wimpled" (p. xvi) so that even its sex is a matter of intuition, an eidolon proper to the imagination of the character who conceived the Benedictine monk and the supernatural machinery of *The Monastery/The Abbot*. Shadow though he calls himself (p. xix), he defends himself lustily in debate with Clutterbuck, who offers, timidly at first, "fluttered" by his "filial awe" (p. xv), the full range of criticisms, past and future, of Scott's work. The Waverley novels, he reports, are at times improbable, unnatural, hastily constructed of a few fine tableaux and characters patched with unconvincing plot-actions, cynically multiplied year upon year "merely for the lucre of gain" (p. xxv). The author's eidolon kindly advises the Captain to stop mouthing critical cant about "flow" and "construction" and attend to the facts, which are: (1) that book writing, composition, is a demonic, instinctual ("perhaps the strongest of all instincts," p. xxvii) enterprise, not a rational one—"A Demon sits on my pen . . . characters expand under my hand, incidents are multiplied; the story lingers, while the materials increase; my regular mansion turns out a Gothic anomaly" (p. xxii); (2) that the public may take him or leave him, and will, and so may and will he them—"I deny there is any call for gratitude, properly so called, either on one side or the other" (p. xxi); and (3) that he is no cynic but, by God, a public benefactor—"a successful author is a productive laborer, and . . . his works constitute as effectual a part of the public wealth—as that which is created by any other manufacture" (p. xxvi).

This canny and candid defense provokes a heated "Are there no bounds to your audacity?" from (Scott) the interlocutor, to which (Scott) the outlaw-eidolon replies sonorously that the bounds he keeps are "the sacred and eternal boundaries of honour and virtue." Where is this boundary? Scott the husband, father, gentleman, and Christian has placed it firmly between himself and his secret ambitions. The eidolon of his ambition has fixed them somewhere on the ambiguous border, as the eidolon's parting shot from Spenser has it, between "Be Bold" and "Be not too Bold" (p. xxix).

Meanwhile the Rev. Dr. Dryasdust, pea green with envy ever since the successful imitations of the author of Waverley produced by Lawrence Templeton and Captain Clutterbuck, worthier scholar and hence more deserving "son" than either, finally gets, or invents, his moment. "I also have seen the vision of the author of Waverley," he replies the same year in his Prefatory Letter to *Perveril of the Peak*, and he gave me a manuscript to edit too (p. xv). Furthermore, says Dryasdust somewhat spitefully, he sought me out, like a gentleman, in my own house, and he showed himself openly, not all muffled and mysterious: "the features, form, and dress of the eidolon . . . seemed to me more precisely distinct than was vouchsafed to you . . . but Heaven forbid I should glory or set up any claim or superiority over the other descendants of our common parent from such decided marks of his preference" (p. xvi).

Dr. Dryasdust looks over the manuscript brought him by the eidolon and begins his criticism the way Clutterbuck had: fictions and "figments" have got the better of close construction and historical veracity—"the old gentleman hath broken all bounds" (p. xvii). The eidolon raised by this critical reverie contrasts with the muffled dwarfish one of *Nigel*. He is definitely a bounds-breaker, a kind of giant: "bulky and tall . . . heavy . . . shaggy" with a large belly, a huge appetite for the Doctor's meat and drink, a taste in comfortable clothes, wine, and a "constitution built for permanence" (p. xviii). He reminds Dryasdust of Dr. Johnson, but the image suggests it is really the author of Waverley as Falstaff, in fact, on his way to join the antiquarians of the Roxburghe Club of London, "one of the most select companies of right English spirits which ever girdled in and hewed asunder a mountainous sirloin and a genuine plum-pudding" (p. xix).

In this form the author of Waverley is especially well prepared to counter the scholar's accusation that he steals and misuses history in his novel—"Tis my vocation, Hal. It is no sin for a man to labour in his vocation" is a quotation often on the author of Waverley's lips. More lyrically, the author of Waverley argues that his dips into the fountain of history do not pollute it but rather make it useful, like "the water we subtract for domestic purposes." He compares the novel to a divining rod—"a valueless twig in itself, but indicator, by its motion" where the fountain of true history is (pp. xxii, xxiii). Like Falstaff he will evade, persuade, and call "cant" upon the narrow Puritan morality which wants to erase "misleading" fiction and rear children on a strict diet of fact. When caught out in a plain lie—"Here you have a Countess of Derby fetched out of her cold grave and saddled with a set of adventures dated twenty years after her death"—he can recover, like Falstaff, with an ironic truth: "She may sue me for damages, as with the case Dido *versus* Vergil" (p. xxv). His ambition, says this huge hill of flesh complaining "do I not bate!" is not exactly to duplicate, far less to compete with, that most famous user and abuser of history, William Shakespeare—"May the Saints forfend that I should be guilty of such unfounded vanity! I only show what has been done when there were giants in the land. We pygmies of the present day may at least, however, do something; and it is well to keep a pattern before our eyes" (p. xxiv).

"Flinging a testy adieu" to the unconvinced scholar, the eidolon bulls his way out of the house rather like a former eidolon escaped the critical Demon of reader Martha Buskbody. He is on his way, he has said, to abandon the role of author for retirement with the bookmen of the Roxburghe Club. When he reappears the next year in the long introduction to *Quentin Durward* it is the beginning of another interesting story-within-the-stories of the Waverley novels—the story of the disclosure of the identity of the eidolon. Admitting that his money and status makes him subject to the vicissitudes of the financial community in a way that an ordinary man might not be, the author of Waverley tells us how he went to France to live on the cheap for a year and met a decayed Marquis with a manuscript on the history of his Scottish ancestor, who turns out to be a fan of that entertaining work, "The Bridle of Lammermoor," by Sir Walter Scott. The misreading of the title undercuts the true disclosure of the author's identity: the Scotsman corrects the Frenchman on both counts. The author of Waverley stops short of offering the Marquis the real (fictional) identity of the novelist, himself, when the Marquis compares the author to "a comedian" or a "family jester"; hearing this, the author "backed out of the candid confession which my vanity had meditated" (p. xxix).

The introductory chapter to *Tales of the Crusaders* (1825) purports to be an account by an Edinburgh reporter hidden under a table at a secret meeting of the multitude of narrators responsible for the novels, mixing in wonderful promiscuity with characters from the novels, and presided over by the eidolon of the author of Waverley. He calls for a motion to incorporate the whole community into a joint-stock company for the continuing production, by machine, of Waverley novels, for all sensible persons have long ago guessed that the novels could not all have been produced by one human hand.[14] Since they won't agree to the incorporation, the mechanization, or to his authority at all, the eidolon, as chairman of the meeting and father of the family, ends by repudiating them all—"I will unbeget you" (p. xxiv)—to write history.

Scott began work immediately on the *Life of Napoleon*, and shortly thereafter on *Woodstock*. Within months the joint stock companies of London and Edinburgh suffered the severe depression which inexorably involved Scott's publishers and himself. The possibility of financial distress and exile dramatized in the introduction to *Quentin Durward* became poignantly real. He then became virtually the machine he had in the introduction to *Tales of the Crusaders* offered to become, recognized himself to have already become, driving himself to produce the writing—simultaneous histories and novels on the average of ten to twenty pages of print a day for the rest of his life—that paid the debt of the industry, both fictional and real, whose Captain he was.

Many of those who were in the "secret" of Scott's authorship became trustees or creditors in a company which sequestered and managed the property, real and "eidolonic," which was Walter Scott. Magnanimity, generosity, the true adherence to the "boundary of honor and virtue," moved Scott to "harness himself" and his Demon of Composition to pay his debts, and moved his friends and creditors to trust him. Without cynicism do we note as well the author of Waverley's admission from his earliest appearances that he literally could not stop composing, that while he knew he *should* desire order, leisure, care, and "evolution" in his narratives, what he *did* desire was multiplicity, haste, profusion, continuation. There is some truth in the sentimental view that Scott "wrote himself to death" between 1826 and 1832 trying to clear that "property"—Abbotsford and the outlaw booty of the eidolon identity beneath it—for his family and his name.[15] On the other hand, he created many an opportunity between 1816 and 1825 for his schizophrenic narrative personas to warn him he was writing himself out, to assure himself he was going to stop or slow down. To assure himself he need *not* stop or slow down.

What the near-bankruptcy and harnessing perhaps gave him, in another sense, was the sanction he craved to take up that outlaw booty, that Demonic eidolon, and call it legal, call it moral, call it Walter Scott. Exactly a year after the Trust had taken over the author of Waverley, in February 1827, Walter Scott was genuinely surprised at a Theatrical Dinner by Lord Meadowbank's proposal to unmask the author in a toast to Walter Scott. But he let it happen on a graceful and surely thankful impulse, and rose in response to "confess" what his eidolon had backed out of confessing to another Lord in the introduction of *Quentin Dur- ward*, to "plead guilty" to the "loud and rapturous applause" (p. 464) of the three hundred who knew of his plight and his harnessed future. A few weeks later, writing the introduction to *Chronicles of the Canon- gate*, he pleaded guilty again with a brief account of the dinner- revelation, and a poignant comparison of his trick to that of a famed Harlequin who lost his power when, in a bid for personal fame, he played unmasked onstage. For Harlequin's power was rooted in his "audacity," his outrage and outrageousness, and his audacity in his anonymity (p. 318).

Scott's personal authorial papers speak movingly during this time of his relief at the ending of the rigid masquerade for which he could never quite account,[16] of his canny understanding that the recognition now might make for a number of financial possibilities. The greatest of these, shaped as he completed *Chronicles of the Canongate* in the fall of 1827, was the "magnum opus," a new edition of all the Waverley novels with introductions and notes which would fully bare both the sources and the process of the now harnessed Demon-composer, Sir Walter Scott, Bart.

This project, which occupied the next and last five years of his life, is a remarkable combination of artistic and personal self-examination, historical scholarship, and self-indulgence. The by-now-familiar images of the writer as fountain, as machine, as demonically possessed, occur regularly; the germs of the stories are exposed in the introductions and elaborated almost obsessively in the notes—one often has the impression that though he could not rewrite these stories, he leapt at the chance to "continue" them.[17] The coda of these magnum opus introductions is always an account of the degree of public favor, the record of the sales chart, on each novel. Scott's humility comes to seem a little suave, perhaps, but one cannot detect here either the contempt for the public or that self-contempt for which Dickens in the next generation indicted Thackeray.

Yet something nervous, tricky, wrathful, not humble, not reconciled—not yet, not ever, quite unmasked—surfaced in two more remarkable alter-egos conceived by the author of Waverley, Walter Scott, for the novels of his last year. One is Paul Pattieson, who visits the resurrected Jeddediah Cleishbotham to haggle with him over and finally to steal and publish *Count Robert of Paris*, the last manuscript of his deceased brother Peter. The other is the imagined editor-narrator of the first fiction to bear the name of Walter Scott, *The Chronicles of the Canongate*, first and second series, published in 1827 and 1828. Scott names him with potent simplicity, Chrystal Croftangry.

Croftangry's story crystalizes Scott's anger and his sublimation beautifully, for he begins his personal narrative as a bankrupt debtor in the prison-sanctuary of the Canongate district. He is freed by the intervention of friends, one of whom collapses into the mental imbecility that was Scott's deepest fear, and occasional fate, when the fountain went dry; he eagerly pursues but finally rejects the opportunity to buy back the Croftangry patrimony, and settles at last, freely at "home," in the prison-sanctuary of the city. Dickens would later inherit and master this topos of the chosen fate of prison in the urban setting which Scott/Croftangry offers here, as he would inherit and master Croftangry's rage at, and addiction to, the new pace of urban life and machinery. To hear the earlier writer condemning the brain-unhinging pace and land-and-peace-destroying ubiquity of mail coaches and roadways on his trip out of the city, and then admit his reliance on them as an escape as he heads back into the city (pp. 349, 366), is to anticipate the later writer on the great Victorian leveler and dynamo, the railroad. To follow Scott's alter-ego editor onto the territory of his patrimony, taken over by speculators, pulled down and rebuilt in bare cheap modern architecture which fell apart even before it could be inhabited, is to anticipate

Dickens's narrator on the Veneerings (p. 359). To see Croftangry's impotent outlaw love of his past explode against his moral commitment to (and personal shuddering at) the visible future, is to see not only Scott grimly riding the Britain of Reform time but also the whole century's rage for (and at) progress and history aborning.

Angry as Croftangry is, at the amoral advancing future, at the violence and illegitimacy of the lost immediate Jacobite and personal past, his solution is archetypal Scott, not Victorian but Romantic. He will not reform or reclaim the corrupted Glentanner estate of the Lairds of Croftangry (passed to them, interestingly, in Elizabethan times through a bastard female).[18] Instead he will go back to an uncorrupted past remoter still, a solider estate because it is a state of mind, a more peaceful and moral form of his identity, of his name. He knows that the legend of the ancestor who tilled the field in the Canongate near the King's palace and received both the property and the name of Croft-an-ri (land from the king) is probably a fiction (pp. 341, 342). But it's the fiction he wants, the deepest possible cover, the secret leaves from which Robin Hood sends his arrows, the bed where John Fowles tells us the British writer embraces his mistress, Loss (*Daniel Martin*, p. 249).

The final loss, embraced with wrath and cunning, is chronicled in the Introduction to *Count Robert of Paris* and *Castle Dangerous*, written in 1831 less than a year before Scott's death. In this last appearance the author of Waverley instinctively makes use of his original alter-ego. Remembering, interestingly, that the young source of manuscripts, Peter Pattieson, was dead, but forgetting that he had killed off the contentious old man who had signed his name to his stories, the author appears again as a deeply disturbed Jeddediah Cleishbotham.

In the invented last mask of peaceful Peter Pattieson's haughty, "seedy," "rapacious," and pugnacious brother, Paul (pp. xiii, xiv), Scott reclaims "audacity"; his Jeddediah Cleishbotham is his usual irritable self enlarged into a virtual paranoiac. Here Scott puzzles over his wrath as he had puzzled in the General Preface to the Waverley novels over his satisfaction. For this Paul, he tells us, has taken over Peter Pattieson's functions in Gandercleugh and seems ready to replace Jeddediah himself in his functions as well. Watching the usurper, Jeddediah is "agitated by a chaos of passions, of which anger was predominant, and for what reason, or against whom, I entertained such tumultuous displeasure, it was not easy for me to determine" (p. xvii). A rumor shakes the community at Gandercleugh, the world's navel: their scholar-writer is an impostor, the source of the marvels is this mysterious stranger. Jeddediah meditates some deed of violence against the young trickster, against the fickle community, for "my anger was directed at all and sundry" (p. xvii), yet he knows his future lies in conciliating both, for "in this world it is not often that the gratification of our angry passions lies in the same road with the advancement of our interest" (p. xix). And so wrath is "arranged . . . narrowed . . . soothed" (p. xviii), leaving that most modern, most Waverleyan of emotions in its place—"anxiety" (p. xix).

Pause for a groan of assent from Fergus MacIvor and Edgar Ravenswood, Rebecca of York. And from Walter Scott, old, sick and famous, who watched houses burn and glass shatter in the Reform agitation which gripped his nation in the last year and a half of his life, and who ate his liver under cover instead of doing what he wanted to do, fight the new world on behalf of old passions in public speeches and political pamphlets. More heads than Scott's thought that the nation would break apart; that men would have to go "out" in "the thirty-one" as they had in "the forty-five." In a striking passage in the *Journal* of 13 October 1831 Scott built a Waverleyan fantasy about it—the crown insists on its rights, the Parliament insists on Reform, the royalists legitimize the FitzClarence children to provide a male heir to rally to, Peers and Populace "seize on the Person of the Princess Vittoria, carrying her North and setting up the banner of England with the Duke of W[ellington] as Dictator—a brave *brave et demi!*." "Well," Scott reflects, cooling, waiting for the Great Cover, "I am too old to fight and therefore should keep the windy side of the Law; besides, I shall be burned out before times come to a decision" (*Journal*, p. 644).

The times came to their decision on July 17, 1832. In London King William IV gave the Royal Assent to the Reform Bill, and the Queen prepared the thirteen-year-old Princess "Vittoria" for the first of several "royal progresses" designed to make her people used to the idea of a Queen. And on that same seventeenth of July, Lockhart reports, Walter Scott tried one last time to get the machine going: "'Now give me my pen, and leave me for a little to myself.' Sophia, [Scott's daughter] put the pen into his hand, and he endeavoured to close his fingers upon it, but they refused their office—it dropped on the paper. He sank back among his pillows, silent tears rolling down his cheeks" (Lockhart's *Life*, p. 637). He died on the twenty-first of September, and his life, like his works, became the environment of the nineteenth-century novelist.

Notes

Introduction

1. *The Journal of Sir Walter Scott*, ed. W. E. K. Anderson (Oxford: Clarendon Press, 1972), p. 398, entry for Dec. 17, 1827, hereafter referred to as *Journal*.

2. J. G. Lockhart, *The Life of Sir Walter Scott, Bart* (1837–38) (reprint, London: J. M. Dent & Co., 1906), p. 643, hereafter cited as Lockhart.

3. Review of the first six volumes of Lockhart's *Life* in *London and Westminster Review* (1838), (reprinted in *The Complete Works of Thomas Carlyle: Critical and Miscellaneous Essays*, 4 vols. [New York: P. F. Collier & Son, 1901], 3:451.

4. Edgar Johnson (*Charles Dickens: His Triumph and His Tragedy* [New York: Simon & Shuster, 1952]) tells the story of Dickens reading Lockhart's *Life* and making his decision to go to America in 1843 (p. 358). A letter of 1841 traces Dickens's fear of "writing himself out" to the example of Scott. The purely commercial language masks, as I think is the case with Scott, a deeper concern with personal exhaustion: "I remember that Scott failed in the sale of his very best works . . . *because he never left off.* . . . I am doing what every other successful man has done. I am making myself cheap" (*The Letters of Charles Dickens*, ed. Madeline House and Graham Storey, 5 vols. [Oxford: Clarendon Press, 1969], 2:365, Dickens's italics).

5. I have examined this at greater length in "Steamboat Surfacing: Scott and the English Novelists," in *Nineteen Century Fiction* (March 1981): 468–76.

6. The first quotation is from "Gas at Abbotsford" (1940) (reprinted in *Collected Essays: Virginia Woolf*, 4 vols., [New York: Harcourt, Brace, 1967], 1:137; the second from "The Antiquary" (1924), reprinted in the same collection, 1:139.

7. Harold Bloom's illuminating and controversial dictum that an Oedipal struggle between a strong predecessor and anxious successors inevitably produces fertile "misreadings" of the former by the latter as the necessary condition of his creative freedom underlies my argument about Scott and his successors in this section and to some extent in the conclusion, where I take up the develop-

ment by Scott of a continuing narrative personna called "the author of Waverley." "Strong poets," says Bloom in *The Anxiety of Influence* (New York: Oxford University Press, 1973), "make [poetic] history by misreading one another, so as to clear imaginative space for themselves" (p. 5). In the first chapter I will argue, in fact, that this anxious separation from and misreading of the overshadowing, forceful Father, *as* a forceful Father, is a primary "swerve" in the character of the young hero of the Waverley novels—this is almost always followed, interestingly enough, by a final psychically necessary swerve back to an uncovered "true" (though to many readers hastily and artificially plotted) reading of the father as an essentially mixed and peace-loving figure.

8. Alexander Welsh, *The Hero of the Waverley Novels* (1963), (reprint, New York: Atheneum, 1968), p. 18.

9. Robert Caserio, *Plot, Story, and the Novel* (Princeton, N.J.: Princeton University Press, 1979), p. 17. Caserio's book is one of several in recent years which participate in the attempt to rehabilitate "narrative reason," sequence, action, plot, and ultimately "reference" for the criticism of narrative. Another important one is George Levine's *The Realistic Imagination* (Chicago: University of Chicago Press, 1981). The movement seems allied with the "counter-attack" by Gerald Graff and others against a perceived postmodernist challenge to literature's traditional role as the "sovereign orderer of reality and our most valuable means of making sense of the world" (*Literature against Itself* [Chicago: University of Chicago Press, 1979], p. 7). The new traditionalist claim that reality *is* "susceptible to comprehension and management" and that literature, above all narrative, is the model for and sign of this activity, has the inevitable effect of restoring Scott to the center of the tradition. For whatever the final nature of "reality" may be, the meeting of it as incomprehensible and the development of alternating structures of "management" called "history" and "dream" is, as Caserio and Levine among others note in their different ways, the key process of the typical Scott story.

10. Anthony Trollope, *Phineas Redux*, World's Classics (London: Oxford University Press, 1952), ch. 61. It is only fair to add that Chaffanbrass does not consider his client "saved" by the timely intrusion of Scott's standard of probability, but must rely in the end on the material evidence of the key that gave the real murderer freedom to attack his victim.

11. It is Robert C. Gordon's thesis that a partly subconscious duplicity on Scott's part about his relationship with his father is responsible for many an ambiguously loved/hated, or loving/undermining, father or pseudofather in Scott's novels, all of them evidence that whatever his conscious respect, "his imagination had its own purposes, and one of these was to put Walter Scott senior in his place" (*Under Which King?* [Edinburgh: Oliver & Boyd, 1969], p. 4).

12. "Sometimes those who have been burned are able only with restrained and painful effort to portray fire. His young people seldom undergo the dreadful hunger and anquished heartache he himself had so painfully known," says Edgar Johnson (*Sir Walter Scott: The Great Unknown*, 2 vols. [New York: Macmillan, 1970], 1:123–24).

13. John Fowles, *Daniel Martin* (New York: New American Library, Inc., 1977), p. 288.

14. What is "Abbotsford" to Scott? To read his biographers and critics is to feel it is the recycled Gothic house itself, with its books and its nooks and above all its collection of weapons and artifacts from medieval and Scottish history. Yet to read Scott's letters and journals is to conceive a vision of Abbotsford as land and river and, above all, *trees*. Seeing his possessions likely to be swept away in the looming bankruptcy of his printing houses Scott admits that "Abbotsford" has been "my Dalilah and so I have often termed it—and now—the recollection of the extensive woods I have planted and the walks I have formed from which strangers must derive both the pleasure and profit will excite feelings likely to sober my gayest moments" (*Journal*, p. 39). Or again, "I have a curious fancy. I will go set two or three acorns and judge by their success in growing whether I will succeed in clearing my way or not," followed two days later by "Rose late in the morning . . . to give the cold and toothache time to make themselves scarce. . . . Today all is quiet but a little swelling and stiffness in the jaw. Went to Chiefswood at one and marked with regret forty trees indispensably necessary for paling. Much like drawing a tooth—but they *are* wanted and will never be better but I am avaricious of grown trees having so few" (*Journal*, pp. 124–25).

15. Johnson's biography describes the fever of projects, and projection, into which Scott launched as soon as he began to see himself feeding his own presses, i.e. Ballantyne's, keeping the machines running: new poems and prose works, reprints, an Annual Register—these were only a few of the forms which the process would take, the process of converting blank paper into "long shelves" of Ballantyne books (Johnson, pp. 306–9).

16. Avrom Fleishman, *The English Historical Novel: Walter Scott to Virginia Woolf* (Baltimore: The Johns Hopkins Press, 1971), pp. 43–44.

17. In *Walter Scott: The Making of the Novelist*, Jane Millgate focuses in on the crucial early years of the "anonymity game" through which Scott constructed a field on which he could both hide and advertise his "novelty." Her book, which appeared too late for me to take full advantage of its many interesting close readings, depicts Scott's movement through the early poems and the first half-dozen Scottish novels as an evolving and highly sophisticated "art of repetition with variation," where the artist, "at some deep level . . . afraid of confronting his own originality," lays every possible stress on the imitation he is engaged in rather than the creation ([Toronto: University of Toronto Press, 1984], pp. 104, x). Her analysis of the "fable of composition" (p. 15) offered in the prefaces and introductions of these poems and novels is similar in many respects to the one I argue in the conclusion of this book: her reading of both the prefaces and the fictions of *Guy Mannering* and *The Bride of Lammermoor* are especially illuminating.

18. *Past and Present* (1842) (reprint, Boston: Houghton Mifflin, 1956), p. 247.

19. In the absence of a modern standard edition of the Waverley novels, I use the Dryburgh Edition, 25 vols (London: Adam & Charles Black, 1892). *Ivanhoe* is vol. 9; the quotation is from Scott's magnum opus "introduction,"

p. xviii. Other Waverley novels will be cited first as footnotes with volume numbers, thereafter in the text with page numbers

20. *Rebecca and Rowena*, vol. 9 of the Biographical Edition of *The Works of William Makepeace Thackeray*, 13 vols. (New York and London: Harper, 1898–99), ch. 7.

21. *Pendennis*, vol. 2 of the Biographical Edition of *The Works of William Makepeace Thackeray*, ch. 18.

22. A good short analysis emphasizing the difference between *Esmond* and *Waverley* occurs in Francis R. Hart's important book, *Scott's Novels: The Plotting of Historic Survival* (Charlottesville: University Press of Virginia, 1966), pp. 18–23.

23. Charles Dickens, *David Copperfield* (reprint, New York: New American Library, 1962), p. 606.

24. George Eliot, *The Mill on the Floss* (Boston: Houghton-Mifflin, 1961) Bk. IV, ch. 3.

25. Ruby Redinger, Eliot's most recent biographer, abstracts the "finishing Scott" episode from John Cross's nineteenth-century biography; Cross has it from Eliot's friend Edith Simcox. Redinger cautions that since Edith Simcox, like ourselves, loved to imagine that a personal incident must be behind significant events in the novels, the anecdote might possibly have its source not in anything Eliot told her friend directly but in her friend's speculations about the sonnet which opens chapter 57 of *Middlemarch*. This describes children who, "when the book and they must part," wrote "the tale, from Tully Veolan. . . . In lines that thwart like portly spiders ran" (*George Eliot: The Emergent Self* [New York: Alfred A. Knopf, 1975], pp. 57–59).

Chapter One

1. Northrup Frye, *The Secular Scripture: A Study of the Structure of Romance* (Cambridge, Mass.: Harvard University Press, 1976), pp. 29–30.

2. Note, for instance, Coleridge's complaint that "we" are utterly indifferent "to the feuds of Norman and Saxon (N.B. what a contrast to our interest in the Cavaliers and Jacobites and the Puritans, Commonwealthmen, and Covenanters from Charles I to the Revolution)" (among marginalia printed in T. M. Raysor, ed., *Coleridge's Miscellaneous Criticism*, reprinted in *Scott: The Critical Heritage*, ed. John O. Hayden [New York: Barnes & Noble, 1970], p. 182), and the anonymous reviewer of the *Eclectic Review* (June 1820) who waved aside Scott's carefully made argument about the necessary artifice of the language he chose for *Ivanhoe's* medieval characters to lamentingly call to mind "how much of the spirit and effect of the dialogue in the preceding tales of the Author of *Waverley*, arise from the recognized peculiarities of provincial idiom, and the comic force of quaint or familiar turns of expression" (reprinted in *Critical Heritage*, p. 189). Scott said in the 1832 General Preface to the Waverley novels that he had hoped to duplicate for Scotland the success of Maria Edgeworth in "introducing her natives to those of her sister kingdom in a more favorable light that they had been placed hitherto," and in procuring "sympathy for their

virtues and indulgence for their foibles" (*Waverley*, p. xiii). Whatever the merits of arguments about the comparative "life" and language of Scottish or chivalric novels, it seems probable that Scott's departure from the safely elegiac regionalist politic of Miss Edgeworth's model made some English readers uncomfortable on more than aesthetic grounds.

3. F. R. Hart's book *Scott's Novels* argues persuasively that the old critical orthodoxy separating the "real" Scottish novels from the "pasteboard" chivalry novels makes little sense. He proposes that Scott moved toward premodern European history in his "quest for the historical picturesque," achieving indeed a "new imaginative freedom in the very remoteness of the new subject matter, in its susceptibility to a more freely symbolic rendering" (p. 151). Hart concentrates on old critical orthodoxy's opposing pairs (i.e. Richard and John) in his analysis of *Ivanhoe*, ignoring the figure of Locksley, or Robin Hood, whom I take to be pivotal, but he does open territory which my argument attempts to extend in his intriguing remark that in chivalry Scott found a romantic "opposition" which is more symbolic and hence, "paradoxically, more permanent" than the Cavalierism-Jacobitism that was closest to home.

4. Scott tells us in the Templeton "introduction" to *Ivanhoe* that he has chosen neither pure authenticity of antique language nor pure modern speech in which to write his historical novel, but rather an indistinct patchwork of terms and phrases already partly familiar as antique language, a deliberately artificial creation. Few things make critics, old or new, more impatient than this created language of *Ivanhoe*. I can only say I find myself adjusting to it perfectly well as the novel passes, though I am properly rebuked by the stout declaration of Robin Mayhew, scenting a "wrong kind of Scott Revival" in the air in the early '70s, that "the demonstration that *Ivanhoe* is 'about' some of the same things as, say *Rob Roy*, does not rescue the prose of its tournaments and catastrophes from being a turgid bore" (*Walter Scott* [Cambridge: Cambridge University Press, 1973], pp. 6, 5).

5. Pistol speaks these words, loftily playing the chivalric hero, as a prologue to the great news he has to deliver to Falstaff in *Henry IV, Part II*, that Henry IV is dead and Falstaff's patron, as he thinks, is no longer Prince Hal but King Henry V. I have quoted here, and will be quoting in future, from the Signet Classic editions of the Henry plays, and later *Hamlet*, and *MacBeth*, ed. by Sylvan Barnet (*Henry IV, Part II* [New York: New American Library, 1965], p. 161).

6. *Henry IV, Part I*, Signet Classic edition (New York: New American Library, 1965), p. 51.

7. Wilmon Brewer compiled an extensive book, *Shakespeare's Influence on Sir Walter Scott* (1925) (reprint, New York: AMS Press, 1974), which does a serviceable job of noting both direct and indirect references. Though the book does not often draw inferences from the data it gathers, and runs mainly to quantifications (i.e. *Waverley* contains thirty-six references to sixteen plays [p. 247]), it contains important reminders about the overall Shakespearean sponsorship of Scott, not just that of the Henrys. More interesting comments have come from David Brown, for instance, who finds in an uncited quotation

from *Richard II* during the progress south of the Prince in *Waverley* a "deftly ironic parallel" between each deposed Prince's subjects' refusal to "cry amen" to them, a parallel reminding us of Scott's continuing support not of usurpation but of "established usurpers" (*Walter Scott and the Historical Imagination* [London: Routledge & Kegan Paul, 1979], p. 16).

8. In this connection G. M. Young once commented that "of all the causes for which men have fought and died, the Protestant succession as by law established was probably the least inspiring" ("Scott and the Historians" in *Sir Walter Scott Lectures, 1940–1948* [Edinburgh: University Press, 1936], p. 86).

9. My sense of Scott's "development," though somewhat different in results, proceeds from the same intuition that animates Graham McMaster's recent treatment of *Scott and Society* (Cambridge: Press Syndicate of the University of Cambridge, 1981), perhaps the best of the recent full-length treatments of Scott. Tracing a path essentially through Scottish novels from *Waverley* to *Redgauntlet*, McMaster takes note of recent efforts to make Scott a cool realist, but demurs: "I believe Scott is driven to the creation of myths, to the forcing of his material into a series of repeated patterns" (p. 4) moving "away from realism towards fantasy, allegory and symbolism" (p. 149).

10. *Old Mortality*, 6:200.

11. Note in *MacBeth* not only the generating image "Will all great Neptune's ocean wash this blood / clean from my hand? No; this my hand will rather / the multitudinous seas incarnadine, / making the green one red" (Signet edition [New York: New American Library, 1963], pp. 63–64), but also the entire characterization of MacBeth's split between desire and act, analogous to what Welsh calls the Waverlean premium on having and prejudice against getting.

12. A. O. Cockshut, like many critics, has seen the plot of *Waverley* "constructed in a circle" of returns to sanity and civility (*The Achievement of Walter Scott* [London: Collins, 1969], p. 115). A more careful reading, I think, is Robert C. Gordon's in *Under Which King?* which notes that Edward "does not come full circle" either psychically or geographically but rather stops short of total return "south" to "sanity" (p. 24).

13. Moments of sheer energy like this, actually few and far between in *Ivanhoe*, occasion Walter Bagehot's wonderfully catty remark that, whatever Scott's intentions, the "boy" inside every Victorian reader who "idolises mediaeval society as the 'fighting time'" will solidify through loving re-readings of *Ivanhoe* the dangerous "impression that the middle ages had the same elements of happiness which we have at present, and that they had fighting besides," the one element of happiness missing from modern life! (general review of Scott's novels written in 1858, reprinted in *Critical Heritage*, pp. 409, 410).

14. Working with Frye's definition of romance forms, Kenneth Sroka follows Scott's treatment of the oak tree symbol through the novel in "The Function of Form: *Ivanhoe* as Romance," in *Studies in English Literature* 19 (1979): 645–60. Evil by this analysis rests with those unsympathetic to (and vice versa) Sherwood forest, with the Normans who are "abusers of the oak" (p. 648). That Ivanhoe's Saxon father, as the one who symbolically uprooted the oak which his disinher-

ited son bears on his shield at Ashby, belongs in the same "class" momentarily with the Normans here, is one of the reasons why David Brown finds a "failure of historical imagination" in Scott when he turns from the Scottish novels. Brown is looking for the kind of "class analysis" that marked Scott's treatment of gentry-peasantry Scotland and finds that Norman as gentry and Saxon as peasantry doesn't "work" consistently in *Ivanhoe* (*Walter Scott and the Historical Imagination*, p. 184).

15. Welsh's famous analysis of Bois Guilbert's death, somewhat more abstract and less attuned to the movement of the novel, I feel, is that this strange phenomenon hints at "some profound law of the Waverley Novels. . . . On behalf of the individual who has sacrificed so much for the preservation of society this romance challenges the potency of death. The hero is threatened, but never dies; and by refusing to kill, he hopes never to experience death" (*The Hero of the Waverley Novels*, p. 226). Hart calls the villain's death "a chivalric form of old Krook's combustion syndrome" (Krook self-destructs in *Bleak House*) (*Scott's Novels*, p. 158).

Chapter Two

1. *Rob Roy*, 4:258.

2. Alexander Welsh calls this, in a less sympathetic and accurate, if memorable, phrase, "this searching about for the police" (*The Hero of the Waverley Novels*, p. 157).

3. We do well to remember, too, as Robert Gordon suggests, that "one reason for not underrating the 'non-Scottish' works . . . is simply that so often . . . they swarm with Scotsmen." (*Under Which King?* p. 128). Reversing the journey, going to the king across the water, *Quentin Durward* finds a territory populated by Scots already romantically self-exiled (i.e., psychically and financially on the make).

4. Critics seem virtually united in their dislike of all the "devices" connected with Rashleigh: Donald Davie, A. O. Cockshut, John Lauber (*Sir Walter Scott* [New York: Twayne, 1966]), all single out the elder Osbaldistone's "substitution" of Rashleigh for Frank as especially unbelievable, forgetting the Hal-Hotspur parallel because Rashleigh, despite his similarly (and not accidentally?) fiery name, is no soldier. For these readers the novel falls apart into an early realistic, a final romantic portion, because no clear unity derives from the "progress" of the protagonist. David Brown, in chapter 5 of *Walter Scott and the Historical Imagination*, reviews the alternative unity theory; that the novel offers a linked structural contrast of south and north, first English, then Scottish. My own analysis expands that of Robert Gordon, for whom "it is the issue of filial responsibility that unifies Rob Roy," contrasting Frank's rebellion against the exaggerated filiality of Diana Vernon, Baillie Nicol Jarvie, and the sons of Rob Roy (*Under Which King?* p. 68).

5. *Quentin Durward*, 16:9.

6. To elaborate the elegantly mercantile rerendering of this concept, D. D. Devlin notes in a chapter on *A Legend of Montrose* and *Rob Roy* that "men of

prudence" like the former novel's Dugald Dalgetty and the latter's Baillie Nicol Jarvie identify "honor" with "interest" in a quasi-Falstaffian way (*The Author of Waverley*, p. 87). Gordon is one of many to note the exquisite and prophetic irony by which *Rob Roy* embodied "the system of values by which Scott lived and wrote and by which he was both to flounder into disaster in 1826 and to redeem himself" (*Under Which King?* p. 77). Eric Quayle's revisionist account of *The Ruin of Sir Walter Scott* (New York: Clarkson N. Petter, 1968) traced the complex history of the edifice, material, commercial, and psychic, built by the "credit" of the author of Waverley until its collapse in the panic of 1826: "Constable and Company had backed the bills of Hurst, Robinson and Company; James Ballantyne and Company had backed the bills of Constable and Company; all three concerns were roped together on a slippery slope of dissolving credit without one solid redoubt to anchor in" (p. 196). Scott's "honor" took over after the collapse of credit refusing to declare bankruptcy he began that process mythically perceived as "writing himself to death" to pay his debts. Honor, since it stayed home, eschewing frays in the streets, approached not homicide but suicide.

7. Francis Hart has studied the three sources of authority—traditional, contractual, and providential—which, sometimes in conflict, sometimes in tenuous alliance, complicate the search for male identity in the Waverley novels, touching on the half-sincere "showmanship" of Louis's authority as an example of the self-manipulation that this entails ("Scott's Endings: The Fictions of Authority," *Nineteenth Century Fiction* [June 1978] : 48–68).

8. Some of the "changes" in Louis are in the eye of the beholder, though. Thomas Crawford calls attention to the tricks Quentin plays on himself while searching for the royal authority in the financial one he sees in front of him: "Quentin Durward manufactures two quite different pictures of Louis XI for himself out of the same features; incognito, the King looks like a money-grubbing merchant, but in his own proper person his wrinkles seem 'the furrows which sagacity had worn while toiling in meditation upon the fate of nations'" (*Scott* [Edinburgh: Oliver and Boyd, 1965], p. 71). The quotation from *Quentin Durward* appears on p. 88.

9. Scott's habit of speaking through his characters "unconsciously" in Shakespearean forms and phrases was documented early on in a brilliant anonymous review of *Woodstock* (*Westminster Review*, April 1826, reprinted in *Critical Heritage*, pp. 290–99). Shakespeare's works, as we shall see in Chapter 5, were virtually a character in *Woodstock*, and Scott does a great deal of direct citing of Shakespeare's works, but the uncited (not all of them, I believe, unconscious) allusions carry great weight too, as in this one from *Henry V*.

10. Jane Millgate has explored this duplicity in an essay which argues that the apparent "frankness" of the first-person narrative hides a strategy by which "autobiography is . . . transformed into a ritual for keeping full understanding at bay"; that the lack of *Great-Expectations*-like self-exploration in the narrative is evidence of deep strains and guilts which remain "unexorcised" and hence cannot be reached by memory or healed by narration ("*Rob Roy* and the Limits

of Frankness," *Nineteenth Century Fiction* [March 1980]: 392). About the hero's two names, Millgate reminds us that Frank is "frank indeed, but the connotations of his surname (Osbaldistone)—bones, bleakness, and stoniness—tell us something rather different about the underlying meaning of the text" (p. 379).

11. "It is hard to say which is more enticing," remarks Alexander Welsh, "her mysterious dedication to the cloister or her availability as a 'man'" (*The Hero of the Waverley Novels*, p. 188). Welsh is one critic who takes her name quite seriously: "With the intuitive sense of poetic justice shared by his critics, Scott makes death the last word for Die" (p. 189).

12. Note, for example, the richly complex response to *Waverley*'s awakening of that memory by the anonymous reviewer of *British Critic* in August 1814: "It is [set in] the year 1745, the last fatal year when the blood of our countrymen was spilt on its own shores, when Briton met Briton on his native land. It has pleased Providence in his mercy to this favored country, for a space of now nearly seventy years, to secure it from the still more fearful and deadly scenes of civil commotion. By the restoration of peace to the whole European world a mighty machine of national strength is suddenly diverted from those external objects to which it has been so long, and so powerfully directed; it is our earnest hope, as it is our most confident trust, that its gigantic force may not, by an unnatural revulsion, be turned inwardly upon itself, and that the same energies which blessed us with victory, and crowned us with glory in our operations abroad, may not inflame us with the ardour of contention, nor curse us with the spirit of discord at home. . . . If the history of those bloody days, which is embodied in this tale, shall by an early and awful warning inspire the nation with a jealous vigilance against the very first symptoms of their recurrence, we shall consider that not even the light pages of fiction have trifled in vain" (reprinted in *Critical Heritage*, pp. 68–69).

13. John P. Farrell, *Revolution as Tragedy: The Dilemma of the Moderate from Scott to Arnold* (Ithaca, N.Y.: Cornell University Press, 1980). pp. 71, 44.

14. One early anonymous reviewer of *Quentin Durward* accused Scott of combining the vicious behavior of William de la Marck with the urban insurrection which forms the main middle action of the story, though it occurred half a generation later than the time of the story, "only for the purpose of an additional gibe at popular revolutions" (review in *New Monthly Magazine*, July 1823, reprinted in *Critical Heritage*, p. 278). Avrom Fleishman contends, interestingly, in a discussion of *Durward* and *Anne of Geierstein*, that the new quasi-urban middle class shown coming to power in those two novels is less an anticipation of the modern bourgeoisie than "a revival of the classical ideal of the Roman Republic" (*The English Historical Novel*, p.60). At some profound level, as I shall argue in Chapter 5, the essential war of opposites in Scott's idea of history is, as it was in Gibbons and other speculative Enlightenment historians, that of Roman and Barbarian.

15. The naked house, I have argued, was a primary topos deep in Scott's own psyche, one that linked "leaves" of novels and planting trees over the hills of Abbotsford as the major enabling act of his life. See for instance the *Journal* for

18 June 1826: "This morning wrote till one-half twelve. . . . Methinks I can make this work answer. Then drove to Huntley Burn. . . . The young woods are rising in a kind of profusion I never saw elsewhere. Let me once clear off these [bankruptcy] encumbrances and they shall wave broader and deeper yet. But to attain this I *must work*" (p. 159, Scott's italics); or more simply, the *Journal* for 2 October 1826: "Wrote my task. Went out at one and wrought in the wood till four": followed by 3 October's comic dilemma: "I wrote my task as usual but strange to tell there is a want of paper. I expect some to-day. In the mean time to avoid all quarrel with Dame Duty I cut up some other leaves into the usual statutory size" (p. 206). Throughout the *Journal* "write" and "wrought" seem interchangeable between the desk and the woods, and so do the necessary "leaves."

16. R. V. Johnson has noticed the incongruity of the pastoral setting of the novel's first few chapters, which in fact constitute "a macabre variant of the mythic pattern of garden, tree and fruit"—the Bohemian as acorn, rather than apple, being a tough nut to crack as the icon of the knowledge of good and evil ("An Assurance of Continuity: Scott's Model of Past and Present in *Quentin Durward*," *Southern Review* [University of Adelaide, Australia] [July 1980]: 83).

17. Francis Hart offers a more ancient, and more modern, iconography for this wanderer, one of Scott's most interesting figures: "In the political terms of a Waverley identity he is 'unaccommodated man,' Quentin's essential plight embodied, like Lear's in Tom o' Bedlam, in a moral-legal wilderness" (*Scott's Novels*, p. 231).

18. "Uncertainties and self-deceptions like this make Quentin a suitable hero for a novel in which Scott is trying to present a changing society which has been unable to develop new theories to support its new practices, and consequently is not sure itself how much or how fast it is changing," comments A. O. Cockshut (*The Achievement of Sir Walter Scott*, p. 93). I count it a nice touch of Scott to place this feudal daydream in the mind of a feudal hero: we shall see in the next two chapters how clearly the domain of politico–social service to "the lady," the domain of the "Queensman," becomes merely the fantasy kingdom for Scott's men.

19. A. N. Wilson, who says he hated *Quentin Durward* when adults made him read it at the age of twelve, admires it now for, among other things, the "deft but marked way in which Quentin Durward's developing sexual awareness is suggested to the reader" (*The Laird of Abbotsford* [Oxford: Oxford University Press, 1980], p. 159).

Chapter Three

1. *Old Mortality*, 6:194.

2. "The Antiquary" in *Collected Essays of Virginia Woolf*, 1:140.

3. E. M. W. Tillyard distinguishes the movement from English/Scots to the third language of artificial premodern English in *The Monastery* ("linguistically

far the strangest of the novels") in "Scott's Linguistic Vagaries,"*Essays Literary and Educational* [London: Barnes & Noble, 1962], p. 99); David Murison, among others, has called the robust Scripture of the Reformation Bible "the second language of Scotland" ("The Two Languages of Scott," in *Scott's Mind and Art,* ed. A. Norman Jeffares [New York: Barnes & Noble, 1969], p. 224); and Robert Hay Carnie notes that it was called "the language of the saints" ("Scottish Presbyterian Eloquence and *Old Mortality,*" *Scottish Literary Journal* 3, no. 3 [December 1976] : 51). In his learned but often surprisingly readable survey of *The Language of Walter Scott,* Graham Tullock elaborates: "It is no accident that Robert Louis Stevenson when he wanted a name for a bad period language called it 'Tushery.' . . . Oaths and exclamations are small, almost meaningless, but unequivocally period elements; in this context they are invaluable . . . tacked on at beginning or end [of the sentence] like a bookend" ([London: Andre Deutsch, 1980], p. 92). "From the purely linguistic point of view," Murison comments, "'tushery' had its good points and results . . . . It added nearly 200 words to the English language . . . by reviving or introducing them from some out-of-the-way original" ("The Two Languages in Scott," p. 218).

4. *The Monastery,* 10:98.

5. Discussing the language "test" scene in *Old Mortality* which I will study in a moment, A. O. Cockshut says in this context that Scott's examination of the "enthusiast's" position "goes beyond and behind the classic Augustan statements about theological fanaticism, recovering the human content of formulae supposed to be dead"; recovery of this content means that "the Gibbonian certainty issuing in the Gibbonian irony [about fanatics] is gone" (*The Achievement of Walter Scott,* pp. 145, 132).

6. *The Abbot,* 11:28.

7. Peter Garside has explored the ambiguous terror of strong language, or any speech at all, in Scott's novels and in his own speech, in a provocatively persuasive series of articles in the *Scottish Literary Journal* ("*Old Mortality*'s Silent Minority," vol. 7, no. 1 [May 1980]; and "Scott's Political Speech," vol. 7, no. 2 [December 1980]). "The constant signalling of the speech-act itself," he says in the first essay (p. 129), makes of *Old Mortality* a virtual source-book not only of radical and moderate speech styles in the seventeenth century but also to those in Scott's own time. Garside's study of both the novel's narrative attitude to the dangers of language and of Scott's own speechmaking shows that Scott at some deep level "identifies language with political disquiet" and hence displays "a desperate desire . . . for an almost literal *quietism,*" a desire which revealed itself ultimately, and paradoxically, Garside argues, in the enormous— but masked—vocalization called the Waverley novels ("Scott's Political Speech," p. 26).

8. In a subtle and enlightening treatment of Morton as the finest of Scott's "conjunctive" heroes, i.e., heroes every detail of whose personal odyssey connects them to the main developments of the intellectual and national history Scott is tracing, Harry Shaw draws attention to the "ideological self-mystifica-

tion" which is a necessary quality of reasoning-to-action not only of the avowed ideologues but of the rationalists like Morton himself (*The Forms of Historical Fiction* [Ithaca, N.Y.: Cornell University Press, 1983], pp. 189–205).

9. Reminding us that Scott has taken pains twice to notify us of the "chill" (of dependence on his uncle) in Morton's soul, Alexander Welsh comments that Morton, like other heroes of Scott, "becomes hot only in the act of verbalizing his indignation" (*The Hero of the Waverley Novels*, p. 250).

10. In linking the White Lady to the mothering, text-interleaving Mary of *The Monastery* and later to the Mary Stuart of *The Abbot*, I am attempting to reinstate in the structure of the double novel a figure which criticism universally has seen as an unassimilated and unsettling decoration. Of this variety of criticism I like best Coleman Parson's picture of Scott, "like an over-confident gardener," "transplanting" the water nymph from *Ondine* into Scottish soil and then "grafting" into the fragile stem elements of sprite, specter, goblin, brownie, and banshee (*Witchcraft and Demonology in Scott's Fiction* [Edinburgh: Oliver & Boyd, 1964], pp. 160–61).

11. In Michel Foucault's *Madness and Civilization: A History of Insanity in the Age of Reason* (1965) (reprint, New York: Random House, 1973), pp. 96–97. "Even the old feasts of fools," says Foucault, anticipating Frye's definition of the purposes of "kidnapped Romance," were theatrical events, and organized into social and moral criticism, whatever they may have contained of spontaneous religious parody" (p. 15).

12. There is, however, an abstractness about this upholding of "life" and its Author which issues both in the indifference to religious form and particular religious feeling which marked Scott's own life and in the curious dance with personal death as a strategy for preserving "life" which Alexander Welsh has noticed in *The Hero of the Waverley Novels*. The series key figure for Welsh is Henry Morton, who spends the last several chapters putatively "dead" and cannot, up to and including the final moment, muster the personal ego to say "I yet live" to the woman he loves (pp. 258–59).

13. The paralyzed and despairing narrator of Ford Maddox Ford's *The Good Soldier* sees the story he has told as an example of his eminently Waverleyan psychic economy, as I have argued in "Steamboat Surfacing: Scott and the Victorians" (p. 485). By the time of Lord Jim and Edward Ashburnham, those two "good soldiers," the strategy of Henry Morton, sinking private woes in public action, is a dead one, of course: Scott hinted at its fragility in the ending of *Old Mortality*, where as Robert Gordon argues, the self-tormentings of the three principal characters in the midst of their apparent successes and reconciliations "testify unmistakeably to the irrelevance of the country's new-found peace for them" (*Under Which King?* p. 66).

14. Scott began but never completed several stories and published several ballads using Thomas the Rhymer, the legendary bard who was supposed to have been held captive by the Queen of Elf-Land somewhere in the Eildon Hills whose three peaks formed part of the significant landscape of his childhood at his grandparents' farm of Sandyknowe. Scott's purchase of the farm and land which

became Abbotsford was partly a way of "owning" a storied glen nearby in which Thomas was said to have walked (Johnson, p. 372).

15. The passing of the world of "faery" becomes a profoundly serious theme to the next generation of novelists. "Never wonder" is the keynote of the new pragmatic society Dickens sees rising in *Hard Times* (1854): in a new species of "Fairy palaces" called factories, says his narrator bitterly, men and women lose in service to machines the last vestige of imaginative curiosity that wasn't beaten out of them in childhood. Caroline Helstone Moore, one of Charlotte Bronte's heroines in *Shirley* (1849), contentedly marries the owner of the Mill which has changed the nature of Fieldhead Hollow, but in the last paragraph of the novel listens in awe and perhaps with some anxiety to her old housekeeper tell how her mother came running in from the fields fifty years before to say "she had seen a fairish (fairy) in Fieldhead Hollow; and that was the last fairish that ever was seen on this countryside."

16. Avrom Fleischman's comment in 1971 is still the case: "Scott's religious position has never been satisfactorily defined, for it was personal, shifting, and self-contradictory" (*The English Historical Novel*, pp. 85–86).

17. Scott dilates in typical Tory fashion on the church as guardian of irrational man several times in the *Journal*, for instance: "The Whigs will live and die in the heresy that the world is ruled by little pamphlets and speeches and that if you can sufficiently demonstrate that a line of conduct is most consistent with men's interest you have therefore and thereby demonstrate [*sic*] that they will at length after a few speeches on the subject adopt it of course. In this case we would have no need of laws or churches for I am sure that there is no difficulty of proving that moral, regular, steady habits conduce to Men's best interest. . . . But of these individuals each has passions and prejudices the gratification of which he prefers not only to the general weal but to that of himself as an individual" (p. 12).

18. This is my argument for the reinstatement in the structure of the novel of Sir Piercie who, along with the White Lady, has been called responsible for the "failure" of *The Monastery* from the first review. Sir Piercie I count no shining success as a character, yet criticism's utter dismissal of him—for instance, Francis Hart's "his central plot importance depends on his role in an ideological struggle to which his folly is unrelated. . . . nor does he stand for any conflux of historic forces" seems off the mark (*Scott's Novels*, p. 192).

19. George Levine has written informatively on "the disenchantment plot" as the ground of the nineteenth-century realistic novel, and on the ambiguous gains that disenchantment brings. Disenchantment for Roland and other Waverley heroes begins with the recognition of enchantment, and the painful process of un-spelling themselves is necessary to the relaxation of the anguish of that discovery; nevertheless the primary reason for disenchantment, as Levine sees Scott shaping the "desire" of the hero, is not so that one can celebrate the destruction of the dream but so that one can attain again the "freedom to dream" (*The Realistic Imagination*, pp. 92, 83).

20. Graham McMaster sees Scott only partly achieving what he intended

with Mary Stuart in *The Abbot*: "Mary seems to be on the verge of symbolising a gayer, more humane and organic, society, which is repressed by a barren, sadistic Protestantism (Lochleven, Lindsay, Ruthven). There is the childlessness of Mary Avenel, the destruction of the Cell of St. Cuthbert, the tearing-down of the garlands of flowers and the stopping-up of the spring of healing water . . . yet it is only faintly sketched in, the novel mostly retreating to the hackneyed, literary theme of 'queen or woman'" (*Scott and Society*, p. 181). I see Scott working more complexly with this "hackneyed" theme.

21. "Roland escapes because he is fictional: Mary cannot because she is historical," says Marian Cusac: "The departure of Mary . . . might be taken as symbolic of the historical figure as he vanishes into his story, leaving the fictional characters still 'alive' and in a sense immortal" (*Narrative Structure in the Novels of Sir Walter* Scott [The Hague: Norton, 1969], p. 43). Mary is a "prince" about to be turned into a legend, a real person about to become 'useful' as a fiction; unlike *Ivanhoe's* Richard, she seems to know it.

Chapter Four

1. *Redgauntlet*, 18:327.
2. *The Pirate*, 13:53.
3. British critic Andrew Hook let this one slip by him in 1972 in the Penguin introduction to *Waverley*: "Scott's triumph became a triumph for the form he wrote in. The novel gained a new authority and prestige, and even more important perhaps, a new masculinity. After Scott the novel was no longer in danger of becoming the preserve of the woman writer and the woman reader. Instead it became the appropriate form for writers' richest and deepest imaginative explorations of human experience" ([Harmondsworth, Middlesex: Penguin Books Ltd., 1972], p. 10). W. M. Parker saw *The Heart of Midlothian* as Scott's "Everest" in his "Preface" to the Everyman edition (London: J. M. Dent & Sons, 1956), p. v. The "Great Tradition" critics of mid-twentieth-century fiction, Leavis, Dorothy Van Ghent, for instance, favored *The Heart of Midlothian* somewhat obliquely, as the best of a bad lot because of the novel's thematic "high seriousness," though they gave it bad marks for aesthetic structure. John O. Hayden notes "some erosion of that longstanding position of favor" for the novel in this century because of some "second thoughts [on] the handling of the moral theme." ("The Big Lie [And a Few Small Ones]," *Scottish Literary Journal* 6, no. 1 [May 1979], p. 34).
4. Nina Auerbach's recent compelling account of the intersection of the fantasies of free mobile womanhood and divine literary "character" in a single generative myth of Victorian religious humanism relies at two of its crucial turning points upon the nineteenth century critical divinization of Scott's female characters, Diana Vernon and Effie Deans. It was these women whom the Victorian imagination first saw virtually stepping out of their texts to become saving icons of power and passion (*Women and the Demon* [Cambridge, Mass.: Harvard University Press, 1982], esp. pp. 190–99).

5. In a fascinating study called *The Feminization of American Culture* (New York: Alfred A. Knopf, 1977), Ann Douglas calls attention to the essentially anti-feminist attempt by "self-designated spokeswomen for the cautious among" nineteenth-century American middle-class women to "manufacture and defend a kind of pseudo-profession through the enunciation of a theory of female 'influence'" (p. 45). She argues that the nineteenth-century theory of the profession of advertising as subliminal formation of desire was in fact this technique or profession of "influence" carried to its extreme, a wresting of this pseudoprofession from women to use against women: "they knew that, in some not-altogether fanciful sense, women would operate as the subconscious of capitalist culture which they must tap, that the feminine occupation of shopping would constitute the dream-life of the nation" (p. 67).

6. Quoted in Parker's "Preface" to *The Heart of Midlothian*, p. viii.

7. Sandra M. Gilbert and Susan Gubar, *The Madwoman in the Attic: The Woman Writer and the Nineteenth-Century Imagination* (New Haven: Yale University Press, 1979), esp. pp. 71–83 and 187–95.

8. Citing Madge's final ballad, James Reed proposes that Madge is a fey and repressed, not a dangerously erotic, madwoman, "of the race of Ophelia, not of Rochester's wife" (*Sir Walter Scott: Landscape and Locality* [London: Athlone Press, 1980], p. 118). Maybe so, at the end, churched and "converted" like Norna her later avatar in *The Pirate*. But for most of her fictional life she does indeed anticipate Rochester's [first] wife.

9. George Eliot's Rosamond, in *Middlemarch*, had perfected the role taught her at Miss Lemon's School, that is, "she even acted her own character, and so well, that she did not know it to be precisely her own" (ch. 12), while *Daniel Deronda's* actress-mother, the Princess Halm-Eberstein, has a nature in which "experience immediately passed into drama, and she acted her own emotions," a talent Eliot calls "sincere acting" (ch. 51).

10. This would make Norna the darkly energizing (and twice abandoned) Sycorax of the island if we expand Graham McMaster's elegant reading of *The Pirate* as Scott's *Tempest* (*Scott and Society*, pp. 182–92). His reading calls attention not only to the primacy of storms and "sea changes" in the narrative but also, interestingly, to a special quality of primitive joy, and sharing of the polymorphous "family" of the island's community, which gives it the fabulous air of Gonzalo's ideal society. Most of the "property," and ideas about individual ownership of property, he notes, are brought to the island by strangers.

11. A figure astonishingly like Scott's fantasy-demon turns up in Doris Lessing's *The Four-Gated City* as the female protagonist's "self-hater," a psychic entity who drives women literally into madness, and whose first words are always, interestingly, an accusation that "she was wicked and bad and disobedient and cruel to her father" (New York: Bantam, 1970), p. 522.

12. *The Heart of Midlothian*, 7:41.

13. Could this be the sense in which we are to understand Harriet Martineau's curious comment on Scott's "moral services": "he has advocated the rights of woman with a force all the greater for his being unaware of the import

and tendency of what he was saying," (essay in *Tait's* Edinburgh magazine [January 1833], reprinted in *Critical Heritage*, p. 340).

14. In this light A. O. Cockshut's otherwise correct reading of Scott as offering in *The Heart of Midlothian* and *Redgauntlet* a "desperate royalism" to counter his picture of "a thoroughly disrupted world" goes astray. "The King" indeed, in both novels, assumes "his high function as a transcendent force for reconciliation"—in the abstract (*The Achievement of Walter Scott*, pp. 97, 163). In *Redgauntlet* the reconciling royal act of grace that frees (or rather declines to recognize) the conspiracy, has real and compromising existence in the political shrewdness of General Campbell; in the earlier novel the act of grace is grounded in the Queen's sexual powerlessness and Lady Suffolk's sexual misbehavior (as was, of course, Effie's "crime").

15. The parricide that woman's self-expression amounts to is hinted at in Effie's final words at her trial; her crime of love did not issue in the murder of her child, she maintains, but nevertheless "I hae been the means of killing my grey-headed father—I deserve the warst frae man, and frae God too" (p. 248).

16. Lars Hartveit has explored at length the careful intertwining in Scott's narrative of the crowd at Wilson's hanging of the national and the purely anarchic impulses which alternately master it, comparing the narrator's balanced sympathy here with the disgust which he exhibits when the same crowd becomes the vulgar "mob" during Effie's trial, and the historian's balance mixed with disgust when the crowd later lynches Porteous. What is missing in Hartveit's account of the various manifestations of "the mob in its search for a scapegoat" (*Dream within a Dream* [New York: Humanities Press, 1970], p. 49) is its final and carefully linked appearance as the tormenters of Madge Wildfire and lynchers of her mother. The first crowd watched Porteous murder (as it thought) Wilson, and attempted to murder Porteous. The second crowd, led by "Madge" (George Staunton-Robertson), murdered the first murderer; the third one compassed the death of the two women guilty of the sexual crime which uneasily shares the moral structure of the novel with the national and religious dilemmas of the "pure" heroine.

17. Jeanie's reiterated "never" to the lawyer's invitation to swear falsely that her sister confided in her has been compared, by Avrom Fleishman among others, to Cordelia's "nothing." Both women are to be commended for refusing to participate in charades of love, of course, yet as Fleishman points out, Scott's heroine, unlike Shakespeare's, needed the "educative relationship" with Madge Wildfire to teach her the wider social uses of the lie, or the mental reservation (*The English Historical Novel*, pp. 89, 90).

18. Summarizing discoveries by Welsh and Fleishman, among others, John Hayden notes that closer examination of the way mercy mediates truth to achieve justice (and justice mediates truth to achieve mercy) in the novel reveals that though Jeannie evades what Hayden calls "The Big Lie" (the end justifies the means), "she tells little ones with astonishing ease" ("The Big Lie [And a Few Small Ones], p. 36).

19. In an interesting reading of the "special critical confusion" about *The*

Heart of Midlothian, A. O. Cockshut notes that this is the only novel in which problems of sexual conduct are at the center of the plot and characterization. "Scott's manifest unwillingness to give the mental processes of Staunton and Effie with the fullness of detail accorded to Jeannie and her father" arise from this: he can only sketch in these processes using the materials of religious and political "Enthusiasm" he has already perfected, making Effie, half-realized analogue to Burley et al., "an Enthusiast of love" (*The Achievement of Walter Scott*, pp. 178, 174).

20. Alexander Welsh elaborated the typology, using particularly the Minna-Brenda example; they are distinguished as the subline from the beautiful, the possessor of intellectual from the possessor of domestic or erotic passion, the female partaker in manly action from the feminine sufferer-survivor (see the section "Blond and Brunette" in *The Hero of the Waverley Novels*, pp. 70–78). Francis Hart refines and diffuses the Minna-Brenda contrast somewhat, necessarily, but somewhat unfairly, taking Welsh's categories more absolutely than he actually drew them, and arguing for Brenda as the more voluptuous and loyal (Welsh's "dark maiden" qualities) personality (*Scott's Novels*, pp. 296–300).

21. Scott had flirted with a genuine incest plot in a novel published the same year, *St. Ronan's Well*; his publisher-critics made him change it. False incest (he had used this before in *The Antiquary*) is closer to the pattern of desire in the Waverley novels as Alexander Welsh phrased it: "the premium on *having* and the prejudice against *getting* have other extensions. . . . It is as if the romance of property were suspicious of any kind of force or energy. The bias against conveyable goods extends even to the sentiment of love. To love something means to want it" (*The Hero of the Waverley Novels*, pp. 120–21). To love/want a woman and find you already have her as a sister is the perfect solution. To assign that sister a lover in the form of a close friend who has made a career of rescuing you is to perform the same rescue from "wanting" for your sister. I belive I just saw the same formula applied in the climax to George Lucas's *Star Wars* trilogy.

22. Many critics have noted the link between the lost causes of Hugh Redgauntlet and Peter Peebles; summarizing this critical history, David Brown continues: "The law . . . is shown to be a parasite of the property system. . . . The effect is to satirise not only Redgauntlet, but also the bourgeois lifestyle of the novel's 'survivors'" (*Walter Scott and the Historical Imagination*, p. 165). Robin Mayhead notes of both *The Heart of Midlothian* and *Redgauntlet* that Scott, "while finding so much to cherish in the monuments of civilization, sometimes turned upon them an alarmed scrutiny. . . . And the monument that worries him the most is the one that he knew best—the law" ("The Idea of Justice" in Jeffares, ed., *Scott's Mind and Art*, p. 173).

Chapter Five

1. This aphorism from Gaston Bachelard's *The Psychoanalysis of Fire* appears as the opening epigraph to Hayden White's important study *Metahistory: The Historical Imagination in Nineteenth Century Europe* (Balti-

more: The Johns Hopkins University Press, 1973). White depicts the nineteenth century's imagination as following a "full circle" from a rebellion against the ironic historical vision of the late Enlightenment through a romantically innocent effort to "constitute history as the ground for a 'realistic' science of man, society, and culture," to an ironic recognition that this process produced "only a host of competing 'realisms'" whose status, like that of all fictions, rests finally on its capacity to offer a coherent and activating vision (p. 432). White earlier notes that the eighteenth-century historians, of whom, on his antiquarian side, Scott was one, lacked an adequate theory of human psychology "in which reason was not set over against imagination as the basis of truth against the basis of error, but in which the continuity between reason and fantasy was recognized" (p. 51). And though Scott appears to work from this discredited eighteenth-century duality, the more acute contemporary criticism of Welch, Hart, and Levine, for instance, has recognized Scott's blurring of the distinction between the "dream" and the "reality" which can be "studied," as a crucial stage in the development of such a theory.

2. *Woodstock*, 21:463. These verses from a ballad called "The Woodstock Scuffle" (1649) are printed as an appendix.

3. Joyce's protagonist finds among his dead priest friend's books *The Abbot*, *The Devout Communicant*, and *The Memoirs of Vidcoq*, and tells us that "I liked the last best because its leaves were yellow" (*The Dubliners* [1916] [reprint, New York: Viking Press, 1969], p. 29). The other quoted words are on p. 32.

4. Francis Hart's *Scott's Novels* is perhaps the most fully argued case for the necessity and linkage of the two "matters": Hart proposes that the matter closest to home, the Jacobite, rather quickly became "too narrow . . . inadequate" for his true theme—the mutated survival of certain human values in the midst of the continuing fall of ancient houses and races. The intent to write "a history" becomes the need to write about "histories": in the key early novel *The Antiquary*, Hart reminds us, "the tragicomedy of Jacobitism" becomes the "tragicomedy of conflicts among antiquaries with conflicting methods and values" (p.249).

5. David Brown argues that the Royalist/Whig division of the seventeenth century is in fact being satirized in the portrayal of opposing political parties or "clubs" in *The Antiquary*, whose two "sides"—royalism now being represented by the Hanoverian monarch, populism by the entrenched middle class—are virtually indistinguishable. Since "politics as the expression of real social conflict has practically ceased to exist" in the time of the Antiquary, the time of Scott's own youth, "only 'history' is left as an arena for argument" (*Walter Scott and the Historical Imagination*, p. 51).

6. James Simmons, *The Novelist as Historian* (The Hague: Mouton, 1973), p. 18.

7. According to Alice Chandler (*A Dream of Order: The Medieval Ideal in Nineteenth Century Literature* [London: Routledge & Kegan Paul, 1971]), Scott gathered up through his own scholarly readings the fruits of the eighteenth century's "second wave" of medievalism and offered the century a fully realized

fictional projection of certain medieval values—material abundance, intense commitments, and above all a vision of communal society where individual heroism and the dream of order were somehow compatible. This influential projection triggered further efforts to dig up confirming, or in some cases disconfirming, documentation for it. Chandler notes, interestingly, that both "waves" of medievalism, one in the early sixteenth century and one in the late seventeenth–early eighteenth century, had double antiquarian and politico-theoretical roots: in early Tudor and post-Cromwellian times the aesthetes had special reason to note the recent destruction of monuments and documents and to engage in protective or restorative activities, while at the same time the apologists for the new governmental and social order found new impetus for the urge to write, or rewrite, history (see pp. 45–51, 15).

8. Georg W. Hegel, "Introduction" to *The Philosophy of History* (New York: Dover Publications, 1956), pp. 9, 38). The Idea, or Spirit, whose nature is freedom, is present in all times as the ground of "reality," Hegel argues, and "the whole process of History, is directed to rendering this unconscious impulse a conscious one" (p. 25).

9. Working also from a reading of Scott through White's *Metahistory*, Richard Waswo has offered a compelling analysis of both Scott's tales and his narrative apparatus as offering "an historiography that gives primary importance to the social nexus of human identity , and to the acts of interpretation on which this depends" ("Story as Historiography in the Waverley Novels," *ELH* 47 [Summer 1980]: 305).

10. Alice Chandler has noted the frequency of the image of the descent into the grave and return in the last medieval novels, but ignores the primacy of the parody-resurrection or empty-tomb image in many of Scott's early and middle novels, including the three under study in this chapter ("Chivalry and Romance: Scott's Medieval Novels," *Studies in Romance* 14 [Spring 1975] : 199).

11. *The Antiquary*, 3:28.

12. In search of *The Antiquary's* "principle of coherence," critics divide over whether moments like Edie's deflation represent an essentially comic governing impulse (Daiches, John Buchan, Robert Gordon, James Reed, David Brown), or a tragicomic, even absurdist one (Francis Hart, Robin Mayhead). Mayhead's reading of the novel as a "very conscious compilation of incongruities" side by side with "wasteful disasters," with a Johnsonian Scott at bottom "brooding over *vanitas vanitatum*" (*Walter Scott*, pp. 90–95), offers compelling coherence, though it seems to me to underrate the perhaps fey whimsey of the treatment of history and historians there. I have seen no readings of the novel which do not take Edie's account of the artifacts at Kinprunes as the truth, "the cold voice of reason" as James Reed phrases it (*Sir Walter Scott: Landscape and Locale*, p. 91). Indeed Reed reminds us that Lockhart thought the incident based on a true and similar incident (quoted on p. 91).

13. Apropos, *The Oxford Dictionary of Nursery Rhymes* contains a famous Scottish rhyme about Aiken Drum, who "lived in the moon" and, interestingly, "played upon a ladle," a mysterious and tasty character whose hat was made of

cream cheese and coat of roast beef. His enemy Willy Wood, who "played upon a razor" and is clearly an Englishman, made short work of these dainties, but choked to death on Aiken Drum's trousers, which were made of haggis bags. "Nothing is known about this song," say the editors, "except that it was current in Scotland in 1821 [Scott published *The Antiquary* in 1816] and that the name Aiken drum appeared in a ballad about the opposing armies before the battle of Sheriffmuir in 1715" (this was the year of the abortive Jacobite revolution which forms the climax of *Rob Roy*, which Scott published in 1817). James Hogg published the ballad "Aikendrum" in his *Jacobite Relics* in 1821, noting that he had held the ballad for several years before his friend, Walter Scott, figured out for him which battle it referred to, noting also that the name Aiken Drum appeared in an "unconnected" old rhyme about a man who lived in the moon. It remains only to add that Hogg's collection also includes a ballad explicitly referring to the Stuart king over the water as the hidden "man in the moon" for us to see the palimpsest of possible inscriptions lurking under the name, Aiken Drum. Edie's emphasis that the artifact in question was a *long* ladle reminds us of the still more ancient folk saying about the man who needed a long spoon to sup with the devil, another hint that Aiken Drum's origin in Edie's story might be in myth or tale, not history (see Iona and Peter Opie, eds., *The Oxford Dictionary of Nursery Rhymes* [Oxford: Clarendon Press, 1962], pp. 52–54; and James Hogg, *The Jacobite Relics of Scotland*, 2d series [Edinburgh: William Blackwood, 1821], pp. 258–59).

14. Robert Gordon remarks of the squabbling historians of *The Antiquary* that "Scott as a historical thinker quite casually and humorously confronts us with a rather sophisticated dilemma, that the impulse to study the past may involve the use of tools that in themselves remove the past farther from us" (*Under Which King?* p. 43). In this context Mary Lascelles distinguishes the sense of history, that is, "an estimate of the speed and direction of political currents which will satisfy future generations," which Scott had partially, from his profoundly influential sense of the past, i.e., the mind's sudden capture, in a flash, of a communal reality extending behind the rationally plotted character in action, "like a terrain lying behind a watershed" (*The Story-Teller Retrieves the Past: Historical Fiction and Fictional History in the Art of Scott, Stevenson, Kipling, and Some Others* [Oxford: Clarendon Press, 1980], pp. 61, 34).

15. There is, of course, autobiographical treasure buried in this "house" too: Francis Hart makes the point that the picture of the old man fighting not to be displaced from his house (and yet Sir Henry Lee is really only the "steward" of that royal treasure-box) rings with the personal story of Scott's bankruptcy and the threat to Abbotsford, which occurred during the writing of the novel (*Scott's Novels*, p. 95). Mary Lascelles makes a similar point about Monkbarns, the purchased house of Jonathan Oldbuck the antiquary, who fills it, as Scott did Abbotsford, with the imported history of his "magpie hoard" of artifacts (*The Story-Teller Retrieves the Past*, pp. 51–52).

16. *The Talisman*, 20:17.

17. Seeing Jonathan Oldbuck as simply the admirer and protector of Lovel,

peripheral to the main plot of Wardour and Glenallen houses fallen and then recovered, Hart misses, I think, the significance of this symbolic act by which the third house, Oldbuck's, is rescued from its potential fall into sterility, in his rightly much admired section on "The Falls and Survivals of Ancient Houses" (*Scott's Novels*, pp. 246–58).

18. Hart's audacious but compelling reading of *Woodstock: The Cavalier*, would make "Cavalierism" the Waverley hero of the novel: "For the first half of the novel the problem is the restoring of Sir Henry [the old and true Cavalier] to Woodstock; for the second half it is the restoring of Charles to his own Cavalier values as embodied in the restored Sir Henry and Woodstock" (*Scott's Novels*, p. 94).

19. Scott, if I am right, slips up here, making Jonathan Oldbuck's spiritual "ancestor" John of the Girnel an early medieval figure, where he later describes him as a Renaissance figure, the last bailiff under the abbots (p. 98).

20. *Count Robert of Paris*, 24:3.

21. It is not the passions but the special chivalric mesh of the three—valor, devotion and love—which Scott, finding his appropriate metaphor, says we can now "only look back on . . . as a beautiful and fantastic piece of frostwork, which has dissolved in the beams of the sun" ("Essay on Chivalry," in *The Miscellaneous Prose Works of Sir Walter Scott, Bart* [Boston: Wells and Lily, 1829], 6:12, 13).

22. Both Welsh and Hart touch obliquely on the Robin Hood–Saladin connection, though Welsh's analysis goes somewhat astray, as Hart notes, trying to make the elegant and silken Saladin the "rough and irregular" "dark hero" of the novel, and Hart's analysis, that the novel enacts through the movement of Saladin's gift-talisman "the transferral of the power of the Saladin polito-symbolic ideal from a mythical or utopian East . . . to a politically sick Europe" ignores what I shall argue in a moment is the deliberate reference to the West's own talisman, Robin Hood, already at work in the sick body politic (see *The Hero of the Waverley Novels*, pp. 63–65 and *Scott's Novels*, pp. 175–80).

Conclusion

1. Mark Weinstein rhetorically asks this question after citing Scott's whimsical self-criticisms in an anonymous review of his own novels, in his "Introduction" to *The Prefaces to the Waverley Novels By Walter Scott*, ed. Mark A. Weinstein (Lincoln: University of Nebraska Press, 1978), p. xii. Weinstein has, lucky for us all, responded to Saintsbury's suggestion that the prefaces be collected and "published as a History of the Waverley Novels by their author" (George Saintsbury, *Sir Walter Scott* [Edinburgh: Oliphant, Anderson, and Ferrier, 1897], p. 69). Weinstein's book includes only a selection of the introductions and magnum opus prefaces.

2. An excellent short treatment of this question can be found in Richard Waswo's "Story as Historiography in the Waverley Novels," *ELH* 47 (Summer 1980). "The most remarkable thing about the whole massive paraphernalia of

Scott's narrative presentation," Waswo notes, "is its incremental appearance throughout his career as a novelist." Every time one would think the fictional self-presentations could or should come to a stop, say in 1827 when Scott admitted to his authorial identity, a new set of self-fictionalizations is generated; when the author cannot stop what seemed to start out as good fun, some more "obscure desire," Waswo proposes, is surely at work (see pp. 305–7).

3. The *Journal* continuously records Scott's dutiful self-reproaches and the inevitable honest aftermath: "regular I will be . . . that I may regain independence I must be saving. But ambition awakes as love of quiet indulgence dies and is mortified within me.—Dark Cuthullin will be renowned or dead" (*Journal* for 4 March 1826, p. 105). Or this less "dark" but more endearing reversal in mid self-deprecation: "Reconsidered the probable downfall of my literary reputation. I am so constitutionally indifferent to the censure or praise of the world that never having abandoned myself to the feelings of self-conceit which my great success was calculated to inspire I can look with the most unshaken firmness upon the event as far as my own feelings are concerned. If there be any great advantage in literary [fame] I have had it and I certainly do not care at losing it. They cannot say but what I *had* the *crown*" (*Journal* for 12 December 1827, p. 393). For George Levine, Scott's was "an enormously ambitious art. . . . Unwilling to imagine himself as serious, he devised a form that radically altered and extended the range of the novel" (*The Realistic Imagination*, p. 82). Or more precisely, perhaps, because he was able to imagine himself as not-serious, he was able to be that radical innovator, exemplifying a canny resolution of the dilemma Levine sees Scott's heroes always facing—the consequence of enacting desires is "the loss of the freedom to dream them" (p. 83).

4. Kenneth Sroka reminds us that Scott's fact-giving "introductions," not to mention his proliferating appendices and "notes," are a "rhetorical device" pretending to side with the eighteenth-century canons of careful fact and reason. When we look more closely at the actual arguments of the prefaces and introductions, as well as at the penchant to begin storytelling once more in the midst of the apparently simple "note," we find Scott actually redressing the balance towards the nineteenth century's primacy of imagination (see "Fact, Fiction, and the Introductions to the Waverley Novels," *Wordsworth Circle* 1 [Autumn 1971]: 143).

5. This is the famous essay in *Quarterly Review*, January 1817, reprinted in *Critical Heritage*, p. 114.

6. "Joseph Andrews was eminently successful; and the aggrieved Richardson, who was fond of praise even to adulation, was proportionally offended, while his group of admirers, male and female, took care to echo back his sentiments, and to heap Fielding with reproach. Their animosity survived his life . . . " "Henry Fielding" (1821) (reprinted in *Sir Walter Scott on Novelists and Fiction*, ed. Ioan Williams [New York: Barnes & Noble, 1968], p. 51).

7. From "Henry Fielding" in *Lives of the Novelists* (reprinted in *Sir Walter Scott on Novelists and Fiction*, p. 55).

8. The preface was published with the New York Edition of James's works in 1907–9, reprinted in *The Art of the Novel*, ed. with introduction by R. P. Blackmur (New York: Charles Scribner's Sons, 1934), p. 321: here he makes his famous comment on "story" as "the spoiled child of art" (p. 315).

9. This exercise in tribal wrath distinguishes *The Lay's* Canto sixth, which begins with the famous lines "Breathes there the man with soul so dead, / who never to himself hath said, / this is my own, my native land" (see *The Complete Poetical Works of Sir Walter Scott*, Cambridge Edition [Boston: Houghton Mifflin, 1900], p. 79).

10. In the Dryburgh Edition the introductions to *Tales of My Landlord*, first series, and to *The Black Dwarf* and *A Legend of Montrose* are printed in vol. 5, where the introduction to *Old Mortality* is printed with *Old Mortality* in vol. 4. This early descriptive material about Jeddediah and Gandercleugh is from the first introduction, p. xi.

11. *The Bride of Lammermoor*, 8:9.

12. Discussing this passage in *The Realistic Imagination*, George Levine claims that Scott's refusal to take himself or his fiction seriously means that though all the *materials* are here assembled for a Carlylian, even a modernist, treatment of the "problem of fiction itself," no such treatment happens, and "we never again hear of Peter's difficulties" (p. 90). Not in *The Bride of Lammermoor*, perhaps, but the prefatory chapter to *Count Robert of Paris* elaborates poignantly on this very problem. Levine's text offers an interesting misreading of Scott here, by the way, substituting "written propaganda" for the novelist's "written memoranda."

13. These two novels with their prefatory epistles, appear as vols. 14 and 15, respectively, in the Dryburgh Edition.

14. The introduction to *Tales of the Crusaders*, along with *The Betrothed* and the important introduction to *Chronicles of the Canongate*, to be discussed shortly, appear as vol. 19 in the Dryburgh Edition.

15. A. O. Cockshut is one of the several who use this phrase (*The Achievement of Walter Scott*, p. 19).

16. But as David Hewitt reminds us, Scott uses not only fiction but also autobiography "for self-defense and not just for self-exploration," wishing here as elsewhere to "control his readers' access to him" (*Scott on Himself* [Edinburgh: Scottish Academic Press, 1981], pp. xi, xvi).

17. Difficulty with revisions may arise from two quite different habits of mind, Mary Lascelles reminds us in "Scott and the Art of Revision" (*Imagined Worlds, Essays Presented in Honour of John Butt*, ed. Maynard Mack and Ian Gregor [London: Methuen, 1968]; one habit is a self-concerned and calculating resolve to take no further trouble with a task, the second, closer to Scott's habit of mind, is an unconcern with self in the obsession to finish the story, "pressing on as though speed alone could capture the visionary impression." Scott seemed to have doubts about whether the original "fabric" of his visions, his stories, could stand "reworking," says Lascelles after her exploration of his minor, but often careful, revisions (p. 41).

18. Frank Jordan, in an otherwise informative reading of "Chrystal Croftangry: Scott's Last Best Mask" (*Scottish Literary Journal* 7 [May 1980]), argues that Croftangry's major creation as an author is the actual teller of the tales from the Canongate, Mrs. Martha Bethune Balliol, and wishes to give Scott credit, in "these days of Women's Liberation," for a "portrait of the artist as female in sex and feminine in temperament" (p. 132). The portrait is indeed admirable, but I would connect it rather to Scott's habitual reflex, as here, to assign the origin of his inheritance and his materials to a female, but to receive the outlawed female property inside the law, inside the narrative, as masculine.

Index

Abbot, The, 49, 76, 92–95, 111–15, 120,
  158, 175, 188, 196
Abbotsford, 1, 7, 200, 207 n. 14, 213
  n. 15. *See also* Secret Leaves
Antiquary, The, 17, 81, 156–60, 164–70,
  188, 190, 191, 223 n. 12
Auerbach, Nina, 218 n. 4
Austen, Jane, 8, 169
Author of Waverley, The, 7, 17, 20, 104,
  152, 168–79, 185–202

Bachelard, Gaston, 221 n. 1
Betrothed, The, 25, 176
Black Dwarf, The, 192
Bloom, Harold, 3, 205 n. 7
Brewer, Wilmon, 209 n. 7
Bridal of Triermain, The, 7
Bride of Lammermoor, The, 5, 190, 192,
  194
Bronte, Charlotte, 119, 217 n. 15
Brown, David, 70, 211 n. 14, 222 n. 5
Bunyan, John, 137–39, 188
Byron, George Gordon, Lord, 1, 12, 75,
  121, 189

Carlyle, Thomas, 2, 8, 16, 195
Caserio, Robert, 3
Castle Dangerous, 202
Cervantes, Miguel de, 196
Chandler, Alice, 222 n. 7
Chivalry, 8, 9, 46, 47, 52, 56, 155,
  176–79
Christianity, 17, 20, 25, 26, 44, 46, 84,
  106, 107, 108, 155–57, 178, 183, 184.
  See also Crusades; Covenanters
Chronicles of the Canongate, 200, 201
Cockshut, A. O., 210 n. 12, 214 n. 18,
  220 n. 14

Community, 3, 4, 8, 71, 132
Count Robert of Paris, 17, 25, 176–79,
  187, 201, 202
Covenanters, 9, 33, 100, 101. *See also*
  Christianity
Crawford, Thomas, 212 n. 8
Crusades, 8, 25, 38, 153, 155, 170. *See
  also* Christianity

Destiny, 1, 6, 50, 115
Devlin, D. D., 211 n. 6
Dickens, Charles, 1–4, 9, 13–16, 151,
  201, 202, 217 n. 15
Douglas, Ann, 219 n. 5

Eliot, George, 2, 16, 119, 219 n. 9

Farrell, John P., 71
Ferrier, Susan, 194
Fielding, Henry, 4, 7, 8, 187–89, 191,
  226 n. 6
Fleishman, Avrom, 6, 26, 213 n. 14
Forbes, Duncan, 70
Ford, Ford Maddox, 216 n. 13
Fortunes of Nigel, The, 49, 188, 196
Foucault, Michel, 94
Fowles, John, viii, 6, 39, 202
French Revolution, 70, 71, 168
Frye, Northrop, 18, 25, 26

Garside, Peter, 70, 215 n. 7
Gender, 7, 17, 24, 65, 66, 77, 106, 113,
  115, 116–19, 142, 175
Gilbert, Sandra, 118
Gordon, Robert C., 206 n. 11
Graff, Gerald, 206 n. 9
Greenwood Myth, 10, 17, 18, 129. *See
  also* Robin Hood; Secret Leaves

Gubar, Susan, 118
Guy Mannering, 118, 188, 190

Hardy, Thomas, 38
Hart, Francis R., 208 n. 22, 209 n. 3,
212 n. 7, 222 n. 4, 224 n. 15
Hartveit, Lars, 220 n. 16
Hayden, John O., 218 n. 3
Heart of Midlothian, The, 123–26, 129–
42, 154, 192, 193
History, 8, 11, 12, 13, 17, 80, 153–58,
163, 173
Honor, 6, 17, 53–56, 76, 212
Hook, Andrew, 218 n. 3
Hume, David, 71

Industrial Revolution, 71
Ivanhoe, 7, 9, 12, 16, 17, 18–26, 37–50,
68, 82, 106, 155, 182, 188, 195, 209
n. 4

James, Henry, 188
Johnson, Edgar, 5
Jordon, Frank, 227 n. 18
Journal of Sir Walter Scott, The, viii,
203, 207 n. 14, 213 n. 15, 214 n. 15,
217 n. 17, 226 n. 3
Joyce, James, 34, 153, 222 n. 3

Kenilworth, 49, 120
Kidnapped Romance, 6, 16, 18, 19, 21,
25. *See also* Romance

Lady of the Lake, The, 7, 72
Language, 7, 17, 22–24, 79, 81–85, 100,
106, 171
Lascelles, Mary, 224 n. 15, 227 n. 17
Lauber, John, 211 n. 4
Lay of the Last Minstrel, The, 5, 7, 189,
190
Law, 1, 118, 126, 129, 130, 131, 147,
152, 189
Lawrence, D. H., 118
Legend of Montrose, A, 192, 194
Lessing, Doris, 219 n. 11
Levine, George, 25, 206 n. 9, 217 n. 19,
226 n. 3, 227 n. 12
Lewis, C. S., 26
Life of Napoleon Buonaparte, 199
Lives of the Novelists, 187
Lockhart, J. G., 1, 203
Loss, 3, 5, 17, 20, 154, 202
Lukacs, Georg, 70

McMaster, Graham, 210 n. 9, 217 n. 20,
219 n. 10
Marmion, 7
Mayhead, Robin, 221 n. 22
Mayhew, Robin, 209 n. 4
Millgate, Jane, 207 n. 17, 212 n. 10
Minstrelsy of the Scottish Border, 5
Monastery, The, 49, 89–92, 105–10, 188,
196

Old Mortality, 60, 81, 86–89, 95–105,
154, 171, 192, 193
Origins, 15, 20, 21, 24, 25, 29, 172

Parson, Coleman, 216 n. 10
Peveril of the Peak, 49, 188, 196, 197
Pirate, The, 13, 106, 119–23, 143–46

Quayle, Eric, 212 n. 6
Quentin Durward, 49–60, 70–79, 80,
178, 199, 200

Redgauntlet, 13, 49, 126–29, 146–52, 175
Red-Handed King, 8, 19, 30, 69, 128,
160, 172
Richardson, Samuel, 187, 189
Rob Roy, 14, 17, 49–60, 61–70
Robin Hood, 31, 32, 39, 41, 44, 69, 93,
131, 169, 177, 180, 183, 202. *See also*
Greenwood Myth; Secret Leaves
Rokeby, 7
Romance, 11, 13, 16, 26–31, 34, 50, 61,
75, 135. *See also* Kidnapped Romance

St. Ronan's Well, 221 n. 21
Secret Leaves, viii, 6, 42, 67, 70, 174,
179. *See also* Greenwood Myth; Robin
Hood
Shakespeare, William, 3, 12, 17, 18, 28,
31, 39, 40, 49, 50, 57, 58, 59, 87, 88,
161, 194, 198, 210 n. 14, 212 n. 9, 220
n. 17
Shaw, Harry, 215 n. 18
Shelly, Mary, 118
Siege of Malta, The, 176
Simmons, James, 155
Smith, Adam, 70
Spencer, Edmund, 82, 197
Sroka, Kenneth, 210 n. 14, 226 n. 4
Steward, Dugald, 71

Tales of the Crusaders, 199
Talisman, The, 17, 25, 162–64, 176–84
Thackeray, W. M., 3, 4, 9, 10–14, 16,
201

Trollope, Anthony, 3
Tullock, Graham, 215 n. 4

Van Ghent, Dorothy, 218 n. 3

Waswo, Richard, 223 n. 9, 225 n. 2
Waverley, 12, 13, 16, 18–37, 49, 51,
   120, 185

Weinstein, Mark, 225 n. 1
Welsh, Alexander, 3, 29, 64, 78, 93,
   117, 216 n. 12, 221 n. 20
White, Hayden, 221 n. 1
Woodstock, 17, 161–62, 170–76, 199
Woolf, Virginia, 2, 3, 81, 167
Wordsworth, William, 1, 4, 187, 188,
   189